HOME REPAIR & REMODEL
COST GUIDE 2006

Marshall & Swift/Boeckh, LLC

Los Angeles, California – Princeton, New Jersey

The information and prices contained in the *Home Repair & Remodel Cost Guide 2006* have been compiled by Marshall & Swift/Boeckh, LLC from sources believed to be reliable and to be representative of current price and cost situations. No warranty, guarantee or representation is made by Marshall & Swift/Boeckh, LLC as to the correctness or sufficiency of any information process or representation contained in the *Home Repair & Remodel Cost Guide 2006,* and Marshall & Swift/Boeckh, LLC assumes no responsibility or liability in connection therewith, nor can it be assumed that the material or prices presented will not be changed due to local or national conditions. Nothing contained in the *Home Repair & Remodel Cost Guide 2006* shall be construed as a recommendation to use any product or process.

Product or brand names used in this book may be trade names or trademarks. Where we believe that there may be proprietary claims to such trade names or trademarks, the name has been used with an initial capital or it has been capitalized in the style used by the name claimant. Regardless of the capitalization used, all such names have been used in an editorial manner without any intent to convey endorsement or other affiliation with the name claimant. Neither the author nor the publisher intends to express any judgment as to the validity or legal status of any such proprietary claims.

ISBN 1-56842-159-1

For information or technical assistance, contact:

Marshall & Swift
P. O. Box 26307
Los Angeles, CA 90026-0307

Sales & Service: (800) 544-2678
Technical Support: (800) 526-2756
Customer Fax: (213) 683-9043
Web site: http://www.marshallswift.com
e-mail: csinquiry@marshallswift.com

TABLE OF CONTENTS

TABLE OF CONTENTS

OPEN THE BOOK AND CLOSE THE SALE

A number of helpful home remodeling and repair books have recently been published. Unfortunately, they all seem to be missing one essential ingredient: the specific costs associated with each repair or remodel! Now, with Marshall & Swift's *Home Repair & Remodel Cost Guide*, anyone can quickly discover just how much it will cost to perform almost any home repair or remodel job.

This easy-to-use, comprehensive guide is updated annually to make sure the information stays current. Designed for realtors, homeowners and appraisers, the *Home Repair & Remodel Cost Guide* is a powerful negotiating tool and a helpful budgeting resource as well as a handy estimating guide.

For realtors, the guide can be confidently used to assist a seller in setting the listing price or asking a buyer to raise his or her offer. Simply by opening this book, realtors can often close the sale. When a home does need a little extra care, the realtor can provide a third-party source without calling in a contractor for an estimate.

With the *Home Repair & Remodel Cost Guide* you can:

- Provide a quick estimate on repairing a fixer-upper

- Improve the accuracy and professionalism of comparative market analyses

- Double-check contractors' figures

- Justify the recommended listing price

- Make comparables more comparable by looking at the specific differences

In addition to removal costs, which are built into the base costs on all items, the guide features financing information, types of available mortgages, home improvement loan payment and depreciation tables. With basic terminology explained, detailed drawings, prices of important components and costs on hundreds of various components, the *Home Repair & Remodel Cost Guide* is an invaluable reference guide for almost anyone.

THE DATA

The research team at Marshall & Swift is constantly gathering, monitoring and developing construction cost data throughout the U.S. and Canada. Therefore, the Marshall & Swift databases reflect the most recent changes in construction technology relating to building, productivity and ultimately, price.

Labor rates are gathered for 22 trades in each of the researched cities. The local multipliers are based on prevailing wages for the trades included.

Material costs are determined through contact with building product manufacturers, dealers, supply houses, distributors and contractors. Crew sizes and productivity rates have been developed by Marshall & Swift's staff of construction experts.

HOME REPAIR & REMODEL

Note: Local and/or economic conditions may dictate necessary adjustments to a particular locale. All costs included in the *Home Repair & Remodel Cost Guide* are based on the Marshall & Swift national averages.

The information and prices contained in the *Home Repair & Remodel Cost Guide* have been compiled by Marshall & Swift/Boeckh, LLC, from sources believed to be reliable and to be representative of current price and cost situations. No warranty, guarantee or representation is made by Marshall & Swift/Boeckh, LLC, as to the correctness or sufficiency of any information, prices or representation contained in the *Home Repair & Remodel Cost Guide,* and Marshall & Swift assumes no responsibility or liability in connection therewith, nor can it be assumed that the material or prices presented will not be changed due to local or national conditions. Nothing contained in the *Home Repair & Remodel Cost Guide* shall be construed as a recommendation to use any product or process.

WHAT THE DATA CONTAINS

1) A replacement cost is described as cost for removing the existing components and replacing them with new materials. Replacement cost includes labor, material and all connections unless otherwise noted. Removal cost includes debris removal to a dumpster within 100 feet of the property. Dumpster rental is not included in the costs.

2) Contractors' overhead and profit.

3) Workers' benefit packages and insurance.

INFLUENCE OF LOCAL CONSTRUCTION PRACTICES

Since construction practices vary from one location to another, some of the specific component costs may differ from those published. These differences generally stem from one or more of the following and should be adjusted accordingly:

1) Local building code regulations.

2) Climatic conditions.

3) Availability of specific materials.

<table>
<tr><td align="center">Corporate Office
915 Wilshire Boulevard, 8th Floor
Los Angeles, CA 90017-3409
(800) 544-2678 or (213) 683-9000
Fax (213) 683-9010</td><td align="center">Princeton Forrestal Center
101 College Road East, 3rd Floor
Princeton, NJ 08540
(800) 451-2367 or (609) 987-8333
Fax (609) 452-5705</td></tr>
</table>

SAMPLE ESTIMATE

To use this guide, simply locate the item you want replaced using the index located in the back of this book, then multiply that cost by your individual location multiplier.

Example:

<u>Work to be performed</u>

1) Paint Living Room
2) Paint Door and Trim
3) Replace Toilet
4) Replace Two Flush, Hollow-core Partition Doors

Location: Princeton, NJ (ZIP 08540)

HOME REPAIR & REMODEL COST GUIDE WORKSHEET

COMPANY: _Acme Real Estate_

AGENT: _B. Jones_

DATE: _January 1, 2005_   PHONE#: _987-555-1234_

PROPERTY ADDRESS: _Princeton, NJ 08540_

SALE PRICE: _$2,162.10_   FOR: _J. Smith_

LINE	Improvement Required (Component)	Quantity		Unit Cost		Local Mult.		Total Cost
1	Paint living room wall	1	X	415	X	1.37	=	$569
2	Paint living room ceiling	1	X	180	X	1.37	=	$ 247
3			X		X		=	$
4	Hollow-core partition door	1	X	220	X	1.27	=	$ 279
5	Paint door and trim (per side)	2	X	65	X	1.27	=	$ 165.10
6	Toilet (floor mounted)	1	X	705	X	1.28	=	$ 902
7			X		X		=	$
8			X		X		=	$
9			X		X		=	$
10			X		X		=	$

NOTES					
	11	Total Base Cost (Total of Lines 1-10)		=	$2,162.10
Living Room = 12' x 15'	12	Depreciation % (If Required)		=	
	13	Depreciation Amount (Line 12 x 11)		=	$
	14	Depreciation Cost (Line 11 - 13)		=	$

NOTE: Space is provided on the back of this worksheet for sketches, computations and additional notes.

SAMPLE ESTIMATE

SKETCHES AND COMPUTATIONS

Additional Notes: _______________________________________

For your convenience, blank worksheets are supplied in the back of this guide.

BATHROOMS

- Accessories Set
- Bathtub
- Bathtub Enclosure
- Bathtub/Shower
- Bidet
- Caulking (Bathtub)
- Faucet
- Medicine Cabinet
- Mirror
- Shower Door
- Showerhead
- Shower (Over Tub)
- Shower Rod
- Shower Stall
- Sink (Built-In)
- Sink (Wall Mounted)
- Toilet Seat
- Toilet (Floor Mounted)
- Toilet (Wall Mounted)
- Vanity (Metal)
- Vanity (Wood)

ROOM METHOD

Costs include replacing the bathroom completely. (New: fixtures, faucets, floor, ceiling and wall finishes.)

Note: If additional fixtures per room are required, add from the Unit Method.

HALF BATH
(1 toilet, 1 bathroom sink)

Room Size	Quality Levels		
(Square Foot Area)	Economy	Standard	Custom
25 Square Feet	$2,300.00	$4,030.00	$6,170.00
30 Square Feet	2,370.00	4,140.00	6,440.00
35 Square Feet	2,440.00	4,310.00	6,670.00
40 Square Feet	2,490.00	4,450.00	6,890.00
45 Square Feet	2,560.00	4,630.00	7,140.00
50 Square Feet	2,640.00	4,760.00	7,370.00
Over 50 Square Feet	2,690.00	4,930.00	7,660.00

FULL BATH
(1 toilet, 1 bathroom sink, 1 bathtub w/shower)

Room Size	Quality Levels		
(Square Foot Area)	Economy	Standard	Custom
50 Square Feet	$3,900.00	$6,550.00	$ 9,430.00
60 Square Feet	4,030.00	6,840.00	9,940.00
70 Square Feet	4,090.00	7,060.00	10,180.00
80 Square Feet	4,160.00	7,250.00	10,500.00
90 Square Feet	4,260.00	7,420.00	10,740.00
100 Square Feet	4,340.00	7,600.00	10,990.00
Over 100 Square Feet	4,410.00	7,790.00	11,280.00

UNIT METHOD

To replace individual items, use the costs below:

COMPONENT	QUALITY LEVELS		
(Price Each)	Economy	Standard	Custom
Accessories Set (paper and tooth-brush holders, soap dish, etc.)	$ 160.00	$ 215.00	$ 325.00
Bathtub	445.00	775.00	1,360.00
Bathtub Enclosure	325.00	390.00	475.00
Bathtub/Shower Combination	1,075.00	1,190.00	1,330.00
Bidet	570.00	745.00	1,020.00
Caulking – Bathtub	65.00	70.00	80.00
Faucet	155.00	210.00	315.00
Medicine Cabinet	130.00	180.00	255.00
Mirror	155.00	240.00	375.00
Shower Door	230.00	335.00	415.00
Showerhead	85.00	120.00	125.00
Shower (over the tub)	215.00	320.00	385.00
Shower Rod	30.00	36.00	41.00
Shower Stall	920.00	1,130.00	1,395.00
Sink – Built-in	325.00	390.00	495.00
Sink – Wall mounted	375.00	460.00	595.00
Toilet Seat	65.00	75.00	110.00
Toilet – Floor mounted	535.00	705.00	940.00
Toilet – Wall mounted	775.00	1,005.00	1,285.00
Vanity – Metal	345.00	405.00	485.00
Vanity – Wood	365.00	430.00	505.00

TYPICAL LAYOUT

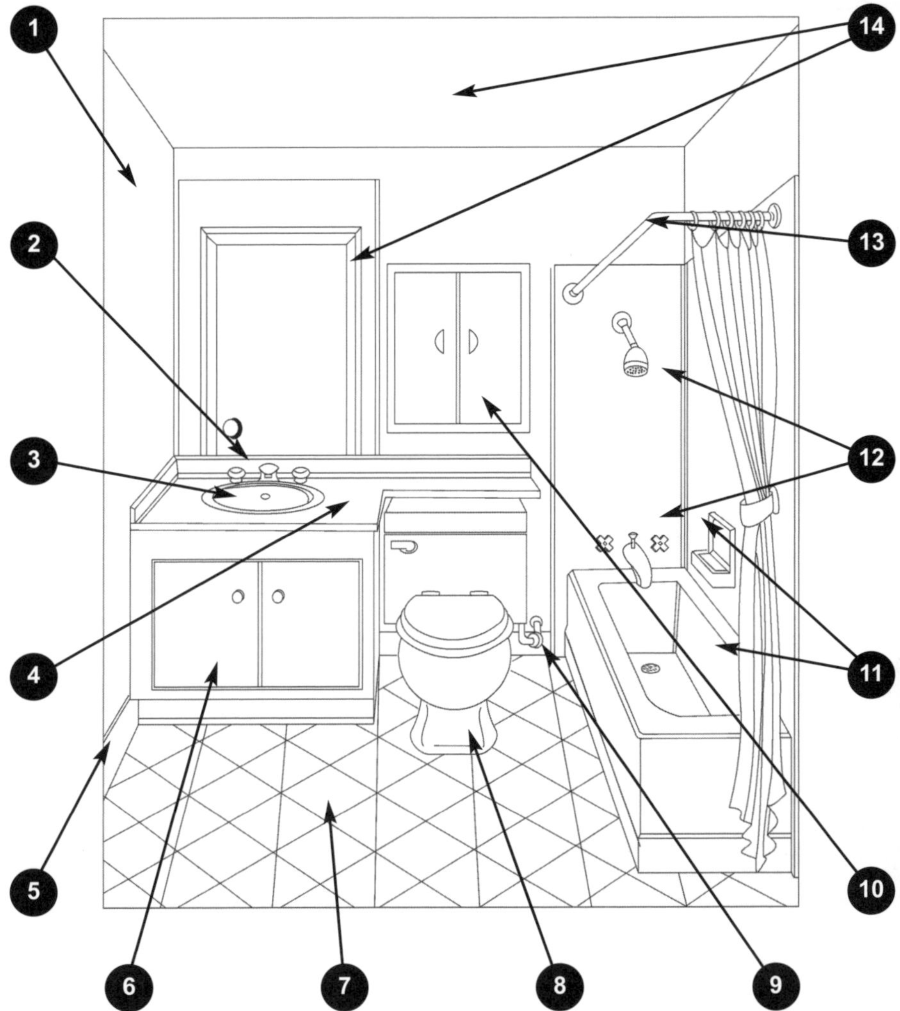

1. Drywall
2. Bathroom Sink Fittings
3. Bathroom Sink
4. Vanity Top
5. Baseboard
6. Vanity Base Cabinet
7. Vinyl Flooring

8. Tank-Type Toilet, 2-Piece
9. Toilet Fittings
10. Medicine Cabinet
11. Fiberglass Tub and Surround
12. Tub and Shower Fittings
13. Curtain Rod
14. Paint

Accessories Set
Minor bathroom attachments, such as paper holder, toothbrush holder, soap dish, etc.

Bathtub
Costs include the bathtub, connection to supply piping, and the drain and overflow.

Bathtub Enclosure
A metal-framed enclosure made with glass or plastic material.

Bathtub/Shower Combination
A one-piece bathtub/shower made of fiberglass. Costs also include the connection to the supply piping and the drain and overflow.

Bidet
Costs include the bidet, faucets and the connection to the supply piping.

Caulking (Bathtub)
A resilient mastic compound between a bathtub and wall or floor surfaces used for waterproofing.

Faucet
A plumbing valve that combines hot and cold water through one outlet.

Medicine Cabinet
A bathroom storage cabinet for medical supplies, toilet articles, etc.

Mirror
A wall-mounted bathroom mirror.

Shower Door
A shower door made of aluminum-framed glass that operates by sliding on a track or swinging on hinges.

Showerhead
A pipe and nozzle through which water is sprayed.

Shower (Over Tub)
Piping, controls and nozzle used to provide water for an over-the-tub shower.

Shower Rod
A steel tube on which shower curtains are hung.

Shower Stall
A prefabricated enclosure for a shower. Costs include the connection to a water supply and drain.

Sink (Built-In)
A built-in bathroom basin. Costs include the connection to a water supply and drain.

Sink (Wall Mounted)
A wall-mounted bathroom basin. Costs include the connection to a water supply and drain.

Toilet Seat
The seat portion of a toilet fixture.

Toilet (Floor Mounted)
A toilet fixture whose base is bolted to the bathroom floor. Costs include the seat (bowl), tank, connection to a water supply and drain.

Toilet (Wall Mounted)
A toilet fixture mounted on a wall. Costs include the seat (bowl), tank, connection to a water supply and drain.

Vanity (Metal)
A metal case used primarily to house a bathroom sink, usually with drawers. Costs do not include the plumbing fixtures.

Vanity (Wood)
A wood case used primarily to house a bathroom sink, usually with drawers. Costs do not include the plumbing fixtures.

CEILING FINISHES

- Acoustical Custom Spray
- Acoustical Panel (Only)
- Acoustical Panel W/ Suspension Grid
- Acoustical Tile (Only)
- Acoustical Tile W/ Furring
- Furring
- Gypsum Board (Standard)
- Gypsum Board (Water Resistant)
- Insulation
- Paint
- Paint (Textured)
- Plaster (Only)
- Plaster (Only) – Thincoat
- Plaster W/ Gypsum, Metal, Or Wood Lath
- Plastic Panels (Only)
- Plastic Panels W/ Suspension Grid
- Plywood Panels
- Repair Existing Plaster
- Stain
- Suspension Grid (Only)
- Wallpaper
- Wood Beams
- Wood Plank

ROOM METHOD – ECONOMY LEVEL

Costs are for replacing (and refinishing) the ceiling completely.

Room size ranges:

Small	(48 Square Feet – 80 Square Feet)	
Medium	(81 Square Feet – 144 Square Feet)	
Large	(145 Square Feet – 200 Square Feet)	
X-large	(201 Square Feet – 275 Square Feet)	

Note: For unusually small or large rooms, use the Unit Method.

Component	Room Size			
(Priced per Room)	**Small**	**Medium**	**Large**	**X-large**
Finishes/Covers:				
Acoustical Custom Spray	$ 70.00	$130.00	$ 185.00	$ 250.00
Acoustical Panel (only)	110.00	175.00	260.00	345.00
Acoustical Panel w/ Suspension Grid	190.00	340.00	510.00	685.00
Acoustical Tile (only)	160.00	280.00	435.00	590.00
Acoustical Tile w/ Furring	260.00	465.00	700.00	965.00
Gypsum Board (standard)	155.00	265.00	405.00	550.00
Gypsum Board (water resistant)	185.00	320.00	500.00	675.00
Paint	65.00	105.00	150.00	210.00
Paint – Texture	55.00	75.00	120.00	170.00
Plaster (only)	265.00	450.00	690.00	1,075.00
Plaster (only) – Thincoat	70.00	125.00	190.00	280.00
Plaster w/ Gypsum Lath	350.00	600.00	925.00	1,260.00
Plaster w/ Metal Lath	395.00	705.00	1,080.00	1,460.00
Plaster w/ Wood Lath	415.00	730.00	1,140.00	1,545.00
Plastic Panels (only)	250.00	420.00	645.00	885.00
Plastic Panels w/ Suspension Grid	320.00	565.00	865.00	1,170.00
Plywood Panels	280.00	505.00	750.00	1,045.00
Stain	60.00	105.00	150.00	210.00
Wallpaper	160.00	275.00	420.00	575.00
Wood Plank	285.00	515.00	775.00	1,070.00
Miscellaneous:				
Ceiling Insulation	$65.00	$120.00	$175.00	$220.00
Repair Existing Plaster	70.00	110.00	170.00	255.00

ROOM METHOD – STANDARD LEVEL

Costs are for replacing (and refinishing) the ceiling completely.

Room size ranges:
- Small   (48 Square Feet – 80 Square Feet)
- Medium (81 Square Feet – 144 Square Feet)
- Large   (145 Square Feet – 200 Square Feet)
- X-large (201 Square Feet – 275 Square Feet)

Note: For unusually small or large rooms, use the Unit Method.

Component	Room Size			
(Priced per Room)	Small	Medium	Large	X-large
Finishes/Covers:				
Acoustical Custom Spray	$ 75.00	$140.00	$ 195.00	$ 270.00
Acoustical Panel (only)	125.00	195.00	315.00	410.00
Acoustical Panel w/ Suspension Grid	215.00	380.00	590.00	795.00
Acoustical Tile (only)	185.00	325.00	475.00	665.00
Acoustical Tile w/ Furring	285.00	515.00	765.00	1,065.00
Gypsum Board (standard)	170.00	280.00	420.00	565.00
Gypsum Board (water resistant)	190.00	335.00	515.00	720.00
Paint	70.00	125.00	180.00	230.00
Paint – Texture	65.00	105.00	145.00	185.00
Plaster (only)	265.00	455.00	720.00	980.00
Plaster (only) – Thincoat	85.00	150.00	200.00	275.00
Plaster w/ Gypsum Lath	360.00	620.00	975.00	1,300.00
Plaster w/ Metal Lath	410.00	720.00	1,120.00	1,495.00
Plaster w/ Wood Lath	435.00	745.00	1,170.00	1,590.00
Plastic Panels (only)	325.00	570.00	855.00	1,175.00
Plastic Panels w/ Suspension Grid	405.00	695.00	1,080.00	1,450.00
Plywood Panels	370.00	635.00	980.00	1,340.00
Stain	65.00	120.00	175.00	220.00
Wallpaper	180.00	315.00	455.00	625.00
Wood Plank	390.00	655.00	1,010.00	1,365.00
Miscellaneous:				
Ceiling Insulation	$ 70.00	$125.00	$180.00	$245.00
Repair Existing Plaster	105.00	155.00	245.00	290.00

ROOM METHOD – CUSTOM LEVEL

Costs are for replacing (and refinishing) the ceiling completely.

Room size ranges:

Small	(48 Square Feet – 80 Square Feet)
Medium	(81 Square Feet – 144 Square Feet)
Large	(145 Square Feet – 200 Square Feet)
X-large	(201 Square Feet – 275 Square Feet)

Note: For unusually small or large rooms, use the Unit Method.

Component	Room Size			
(Priced per Room)	**Small**	**Medium**	**Large**	**X-large**
Finishes/Covers:				
Acoustical Custom Spray	$ 85.00	$150.00	$ 215.00	$ 315.00
Acoustical Panel (only)	150.00	255.00	385.00	525.00
Acoustical Panel w/ Suspension Grid	240.00	410.00	640.00	855.00
Acoustical Tile (only)	210.00	360.00	570.00	755.00
Acoustical Tile w/ Furring	335.00	565.00	870.00	1,180.00
Gypsum Board (standard)	175.00	300.00	450.00	615.00
Gypsum Board (water resistant)	205.00	365.00	560.00	755.00
Paint	80.00	140.00	195.00	275.00
Paint – Texture	65.00	120.00	175.00	230.00
Plaster (only)	275.00	475.00	745.00	1,035.00
Plaster (only) – Thincoat	90.00	155.00	245.00	290.00
Plaster w/ Gypsum Lath	375.00	640.00	995.00	1,345.00
Plaster w/ Metal Lath	415.00	730.00	1,135.00	1,540.00
Plaster w/ Wood Lath	445.00	780.00	1,200.00	1,635.00
Plastic Panels (only)	425.00	750.00	1,180.00	1,595.00
Plastic Panels w/ Suspension Grid	550.00	970.00	1,475.00	1,995.00
Plywood Panels	480.00	820.00	1,250.00	1,720.00
Stain	75.00	130.00	190.00	255.00
Wallpaper	190.00	340.00	510.00	685.00
Wood Plank	485.00	835.00	1,290.00	1,775.00
Miscellaneous:				
Ceiling Insulation	$ 75.00	$130.00	$185.00	$255.00
Repair Existing Plaster	125.00	200.00	325.00	440.00

UNIT METHOD

To replace and refinish individual items, use the costs below:

COMPONENT	QUALITY LEVELS		
(Price per Square Foot)	Economy	Standard	Custom
Finishes/Covers:			
Acoustical Custom Spray	$1.20	$1.25	$1.40
Acoustical Panel (only)	1.55	1.80	2.30
Acoustical Panel w/ Suspension Grid	2.90	3.45	3.75
Acoustical Tile (only)	2.55	2.85	3.35
Acoustical Tile w/ Furring	4.15	4.65	5.10
Gypsum Board (standard)	2.20	2.60	2.65
Gypsum Board (water resistant)	3.00	3.05	3.15
Paint	.85	1.10	1.30
Paint – Texture	.70	.80	1.10
Plaster (only)	3.95	4.15	4.45
Plaster (only) – Thincoat	1.20	1.25	1.30
Plaster w/ Gypsum Lath	5.40	5.50	5.75
Plaster w/ Metal Lath	6.20	6.35	6.55
Plaster w/ Wood Lath	6.55	6.75	7.05
Plastic Panels (only)	3.80	4.85	6.75
Plastic Panels w/ Suspension Grid	5.00	6.30	8.05
Plywood Panels	4.40	5.70	7.30
Stain	0.85	1.10	1.20
Wallpaper	2.50	2.65	2.90
Wood Plank	4.65	5.85	7.45
Miscellaneous:			
Insulation – Ceiling	$1.10	$1.20	$ 1.25
Repair Existing Plaster	1.05	1.30	1.85
Wood Beams – 4" x 6" (priced per linear foot)	7.40	9.50	11.85
Suspension Grid (only)	1.60	1.65	1.75
Furring	1.55	1.70	1.85

TYPICAL CEILING SYSTEM

DRYWALL

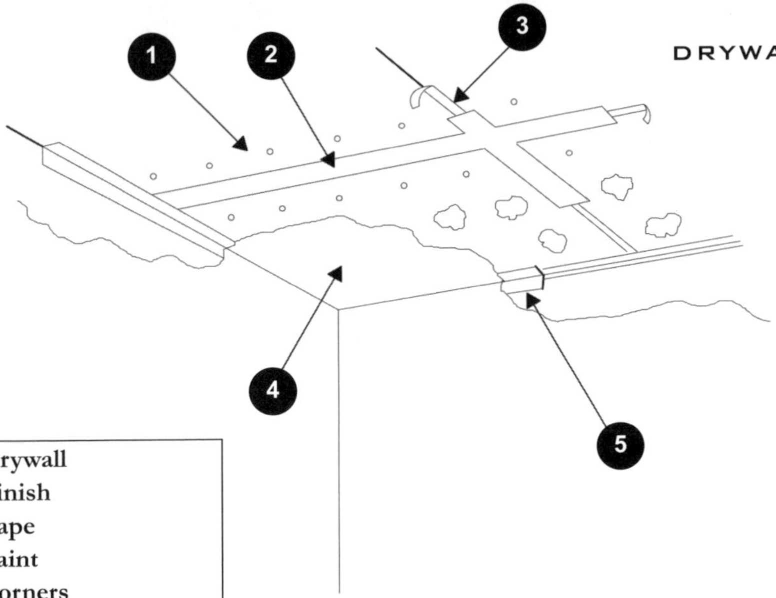

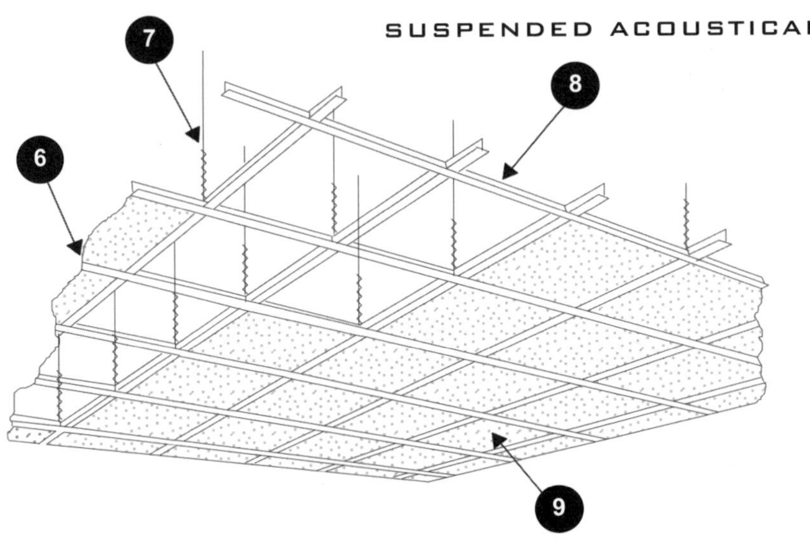

1. Drywall
2. Finish
3. Tape
4. Paint
5. Corners
6. Carrier Channels
7. Hangers
8. Suspension Systems
9. Ceiling Board

SUSPENDED ACOUSTICAL

COMPONENT DESCRIPTIONS

Acoustical Custom Spray
A thin finish coat sprayed onto a ceiling surface. The coat has a granular texture similar to that of acoustical plaster.

Acoustical Panel (Only)
A ceiling cover of a sound-resistant material in panel form. Costs include installed panels only.

Acoustical Panel With Suspension Grid
Costs include the grid system plus panels, which are made of a sound-resistant material.

Acoustical Tile (Only)
A ceiling cover of a sound-resistant material in tile form, usually 12" x 12". Costs include the installed tile only.

Acoustical Tile With Furring
Acoustical tiles applied over furring strips that are fastened to the ceiling.

Furring
Spaced strips of metal or wood that are fastened to the ceiling so that a finished surface can be attached.

Gypsum Board (Standard)
A common ceiling cover of sheets, typically 4' x 8', 1/2" to 5/8" thick. It is also known as sheetrock or drywall. Costs include fill, sand and finishing of taped joints and fastening spots.

Gypsum Board (Water Resistant)
Gypsum board which has been treated to resist the passage of water and moisture.

Insulation
A composite of various types of insulation used above the ceiling. A material with a high resistance to heat flow.

Paint
Costs include primer and finish coats applied to the ceiling.

Paint (Textured)
Primer and finish coats of a heavy-bodied paint applied to the ceiling.

Plaster (Only)
A fine, gypsum-powdered material that provides a good surface finish.

Plaster (Only) – Thincoat
A ceiling cover of a thin mixture, normally applied over gypsum board to provide a desired surface texture.

Plaster W/ Gypsum, Metal, Or Wood Lath
A plaster ceiling cover that is applied with gypsum, metal, or wood lath.

Plastic Panels (Only)
Panels of plastic used as a ceiling cover. The costs are for the installed panel only.

Plastic Panels W/ Suspension Grid
Plastic panels installed in a suspended-grid system.

Plywood Panels
A hardwood ceiling cover made of plywood panels.

Repair Existing Plaster
The repair of hairline cracks, peeling, etc., in a plaster ceiling. Used for small repair areas only.

Stain
A wax-based stain applied as a protective coating on interior wood ceilings.

Suspension Grid (Only)
A suspension-grid system used for supporting ceiling panels or lighting fixtures. Costs include the grid system only.

Wallpaper
A ceiling cover of quality paper.

Wood Beams
A nonstructural, wood or synthetic member that horizontally spans the ceiling and is used for ornamentation.

Wood Plank
A ceiling cover of individual long pieces of wood.

DOORS

- FRAME
- GARAGE DOORS
- GARAGE DOOR
  OPENERS — ELECTRIC
- HARDWARE
- METAL DOORS
- MISCELLANEOUS DOORS
- PAINT
- SCREEN DOORS
- STAIN
- STORM DOORS
- THRESHOLD
- TRIM
- WOOD DOORS

UNIT METHOD – EXTERIOR DOORS

Costs are for replacement of doors unless otherwise noted.
Complete doors include: door, frame and hardware.

| Component | Quality Levels | | |
(Priced as Shown)	Economy	Standard	Custom
Garage (overhead) Doors:			
Metal (sectional) – Complete	$740.00	$ 820.00	$ 895.00
Metal (single leaf) – Complete	720.00	795.00	875.00
Plastic (sectional) – Complete	925.00	1,000.00	1,070.00
Wood (sectional) – Complete	740.00	800.00	845.00
Wood (single leaf) – Complete	645.00	765.00	930.00
Miscellaneous Items:			
Entry Door Frame – Metal (per door)	$160.00	$175.00	$185.00
Entry Door Frame – Wood (per door)	130.00	155.00	185.00
Entry Door Hardware – per Door	85.00	105.00	110.00
Entry Door Trim – per Linear Foot	3.35	3.70	4.15
Entry Door Trim – per Side	65.00	70.00	75.00
Garage Door Opener – Electric	575.00	650.00	740.00
Paint Entry Door – per Side	50.00	55.00	60.00
Paint Entry Door and Trim – per Side	55.00	60.00	65.00
Paint Garage Door – per Side	85.00	90.00	110.00
Stain Entry Door – per Side	65.00	70.00	75.00
Stain Entry Door and Trim – per Side	70.00	80.00	90.00
Threshold – per Door	23.00	28.00	34.00

UNIT METHOD – EXTERIOR DOORS

Costs are for replacement of doors unless otherwise noted.
Complete doors include: door, frame and hardware.

Component	Quality Levels		
(Priced per Door)	**Economy**	**Standard**	**Custom**
Wood Entry Doors:			
Custom – Complete	$1,250.00	$1,515.00	$1,795.00
Custom – Door and Hardware	1,125.00	1,350.00	1,630.00
Custom – Door Only	1,050.00	1,255.00	1,540.00
Custom (stock) – Complete	710.00	880.00	1,055.00
Custom (stock) – Door and Hardware	750.00	925.00	1,105.00
Custom (stock) – Door Only	685.00	825.00	1,010.00
Standard (stock) – Complete	570.00	725.00	950.00
Standard (stock) – Door and Hardware	435.00	575.00	760.00
Standard (stock) – Door Only	365.00	490.00	680.00
Metal Entry Doors:			
Standard – Complete	$655.00	$785.00	$930.00
Standard – Door and Hardware	470.00	605.00	740.00
Standard – Door Only	405.00	520.00	670.00
Miscellaneous Entry Doors:			
Aluminum Storm – Complete	$ 290.00	$ 360.00	$ 450.00
Dutch – Complete	585.00	765.00	1,025.00
Dutch – Door and Hardware	455.00	610.00	835.00
Dutch – Door Only	375.00	535.00	745.00
French – Complete	605.00	740.00	925.00
Screen Door – Complete	160.00	200.00	265.00
Sliding Aluminum/Vinyl – Complete	985.00	1,125.00	1,255.00
Sliding Screen – Complete	105.00	125.00	150.00
Sliding Wood – Complete	1,840.00	2,225.00	2,685.00
Wood Storm – Complete	310.00	365.00	415.00

UNIT METHOD – INTERIOR DOORS

Costs are for replacement of doors unless otherwise noted.
Complete doors include: door, frame and hardware.

Component	Quality Levels		
(Priced per Door)	Economy	Standard	Custom
Wood Doors:			
Closet, Bifold – Complete	$195.00	$235.00	$285.00
Closet, Mirror – Complete	375.00	435.00	525.00
Closet, Sliding – Complete	190.00	210.00	230.00
Flush HC (hardwood veneer) – Complete	395.00	455.00	515.00
Flush HC (hardwood veneer) – Door & Hardware	355.00	405.00	470.00
Flush HC (hardwood veneer) – Door Only	310.00	360.00	405.00
Flush HC (softwood veneer) – Complete	270.00	305.00	360.00
Flush HC (softwood veneer) – Door & Hardware	230.00	275.00	350.00
Flush HC (softwood veneer) – Door Only	190.00	220.00	275.00
Flush Solid Core – Complete	375.00	455.00	545.00
Flush Solid Core – Door & Hardware	255.00	350.00	405.00
Flush Solid Core – Door Only	220.00	285.00	355.00
French – Complete	430.00	505.00	585.00
French – Door & Hardware	340.00	390.00	455.00
French – Door Only	290.00	340.00	390.00
Pocket – Complete	370.00	430.00	510.00
Pocket – Door & Hardware	215.00	260.00	330.00
Pocket – Door Only	170.00	210.00	255.00
Raised Panel – Complete	405.00	425.00	515.00
Raised Panel – Door & Hardware	220.00	260.00	305.00
Raised Panel – Door Only	190.00	210.00	240.00
Miscellaneous:			
Door Frame – per Door	$105.00	$120.00	$130.00
Door Hardware – per Door	55.00	60.00	70.00
Door Trim – per Linear Foot	3.05	3.50	3.75
Door Trim – per Side	70.00	75.00	80.00
Paint Door – per Side	40.00	46.00	51.00
Paint Door and Trim – per Side	55.00	65.00	70.00
Stain Door – per Side	65.00	70.00	75.00
Stain Door and Trim – per Side	75.00	80.00	85.00
Threshold – per Door	28.00	31.00	33.00

DETERMINING DOOR HANDEDNESS

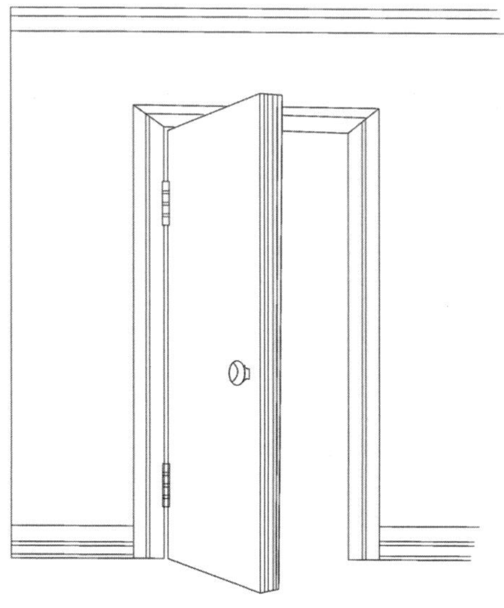

RIGHT-HAND DOOR

If a door opens toward you and the knob is to the right, the door is right-handed.

LEFT-HAND DOOR

If a door opens toward you and the knob is on the left, the door is left-handed.

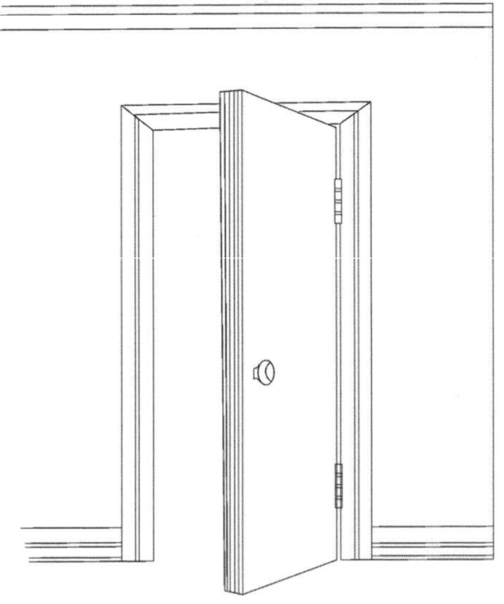

TYPICAL LAYOUT

INTERIOR DOOR SYSTEM

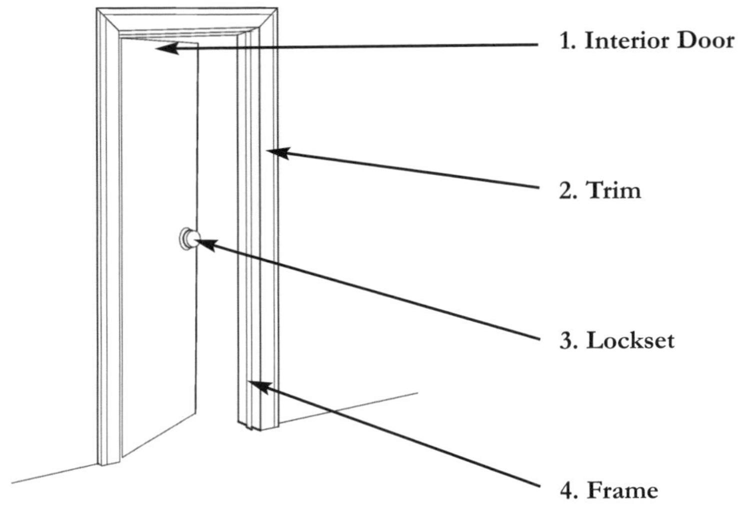

EXTERIOR DOOR SYSTEM

COMPONENT DESCRIPTIONS

EXTERIOR DOORS

Aluminum Storm Door (Complete)

An auxiliary door placed outside of an existing door. Costs also include the hardware closer and chain.

Dutch Door (Complete)

A door cut horizontally through the lock rail so that the upper or lower part of the door can be opened independently. The costs also include the frame and hardware.

Dutch Door And Hardware

A Dutch door including hardware, but excluding the frame.

Dutch Door (Only)

A door cut horizontally through the lock rail so that the upper or lower part of the door can be opened independently.

Entry Door Frame

A surrounding door framing unit that includes the jambs, stops, etc. Does not include threshold and trim.

Entry Door Hardware

Double-locking hardware with dead bolt and hinges.

Entry Door Trim

Any visible wood member around the exterior perimeter of the door.

French Door (Complete)

An exterior door having a top rail, bottom rail and stiles with glass panes throughout its entire area. Costs include the door, frame and hardware.

Garage Door (Overhead Single Leaf)

A swing-up garage door of single-leaf construction.

Garage Door (Overhead Sectional)

A garage door consisting of more than one section.

Garage Door Opener

An electric-powered mechanism for opening or closing a garage door.

Metal Standard Entry Door (Complete)

An exterior door of metal construction with an insulating core. The costs include the door frame and hardware.

Metal Standard Entry Door And Hardware

An exterior metal door including hardware, but excluding the frame.

Metal Standard Entry Door (Only)

An exterior metal door of metal construction with an insulating core.

Paint Door

Costs include primer and finished coats applied to the doors.

Screen Door (Complete)

An auxiliary mesh-cloth wood or aluminum entry door.

COMPONENT DESCRIPTIONS

Sliding Door (Aluminum or Vinyl – Complete)
A sliding aluminum or vinyl door with double glass. Costs include hardware and frame.

Sliding Door Screen (Complete)
An auxiliary mesh-cloth framed door mounted on a track sliding horizontally.

Sliding Door (Wood – Complete)
A sliding wood door with double glass. Costs include hardware and frame.

Stain Door
A protective stain used on wood doors.

Threshold
A strip fastened to the floor beneath the door to cover the floor material joint and to provide weather protection.

Wood Custom Entry Door (Complete)
A prefabricated, highly decorative wood door of custom size. Costs include frame and hardware.

Wood Custom Entry Door And Hardware
A custom door including hardware, but excluding the frame.

Wood Custom Entry Door (Only)
A prefabricated, highly decorative wood door of custom size.

Wood Custom Stock Entry Door (Complete)
A high-quality prefabricated door in standard sizes, including frame and hardware.

Wood Custom Stock Entry Door & Hardware
A custom-stock door including hardware, but excluding the frame.

Wood Custom Stock Entry Door (Only)
A high-quality prefabricated wood door in standard sizes.

Wood Standard Stock Entry Door (Complete)
A smooth-surfaced, solid core, solid hardwood door. Costs include frame and hardware.

Wood Standard Stock Entry Door & Hardware
A standard stock door including hardware, but excluding the frame.

Wood Standard Stock Entry Door (Only)
A smooth-surfaced, solid core, solid hardwood door.

Wood Storm Door (Complete)
An auxiliary door placed outside of an existing door. Costs include hardware, closer and chain.

INTERIOR DOORS

Closet Bifold (Complete)
A double-folding closet door. Costs also include hardware and frame.

Closet Mirror (Complete)
A mirrored-surface door. Costs also include hardware and frame.

Closet Sliding (Complete)
A door mounted on a track that slides parallel to the wall. Costs also include the hardware and frame.

Door Frame
An assembly of two upright members and head over a doorway, enclosing the doorway and providing support on which to hang the doors.

COMPONENT DESCRIPTIONS

Door Hardware
> A complete hardware system including accessories such as knobs, escutcheons, plates, hinges, etc.

Door Trim
> The interior wood trim of an exterior door or the wood trim on either side of an interior door.

Flush HC Wood Door (Complete)
> An interior hollow-core door with either a hardwood or a softwood face. Costs also include the frame and hardware.

Flush HC Wood Door (Only)
> A hollow-core door with hardware, but excluding the frame.

Flush HC Wood Door (Only)
> An interior hollow-core door with either a hardwood or softwood face.

Flush Solid-Core Wood Door (Complete)
> An interior door with a solid core, usually made of wood. Costs also include the frame and hardware.

Flush Solid-Core Wood Door And Hardware
> An interior solid-core door with hardware, but excluding the frame.

Flush Solid-Core Wood Door (Only)
> An interior door with a solid core usually made of wood.

French Door (Complete)
> An interior door having a top rail and stiles, with glass panes throughout. Costs include hardware and frame.

French Door & Hardware
> A French door including hardware, but excluding the frame.

French Door (Only)
> An interior door having a top rail and stiles, with glass panes throughout.

Paint Door
> Costs include one coat of primer and one finish coat.

Pocket Door (Complete)
> A door that, when opened, slides into a framed wall recess. Costs include the frame and hardware.

Pocket Door & Hardware
> A pocket door with hardware, but excluding the frame.

Pocket Door (Only)
> A door that, when opened, slides into a framed wall recess.

Raised-Wood Panel Door (Complete)
> A door having stiles, rails and sometimes muntins that form one or more frames around recessed or raised panels. Costs include frame and hardware.

Raised-Wood Panel Door And Hardware
> A raised-wood panel door with hardware, but excluding the frame.

Raised-Wood Panel Door (Only)
> A door having stiles, rails and sometimes muntins that form one or more frames around recessed or raised panels.

Stain Door
> A protective stain used on wood doors.

Threshold
> A strip fastened to the floor beneath a door to cover the joint where two types of flooring material meet.

ELECTRICAL

- **Antenna (TV/Radio)**
- **Cable (Wire)**
- **Candelabra**
- **Ceiling Fans**
- **Conduits**
- **Distribution Subpanel**
- **Doorbell/Buzzer**
- **Door Chimes**
- **Exterior Fixtures**
- **Fire Alarms**
- **Fluorescent Fixtures**
- **Grounding Rod**
- **Incandescent Fixtures**
- **Intercoms**
- **Lightning Arrester**
- **Outlet Box**
- **Panelboard (Circuit Breakers)**
- **Photocell Device**
- **Receptacles**
- **Security Alarms**
- **Service (1 Phase)**
- **Spotlight (Decorative)**
- **Switches**
- **Telephones**
- **Thermostats**
- **Timer**
- **Track Lighting**
- **Wiring**

UNIT METHOD

The cost of electrical fixtures (e.g. light fixtures, outlets, switches, etc.) includes the cost of direct connection to an existing electrical outlet or hardwiring to an existing electrical box and power source. If you need to run new service or replace or repair existing service connections, use appropriate components in addition to the fixture.

To replace individual items use the costs below:

Component	Quality Levels		
(Priced Each)	Economy	Standard	Custom
Lighting Fixtures:			
Candelabra	$375.00	$540.00	$780.00
Ceiling Fan – w/ Light	405.00	540.00	735.00
Exterior – Decorative	160.00	215.00	315.00
Exterior – Plain	70.00	80.00	125.00
Exterior – Security	320.00	460.00	710.00
Fluorescent – 4' Long (strip)	75.00	110.00	140.00
Fluorescent – 4' Long (surface mounted)	130.00	150.00	185.00
Fluorescent – Decorative	195.00	230.00	260.00
Fluorescent – Recessed	160.00	210.00	280.00
Incandescent – Decorative	160.00	210.00	285.00
Incandescent – Plain	75.00	105.00	130.00
Incandescent – Recessed	145.00	160.00	190.00
Spotlight – Decorative	160.00	215.00	325.00
Track Lighting – 4' Section	120.00	130.00	140.00
Track Lighting – 8' Section	160.00	180.00	190.00
Miscellaneous Items:			
Antenna – TV/Radio	$ 140.00	$ 175.00	$ 195.00
Ceiling Fan	250.00	340.00	455.00
Doorbell/Buzzer	55.00	65.00	70.00
Door Chime	105.00	130.00	175.00
Doorbell/Buzzer/Chime – Transformer	60.00	70.00	80.00
Fire Alarm Control Panel	1,765.00	2,260.00	2,925.00
Fire Alarm Station	130.00	155.00	200.00
Intercom Speaker	130.00	155.00	190.00
Intercom Station	110.00	140.00	175.00
Intercom Station w/ Radio	540.00	685.00	875.00
Lightning Arrester	495.00	620.00	775.00
Photocell Device	80.00	105.00	125.00
Security Alarm Base	375.00	550.00	705.00
Security Alarm Points	50.00	65.00	105.00
Telephone	130.00	155.00	190.00
Telephone Base Station	415.00	520.00	640.00
Telephone/TV Outlet	65.00	70.00	80.00
Thermostat	80.00	105.00	120.00
Thermostat – Programmable	150.00	180.00	195.00
Timer	120.00	145.00	185.00

UNIT METHOD

To replace individual items use the costs below:

Component (Price Each Unless Otherwise Shown)	
Outlets, Switches and Receptacles:	
Outlet Box (w/ nonmetallic sheathed cable)	$ 75.00
Outlet Box (w/ conduit – flexible)	75.00
Outlet Box (w/ conduit – rigid)	115.00
Outlet Box – Exterior (w/ cable)	100.00
Outlet Box – Interior (w/ 110 volt cable)	90.00
Outlet Box – Interior (w/ 220 volt cable)	95.00
Receptacle – 110 Volt	65.00
Receptacle – 220 Volt	95.00
Receptacle – Exterior	90.00
Switch – Wall	65.00
Switch – 3-way	110.00
Switch – Dimmer	70.00
Switch – Exterior	90.00
Service and Service Wiring:	
Cable (wire) (per linear foot)	$ 3.25
Conduit – Flexible (per linear foot)	5.20
Conduit – Rigid (per linear foot)	10.65
Distribution – Subpanel	485.00
Grounding Rod	215.00
Panelboard (circuit breakers)	1,160.00
Service – 1 Phase	2,330.00
House Wiring (Priced per Linear Foot):	
Wiring – 110 Volt	$3.60
Wiring – 220 Volt	6.60
Wiring – Coaxial (TV/radio)	2.75
Wiring – Low Voltage (doorbell/thermostat)	1.15

Bathroom (Mirrors)

Use incandescents or warm white fluorescents on each side of the mirror, about 30 inches apart. Install an incandescent or fluorescent ceiling fixture as well. (For mirrors 36 inches or wider, install three or four incandescents in a 22-inch-minimum-width fixture, or install a 36- to 48-inch diffused fluorescent fixture along the top of the mirror.)

Bathroom (Shower Light)

Use an incandescent in a wet-location ceiling fixture.

Bathroom (Toilet Compartment)

Install either a ceiling or wall fixture with an incandescent or fluorescent lamp.

Bedroom (General)

Install a ceiling fixture or track lighting of wattage sufficient to provide uniform lighting. Install small ceiling lights in large closets.

Bedroom (Reading in Bed)

Provide an individual incandescent or fluorescent lamp with the bottom of the shade at eye level and 22 inches to the side of the center of the book. As an option, headboard track lighting should provide one incandescent bulb for each person, mounted 30 inches above mattress level.

Dining Room (Chandelier)

Provide a total of 300 watts of incandescent lamps. The bottom of the chandelier should be at least 12 inches narrower than the table and 30 inches above the surface.

Entrance (Foyer)

In small areas, use incandescent or fluorescent. For larger areas, use incandescent. Consider wall lamps or a chandelier.

Entrance (Outside)

Flank the door with a pair of incandescent wall fixtures 66 inches above standing level at the door. If only one fixture is possible, mount it at the lock side of the door.

Hallway (Ceiling or Wall)

Install at least one fixture every 10 feet. Recessed or track accent lighting for wall art is acceptable.

Kitchen (Ceiling)

Install either incandescent or fluorescent ceiling fixtures sufficient for general lighting.

Kitchen (Sink and Range)

Install, over the front edge of the counter, two downlights with reflective flood lamps spaced 18 inches apart. Range hoods require incandescents.

Kitchen (Under Cabinet)

Mount as close to the cabinet front as possible. Cover at least two-thirds of the total counter length.

Kitchen (Dinette)

Install a pendant incandescent or fluorescent over the table or counter.

Living & Family (General)

Install a combination of accent and wall-washing track lighting.

Living & Family (Music Stand)

Install one reflective or parabolic reflector flood lamp, in a recessed or track fixture, 12 inches to the left and 24 inches in front of the music.

Living & Family (Television)

Provide low-level lighting to avoid reflections from the screen.

Living & Family (Game Table)

Install one recessed incandescent or fluorescent fixture over each half of the table. For a card or pool table, mount a single shaded pendant 36 inches above the center of the table.

Living & Family (Bar)

Install recessed or track reflector bulbs, 16 to 24 inches apart, over bars.

Site (Vegetation)

Light trees and bushes with spotlights mounted on walls or from ground level. Do not allow light to shine at neighboring houses.

Stairs

Provide fixtures at both top and bottom. Control them from each location with three-way switches.

Study (Desk)

Position one incandescent or fluorescent lamp with the bottom of the shade 15 inches above the desk and 12 inches from the front edge.

Track (Accent)

Ceiling-mounted fixtures should be positioned at a 30-degree angle to prevent light from shining in anyones eyes. Usually, one fixture is required for each object being accented. To locate the ceiling fixture, the distance from the wall should be 60 percent of the vertical distance from the center of the object to the ceiling.

TYPICAL WIRING LAYOUT

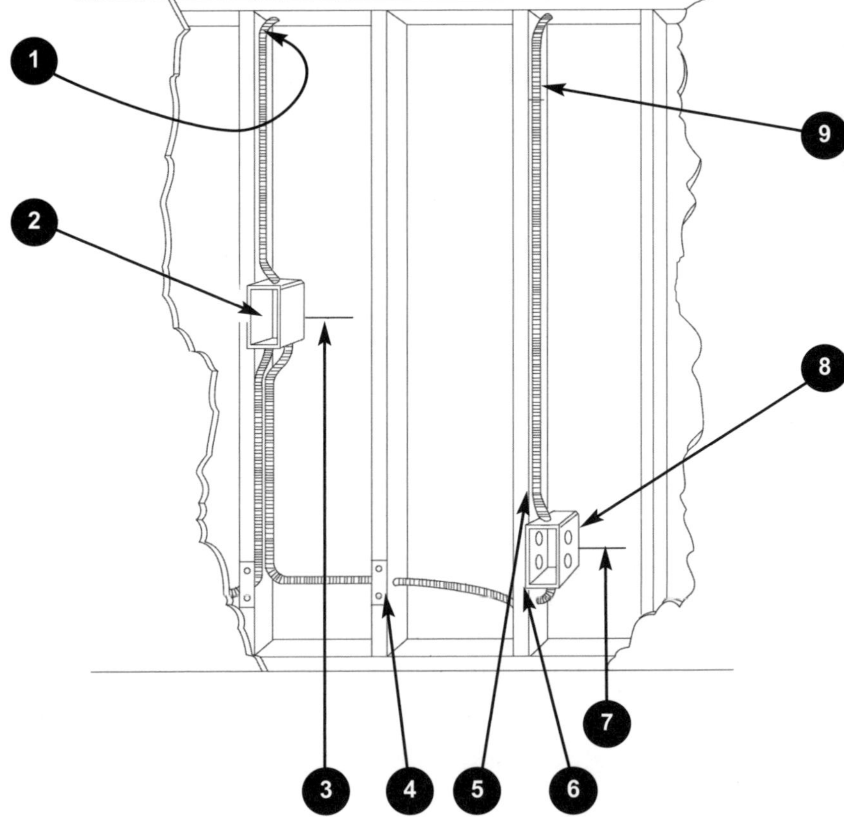

1. Bend Radius

2. Switch Box

3. Box Height 44" – 48"

4. Steel over Cable if within 1 ½" of Stud Face

5. Staple within 8" of Box

6. Hole 1 ½" from Stud face

7. Metal Box Height 12" – 18"

8. Outlet Metal Box

9. Staple Cable every 4' 6" minimum

COMPONENT DESCRIPTIONS

Antenna (TV/Radio)
A roof-mounted antenna including the cable and connectors.

Cable (Wire)
Insulated interior or exterior wires bound together and covered with a nonmetallic sheath. Also known as Romex.

Candelabra
A fixture with multiple lights suspended from the ceiling. Costs include the lamps.

Ceiling Fan
A fan fixture suspended from the ceiling.

Ceiling Fan With Light
A combination fan/light fixture suspended from the ceiling.

Conduit (Flexible)
A metal raceway made of an easily bent construction. Costs include the fittings, elbows, clamps and wiring.

Conduit (Rigid)
A raceway of metal pipe of standard thickness that permits the cutting of standard threads or connectors. Costs include the fittings, elbows, clamps and wiring.

Distribution Subpanel
An assembly of busses and connections, overcurrent devices, switches and control apparatus, constructed for installation as a complete unit. Costs include the cabinet.

Doorbell/Buzzer
A doorbell or buzzer unit. Costs do not include the transformer.

Door Chime
A chime unit. Costs do not include the transformer.

Doorbell/Chime Transformer
A small transformer which supplies low-voltage power for operating a doorbell, buzzer or chime.

Exterior Fixture (Decorative)
An exterior light fixture with decorative features, such as an entrance light. Costs include the lamp.

Exterior Fixture (Plain)
An exterior nondecorative lighting unit. Costs include the lamp.

Exterior Fixture (Security)
An outdoor, wall-mounted light fixture for security lighting, and usually mounted to prevent vandalism. These may sometimes have a high-intensity bulb. Costs include the lamp.

Fire Alarm Control Panel
The base control unit of a fire security system that can include a built-in local alarm and/or a remote signaling transmitter.

Fire Alarm Station
A remote signaling device that is hardwired to a control panel.

Fluorescent Fixture (4'-Long Strip)
A 4'-long lighting fixture, having either one or two tubes, typically hung from the ceiling. Costs include the tubes.

Fluorescent Fixture (4'-Long Surface Mount)
A 4'-long lighting fixture, having either one or two tubes mounted directly to the ceiling.

Fluorescent Fixture (Decorative)
A complete lighting fixture with a louver or diffusing panel, a decorative enclosure and the necessary tubes.

Fluorescent Fixture (Recessed)
A fluorescent fixture set into the ceiling so that the lower edge of the fixture is flush with the ceiling. Costs include the tubes.

Grounding Rod
A polarity-type rod used to provide protection to an electrical system.

Incandescent Fixture (Decorative)
A decorative lighting fixture that uses an incandescent bulb. Costs include the lamp.

Incandescent Fixture (Plain)
An incandescent light fixture, either wall or ceiling surface mounted. Costs include the lamp.

Incandescent Fixture (Recessed)
An incandescent fixture set into a ceiling so that the lower edge of the fixture is flush with the ceiling.

Intercom Speaker
A remote speaker of an intercom system that receives from base or remote stations, but cannot transmit.

Intercom Station
A remote station of an intercom system that both transmits and receives.

Intercom Station With Radio
The base station of a radio/intercom system.

Lightning Arrester
A roof-mounted device to provide lightning protection.

Outlet Box
An outlet box with connectors for attaching to the conduit. Costs do not include receptacles or switches.

Panelboard (Circuit Breakers)
An assembly of buses and connections, overcurrent devices, switches and control apparatus, all of which is constructed as a unit that includes the cabinet.

Photocell Device
A switching device incorporated into an electric circuit that is light controlled.

Receptacle (110 Volt)
A device installed in an outlet box to receive two plugs for the supply of electricity to appliances or equipment.

Receptacle (220 Volt)
A 220-volt contact device installed at the outlet for the connection of a single attachment such as a dryer or range.

Receptacle (Exterior)
A plug-in device installed in an outside outlet.

Security Alarm Base
The base control unit of a security system that can include a built-in local alarm and an internal standby battery.

Security Alarm Points
A remote sensor device to activate an alarm.

Service (1 Phase)
A 200-amp distribution panel with a main switch or circuit breaker. Costs include the waterhead and lead-in.

Spotlight (Decorative)
A decorative light fixture that projects a direct beam of light.

Switch (Dimmer)
An electrical control device that varies the output of an electrical light fixture.

Switch (Exterior)
An exterior weatherproof device used to connect and disconnect an electrical circuit.

Switch (3-Way)
A wall-mounted device used to open or close a circuit or to change the connection of a circuit.

Switch (Wall)
A wall-mounted device used to open or close an electrical circuit.

Telephone
A wall-mounted telephone unit with a connection to an outlet. Costs do not include the wiring or outlet.

Telephone Base Station
The base station for a built-in, in-house telephone system. Costs do not include the wiring, outlet or remote telephones.

Telephone/TV Outlet
An outlet including jack, connections and cover for a telephone or television line. Costs do not include the wiring.

Thermostat
A device activated by temperature changes that controls the furnace and/or air-conditioning output limits. Costs do not include the wiring.

Thermostat (Programmable)
A device that contains a clock system to determine the time periods in which the heating/cooling system controls can be activated. Costs do not include the wiring.

Timer
A device that manually controls the length of time an electrical circuit will remain on or off.

Track Lighting
A system of lights attached to a section of track and affixed to a wall, ceiling or beam. Costs include the lamps.

Wiring (110 Volt)
Electrical wiring/conductors carrying 110 volts of power.

Wiring (220 Volt)
Electrical wiring/conductors carrying 220 volts of power.

Wiring Coaxial (TV/Radio)
A coaxial transmission line used in the transmission of television or radio signals. Costs include the wire and terminal connectors.

Wiring Low Voltage (Doorbell/Thermostat)
A circuit designed for low voltage, such as a doorbell circuit or thermostat.

EXTERIOR WALLS

- ALUMINUM SIDING
- ASBESTOS SIDING
- BATTEN SIDING STRIPS
- BRICK (SOLID)
- BRICK VENEER
- CAULKING
- COLUMNS (WOOD)
- CONCRETE
- FURRING
- HARDBOARD BOARDS
- HARDBOARD PANELS
- INSULATION
- MASONRY BLOCK
- PAINT
- PLYWOOD (TEXTURED)
- REPOINT MASONRY
- SANDBLASTING
- SANDING
- SHEATHING
- SHINGLES (MISCELLANEOUS)
- STAIN
- STONE VENEER
- STUCCO
- STUD FRAMING
- TRIM (WOOD/METAL)
- VINYL SIDING
- WATERPROOFING
- WOOD SHAKES
- WOOD SHINGLES
- WOOD SIDING

UNIT METHOD

Costs are for replacement of exterior wall materials unless otherwise noted. All square foot costs are based on the area of the exterior wall.

Component	Quality Levels		
(Priced Per Square Foot Unless Otherwise Shown)	Economy	Standard	Custom
Architectural – Facades:			
Aluminum Siding	$ 4.15	$ 4.50	$ 4.70
Asbestos Siding	3.25	3.45	3.55
Brick Veneer	16.90	17.40	17.95
Hardboard – Boards	3.10	3.40	3.60
Hardboard – Panels	2.45	2.75	3.05
Plywood – Textured	2.70	2.75	2.95
Shingles – Miscellaneous	3.40	2.45	3.75
Stone Veneer – Imitation	9.40	10.10	10.60
Stone Veneer – Natural	23.05	26.80	31.35
Stucco – On Framing	4.45	4.65	5.25
Stucco – On Masonry	2.40	2.55	2.80
Vinyl Siding	3.45	3.60	3.85
Wood Siding – Bevel	5.10	5.45	5.70
Wood Siding – Clapboard	7.25	7.45	7.75
Wood Shakes	3.75	4.35	4.85
Wood Shingles	3.75	4.05	4.85
Architectural – Miscellaneous:			
Batten Siding Strips (per linear foot)	$ .85	$ 1.05	$ 1.10
Column – Wood (per linear foot)	120.00	135.00	170.00
Column – Wood (per column, 1 story)	1,110.00	1,335.00	1,630.00
Column – Wood (per column, 2 story)	1,990.00	2,410.00	2,925.00
Trim – Wood/Metal (per linear foot)	2.70	2.90	3.50

UNIT METHOD

Costs are for replacement of exterior wall materials unless otherwise noted. All square foot costs are based on the area of exterior wall.

Component (Priced per Square Foot Unless Otherwise Shown)	
Finishes:	
Paint – Epoxy/Urethane	$2.30
Paint – Gutters/Downspouts (per linear foot)	.65
Paint – Masonry	1.05
Paint – Masonry, Waterproof	.70
Paint – Ornamental Iron	1.20
Paint – Removal	2.30
Paint – Stucco	1.30
Paint – Wood Siding	1.25
Paint – Wood Trim (per linear foot)	1.05
Sanding	.55
Sandblasting	6.15
Stain – Wood	.70
Structural Walls:	
Brick – Solid	$24.80
Concrete	23.15
Furring	1.55
Masonry Block	12.90
Sheathing	2.05
Stud Framing	2.90
Miscellaneous:	
Caulking (per linear foot)	$4.35
Insulation – Batt	1.05
Insulation – Blown-in	.80
Insulation – Rigid	1.40
Repoint Masonry	4.15
Waterproofing – Building Paper	.25
Waterproofing – Cement Parging	2.15
Waterproofing – Hot Mopped	.65
Waterproofing – Plastic Sheeting	.35

TYPICAL MATERIALS

MATERIAL	COST RANGE
Aluminum	Medium
Hardboard	Low
Horizontal Wood	Medium to High
Plywood	Low
Shingles	High
Stucco	Low to Medium
Vertical Wood	Medium
Vinyl	Low to Medium

EXTERIOR WALL TERMINOLOGY

FRAME SYSTEM

1. Framing (studs)

2. Metal Lath

3. Sheathing

4. Stucco

5. Windows

6. Doors

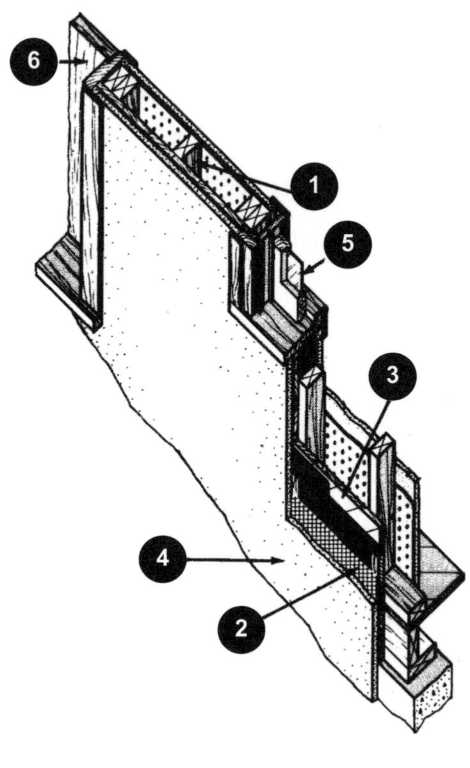

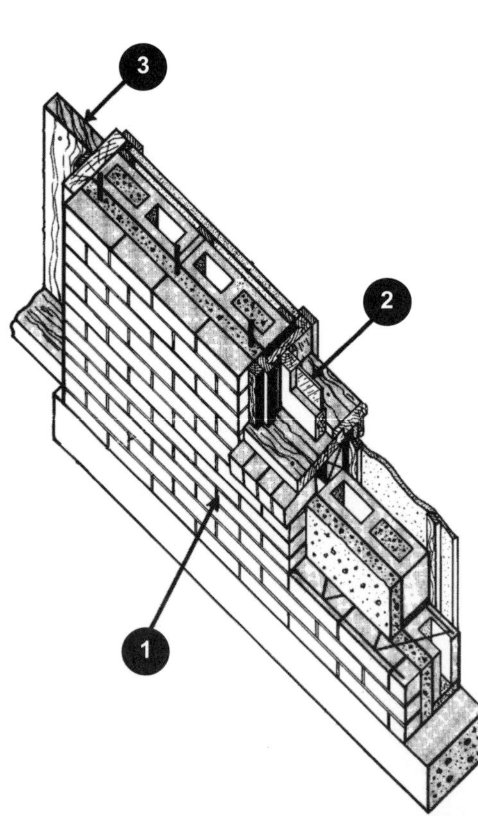

MASONRY SYSTEM

1. Common Brick with Block Backup

2. Windows

3. Doors

TYPICAL SYSTEMS

BRICK OR STONE VENEER

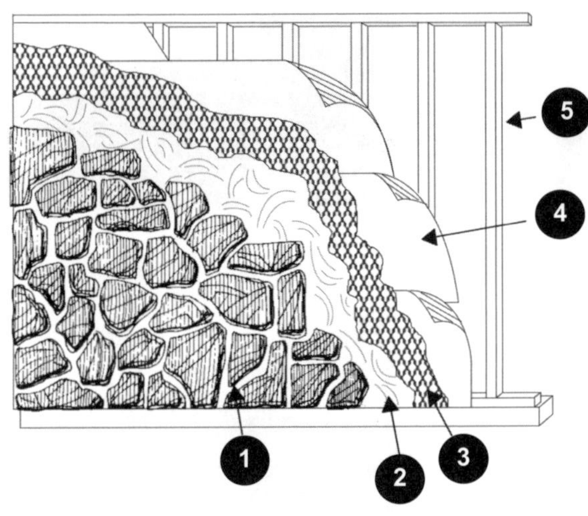

1. Brick or Stone

2. Scratch Coat

3. Metal Lath

4. Building Paper

5. Stud

ALUMINUM OR VINYL SIDING

1. Trim

2. Building Paper

3. Aluminum or
   Vinyl Horizontal Siding

4. Stud

5. Backer, Insulation Board

BRICK WALL PATTERNS

Running -5

English

Common

Dutch

Common with Flemish Headers

Flemish Cross

Garden Wall

Flemish

STONE WALL PATTERNS

LOCAL STONE

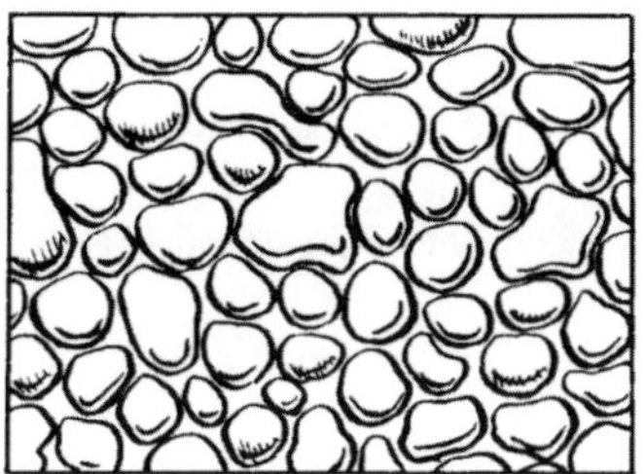

Cobble

Rubble

ASHLAR FACING

Coursed Saw Bed

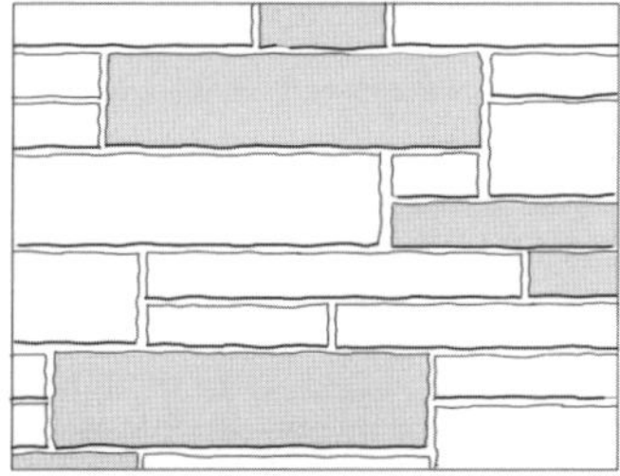

Random Rough Bed

Aluminum Siding
An exterior wall covering typically composed of 1" x 8" aluminum cladding applied over a stud wall.

Asbestos Siding
An exterior wall covering composed of asbestos siding applied over a stud wall.

Batten Siding Strips
1" x 2" wood strips nailed vertically to siding sheets at the butted joints.

Brick (Solid)
An exterior wall consisting of concrete or clay bricks.

Brick Veneer
A nonbearing outside wall facing of brick providing a decorative surface.

Caulking
Installation of a resilient mastic compound used to seal cracks, fill joints, prevent leakage and/or provide waterproofing.

Columns (Wood)
An architectural, hollow or solid wood column that serves as ornamentation. May or may not be load bearing.

Concrete
An exterior wall of reinforced concrete.

Furring
Wood strip spacers that are fastened to a wall to provide a flat plane upon which siding or other surface material may be installed.

Hardboard Boards
An exterior wall covering typically composed of 1" x 12" hardboard applied over a stud wall.

Hardboard Panels
An exterior wall covering typically composed of 4' x 8' hardboard sheets applied over a stud wall.

Insulation (Batt)
A flexible blanket or roll-type insulation installed between studs in frame construction.

Insulation (Blown-In)
A cellulose insulation material blown in between the wall spaces of a frame construction.

Insulation (Rigid)
A structural building board applied to walls to resist heat transmission.

Masonry Block
An exterior wall consisting of concrete masonry units.

Paint
Costs include primer and finish coats applied to the exterior wall.

Plywood (Textured)
An exterior wall covering of textured plywood (T1-11) panels applied over a stud wall.

Repoint Masonry
The removal and replacement of mortar from between the joints of masonry units.

Sandblasting
The use of sand, propelled by an air-blast unit, to remove dirt, rust, paint, or to decorate the surface with a semirough texture.

Sanding
The removal of damaged wall finish by sanding.

COMPONENT DESCRIPTIONS

Sheathing
Plywood sheets attached to stud framing to provide backing to exterior wall materials and add to frame rigidity.

Shingles (Miscellaneous)
An exterior wall comprised of pieces of any number of materials, (wood, fiberglass, cement asbestos, etc.), applied over a stud wall.

Stain
A protective coating applied to exterior wood.

Stone Veneer (Imitation)
A nonbearing outside wall facing of synthetic stone, providing a decorative surface.

Stone Veneer (Natural)
A nonbearing outside wall facing of thin natural stone, providing a decorative surface.

Stucco (On Framing)
An exterior wall covering of stucco applied to a stud wall, including lath, wire or plaster.

Stucco (On Masonry)
An exterior wall covering of stucco applied to a masonry surface.

Stud Framing
An exterior wall constructed using wood studs, plates, firestops, and bracing.

Trim (Wood/Metal)
Any visible finishing component, usually of metal or wood (cornices, fascias, etc.).

Vinyl Siding
An exterior wall covering of typically 1" x 8" extruded vinyl applied over a stud wall.

Waterproofing (Building Paper)
A water-impervious paper, such as tarpaper, applied to a wall to prevent the passage of moisture.

Waterproofing (Cement Parging)
The coat of portland cement mortar applied to the earth side of a foundation or basement walls to provide dampproofing on masonry facing.

Waterproofing (Hot Mopped)
The use of one or more hot-applied coatings or layers of a material to an exterior wall to prevent the passage of moisture.

Waterproofing (Plastic Sheeting)
The use of a plastic sheet applied to a wall to prevent the passage of moisture.

Wood Shakes
An exterior wall covering comprised of any thick, hand-split shingle or clapboard, usually edge-grained, applied over a stud wall.

Wood Shingles
An exterior wall covering of wood shingles laid at either 7 ½" or 11 ½" exposure to weather.

Wood Siding (Bevel)
An exterior wall covering typically consisting of ½" x 8" wood boards whose beveled cross sections enable each board to overlap one another.

Wood Siding (Clapboard)
An exterior wall covering comprised typically of 1" x 8" wood boards applied over a stud wall.

FLOOR FINISHES

- Asphalt Tile
- Brick Pavers
- Carpet
- Carpet Pad
- Ceramic Tile
- Floor Sheathing
- Floor Sleepers
- Linoleum
- Marble
- Quarry Tile
- Regrout Tile Floor
- Resilient
- Rubber Tile
- Sand And Finish Floor
- Slate
- Underlayment – Hardboard
- Vinyl Tile
- Wood
- Wood Parquet Tile

ROOM METHOD

QUALITY LEVEL – ECONOMY

Costs are for replacing (and refinishing) the floor completely.

Room size ranges:
- Small   (48 Square Feet – 80 Square Feet)
- Medium   (81 Square Feet – 144 Square Feet)
- Large   (145 Square Feet – 200 Square Feet)
- X-large   (201 Square Feet – 275 Square Feet)

Notes:
1) For unusually small or large rooms, use the Unit Method.
2) Normal waste is built into costs.

Component (Priced per Room)	Room Sizes			
	Small	Medium	Large	X-Large
Finishes/Covers:				
Asphalt – Tile	$ 180.00	$ 315.00	$ 450.00	$ 605.00
Brick Pavers	600.00	1,035.00	1,595.00	2,105.00
Carpet – Indoor/Outdoor	200.00	355.00	550.00	735.00
Carpet – Synthetic	215.00	385.00	595.00	805.00
Carpet – Wool	460.00	815.00	1,275.00	1,725.00
Carpet Pad	60.00	85.00	130.00	170.00
Ceramic Tile	615.00	1,040.00	1,480.00	1,945.00
Linoleum	265.00	455.00	710.00	940.00
Marble	1,745.00	3,040.00	4,655.00	6,305.00
Quarry Tile	595.00	1,045.00	1,600.00	2,165.00
Resilient	210.00	375.00	575.00	770.00
Rubber Tile	345.00	600.00	925.00	1,250.00
Slate	645.00	1,135.00	1,745.00	2,345.00
Vinyl Tile	320.00	540.00	810.00	1,100.00
Wood – Hardwood (unfinished)	470.00	870.00	1,315.00	1,800.00
Wood – Softwood (unfinished)	430.00	740.00	1,150.00	1,570.00
Wood Parquet Tile (unfinished)	355.00	595.00	920.00	1,245.00
Finishes – Miscellaneous:				
Sand and Finish New Floor	$125.00	$195.00	$315.00	$410.00
Sand and Finish Damaged Floor	140.00	240.00	355.00	470.00
Regrout Tile Floor	130.00	195.00	285.00	380.00
Miscellaneous:				
Floor Sleepers	$ 70.00	$100.00	$150.00	$210.00
Floor Sheathing (boards)	130.00	235.00	360.00	485.00
Floor Sheathing (plywood)	120.00	210.00	320.00	425.00
Underlayment – Hardboard	115.00	200.00	305.00	400.00

ROOM METHOD

QUALITY LEVEL – STANDARD

Costs are for replacing (and refinishing) the floor completely.

Room size ranges:

Small	(48 Square Feet – 80 Square Feet)
Medium	(81 Square Feet – 144 Square Feet)
Large	(145 Square Feet – 200 Square Feet)
X-large	(201 Square Feet – 275 Square Feet)

Notes:
1) For unusually small or large rooms, use the Unit Method.
2) Normal waste is built into costs.

Component	Room Sizes			
(Priced per Room)	Small	Medium	Large	X-Large
Finishes/Covers:				
Asphalt – Tile	$ 190.00	$ 340.00	$ 495.00	$ 660.00
Brick Pavers	720.00	1,260.00	1,940.00	2,555.00
Carpet – Indoor/Outdoor	215.00	385.00	595.00	800.00
Carpet – Synthetic	240.00	415.00	640.00	875.00
Carpet – Wool	510.00	885.00	1,375.00	1,855.00
Carpet Pad	65.00	105.00	150.00	190.00
Ceramic Tile	685.00	1,150.00	1,665.00	2,175.00
Linoleum	340.00	590.00	885.00	1,190.00
Marble	2,200.00	3,840.00	5,910.00	8,020.00
Quarry Tile	640.00	1,130.00	1,735.00	2,335.00
Resilient	320.00	550.00	835.00	1,140.00
Rubber Tile	355.00	620.00	955.00	1,305.00
Slate	835.00	1,475.00	2,260.00	3,065.00
Vinyl Tile	380.00	650.00	1,000.00	1,325.00
Wood – Hardwood (unfinished)	485.00	835.00	1,290.00	1,775.00
Wood – Softwood (unfinished)	450.00	760.00	1,175.00	1,605.00
Wood Parquet Tile (unfinished)	405.00	695.00	1,075.00	1,490.00
Finishes – Miscellaneous:				
Sand and Finish New Floor	$130.00	$215.00	$340.00	$450.00
Sand and Finish Damaged Floor	155.00	260.00	390.00	540.00
Regrout Tile Floor	140.00	215.00	325.00	415.00
Miscellaneous:				
Floor Sleepers	$ 80.00	$120.00	$190.00	$255.00
Floor Sheathing (boards)	135.00	255.00	375.00	520.00
Floor Sheathing (plywood)	130.00	235.00	345.00	460.00
Underlayment – Hardboard	125.00	215.00	335.00	435.00

ROOM METHOD

QUALITY LEVEL – CUSTOM

Costs are for replacing (and refinishing) the floor completely.

Room size ranges:
- Small   (48 Square Feet –   80 Square Feet)
- Medium   (81 Square Feet – 144 Square Feet)
- Large   (145 Square Feet – 200 Square Feet)
- X-large   (201 Square Feet – 275 Square Feet)

Notes:
1. For unusually small or large rooms, use the Unit Method.
2. Normal waste is built into costs.

Component (Priced per Room)	Small	Medium	Large	X-Large
Finishes/Covers:				
Asphalt – Tile	$ 210.00	$ 360.00	$ 565.00	$ 730.00
Brick Pavers	870.00	1,530.00	2,360.00	3,105.00
Carpet – Indoor/Outdoor	250.00	420.00	650.00	885.00
Carpet – Synthetic	260.00	450.00	710.00	965.00
Carpet – Wool	540.00	955.00	1,465.00	1,985.00
Carpet Pad	70.00	120.00	175.00	220.00
Ceramic Tile	790.00	1,340.00	1,930.00	2,515.00
Linoleum	415.00	725.00	1,085.00	1,455.00
Marble	2,805.00	4,905.00	7,520.00	10,205.00
Quarry Tile	705.00	1,230.00	1,880.00	2,545.00
Resilient	350.00	605.00	945.00	1,265.00
Rubber Tile	375.00	645.00	1,005.00	1,360.00
Slate	1,120.00	1,945.00	2,980.00	4,035.00
Vinyl Tile	450.00	790.00	1,220.00	1,610.00
Wood – Hardwood (unfinished)	545.00	955.00	1,455.00	1,985.00
Wood – Softwood (unfinished)	480.00	820.00	1,250.00	1,720.00
Wood Parquet Tile (unfinished)	470.00	805.00	1,235.00	1,695.00
Finishes – Miscellaneous:				
Sand and Finish New Floor	$145.00	250.00	$375.00	$515.00
Sand and Finish Damaged Floor	175.00	290.00	450.00	610.00
Regrout Tile Floor	180.00	285.00	415.00	550.00
Miscellaneous:				
Floor Sleepers	$ 95.00	$150.00	$225.00	$310.00
Floor Sheathing (boards)	160.00	270.00	405.00	550.00
Floor Sheathing (plywood)	140.00	245.00	370.00	485.00
Underlayment – Hardboard	130.00	235.00	360.00	480.00

UNIT METHOD

To replace (and refinish) individual items, use the costs below:

Note: Normal waste is built into costs.

Component	Room Sizes		
(Priced per Square Foot Unless Otherwise Shown)	Economy	Standard	Custom
Finishes/Covers:			
Asphalt – Tile	$ 2.65	$ 2.90	$ 3.35
Brick Pavers	9.25	11.30	13.65
Carpet – Indoor/Outdoor	3.25	3.45	3.80
Carpet – Stair (per riser)	17.00	30.00	36.00
Carpet – Synthetic	3.45	3.75	4.10
Carpet – Wool	7.30	7.85	8.50
Carpet Pad	0.75	0.85	1.10
Ceramic Tile	9.75	10.80	12.55
Linoleum	4.15	5.25	6.45
Marble	27.05	34.30	43.85
Quarry Tile	9.40	10.05	10.85
Resilient	3.40	4.70	5.40
Rubber Tile	5.35	5.65	5.85
Slate	11.40	13.60	16.00
Vinyl Tile	4.70	5.90	7.15
Wood – Hardwood (unfinished)	6.55	7.45	8.45
Wood – Softwood (unfinished)	6.55	6.85	7.30
Wood Parquet Tile (unfinished)	5.35	6.30	7.10
Finishes – Miscellaneous:			
Sand and Finish New Floor			$1.95
Sand and Finish Damaged Floor			2.40
Regrout Tile Floor			2.00
Miscellaneous:			
Floor Sleepers			$1.15
Floor Sheathing (boards)			2.40
Floor Sheathing (plywood)			2.25
Underlayment – Hardboard			2.00

TYPICAL FLOORING SYSTEM

1. Underlayment Panels (if required)

2. Provide $^1/_{32}$" Space Between Panel Edges

3. Subfloor

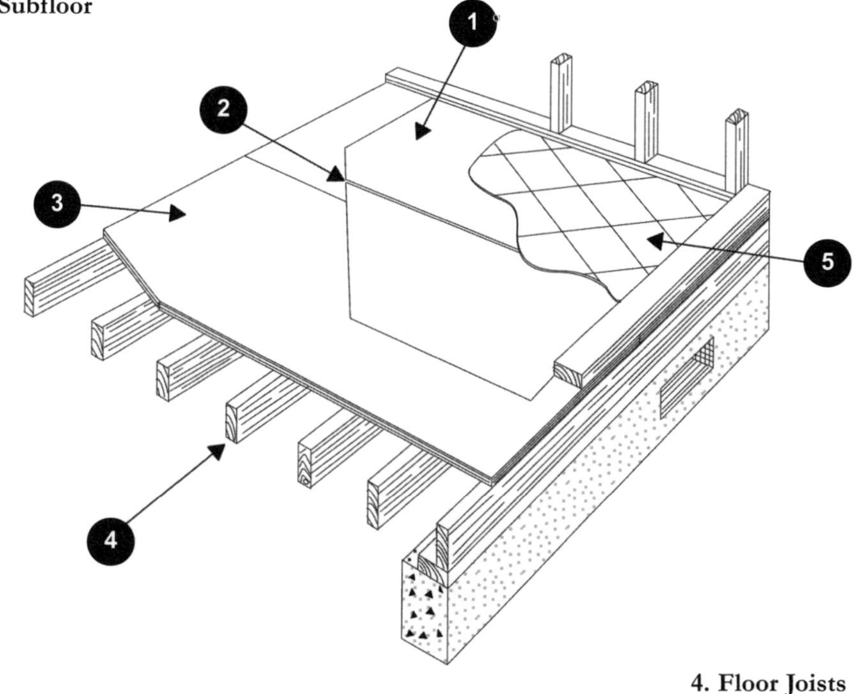

4. Floor Joists

5. Flooring Material

Asphalt Tile

A floor surfacing unit composed of asbestos fibers, mineral fillers and pigments.

Brick Pavers

A floor surface of rectangular-shaped blocks of special fired clay.

Carpet (Indoor/Outdoor)

Carpeting constructed from synthetic material. Designed to be used either inside or outside a building.

Carpet (Stair)

The material and installation of carpeting on stairs.

Carpet (Synthetic)

Carpeting constructed of synthetic materials such as polypropylene, nylon and acrylic.

Carpet (Wool)

Carpeting constructed of animal fiber.

Carpet Pad

Rolls of urethane or similar material, used as cushioning under carpet.

Ceramic Tile

A floor surface unit whose body is made of vitrified clay, either mud set or mastic set.

Floor Sheathing (Boards)

Wood boards which provide a base for the application of a floor surface.

Floor Sheathing (Plywood)

Structural plywood that provides a base for the application of a floor surface.

Floor Sleepers

Horizontal wood members that are laid on a concrete slab and to which the flooring is attached.

Linoleum

A resilient floor surfacing material manufactured in large sheets. Thickness ranges from .125" to .220".

Marble

A floor surfacing constructed of natural marble.

Quarry Tile

A floor surface manufactured from natural clay or shales, usually unglazed. The tiles are normally 6" or more in surface area and approximately $\frac{1}{2}$" to $\frac{3}{4}$" thick.

Regrout Tile Floor

Reapplying cement mortar between tile joints on a floor surface.

COMPONENT DESCRIPTIONS

Resilient

A resilient floor covering classification that includes, but is not limited to, asphalt, cork, rubber and vinyl.

Rubber Tile

A floor surfacing unit composed of rubber.

Sand And Finish Damaged Floor

Removal of old floor finish through sanding, and the application of a new finish.

Sand And Finish New Floor

Sanding and applying the initial finish to a newly laid wood floor.

Slate

A floor surfacing made of thin tiles of slate, usually mud set or mastic set.

Underlayment (Hardboard)

Hardboard applied over the existing floor cover allowing installation of a new floor surface.

Vinyl Tile

A floor surface unit, usually 12" x 12", composed principally of polyvinyl chloride set in mastic.

Wood (Hardwood)

A floor covering made of hardwoods (oak, beech, birch, pecan, etc.).

Wood (Softwood)

A floor covering made of softwoods (pine, fir, etc.).

Wood Parquet Tile

A floor covering of inlaid hardwood (tongued, grooved and end-matched), of short lengths or individual pieces, and usually set in geometric patterns.

HEATING/AIR CONDITIONING

- Air Conditioner
- Air Duct
- Air Exchanger
- Air Intake Grille
- Air Purifier
- Air Register
- Blower (Ventilation)
- Boiler (Hot Water)
- Chimney (Metal)
- Dehumidifier
- Exhaust Fan
- Expansion Tank
- Fan
- Furnace
- Heat Pump System
- Heater
- Humidifier
- Oil Tank
- Package Unit
- Pipe
- Radiant Ceiling Heat
- Radiant Floor Heat
- Radiator
- Thermostat
- Vent (Dryer)
- Vent Stack
- Ventilator (Attic)

Electric-powered Heating Systems:

The cost of the heating unit or boiler does not include the cost of thermostats, piping, ducting or other equipment necessary to distribute the heat generated throughout the building. You must price these items individually using this section.

The power connection for an electric heating unit or device includes direct connection to an existing electrical box and power source located near the installation location. If you need to run new service or repair or replace existing service connections, you must use the appropriate components from the Electrical section.

Gas-fired Heating Units:

The cost of the heating unit or boiler does not include the cost of thermostats, piping, ducting or other equipment necessary to distribute the heat generated throughout the building, or the cost of flues, chimneys or stacks to remove heat and products of combustion from the chamber. You must price these items individually using this section.

The cost associated with the installation of the unit is limited to a direct connection to existing gas and electrical utilities located at the installation site. If you need to run new gas or electrical service or replace or repair existing service connections, use appropriate components in addition to the boiler or heating unit.

Oil-fired Heating Units:

The cost of the heating unit or boiler does not include the cost of thermostats, piping, ducting or other equipment necessary to distribute the heat generated throughout the building, or the cost of flues, chimneys or stacks to remove heat and products of combustion from the chamber. You must price these items individually using this section.

The cost associated with the installation of the unit is limited to a direct connection to an existing oil supply and electrical utilities located at the installation site. If you need to run electrical service, to install a new oil storage tank and/or supply piping, or replace or repair existing oil or electrical connections, use appropriate components in addition to the boiler or heating unit.

Hot Water Heating Systems:

The cost of hot water heating systems, regardless of the fuel, involves additional piping and equipment costs that are not included in the cost of the boiler and heating unit. When repair or replacement is required, you must select and enter appropriate components separately.

Air-Conditioning Systems:

The cost of the air-conditioning unit does not include the cost of thermostats, piping, pipe insulation, ducting, duct insulation or other equipment needed to distribute the cooled air generated throughout the building. You must price these items individually using this section.

The power connection for an electric air-conditioning unit or device includes direct connection to an existing electrical box and power source located near the installation location. If you need to run new service or repair or replace existing service connections, you must use appropriate components from the Electrical section.

Ventilation Equipment:

The cost of ventilation equipment (fans, blowers, humidifiers, etc.) includes the cost of direct connection to an existing electrical outlet or hardwiring to an existing electrical box and power source. If you need to run new service or replace or repair existing service connections, use appropriate components in addition to the fixture.

UNIT METHOD

To replace individual items, use the costs below:

Component (Priced Each Unless Otherwise Shown)	
Equipment – Heating:	
Boiler – Hot Water (electric)	$8,510.00
Boiler – Hot Water (gas)	4,285.00
Boiler – Hot Water (oil)	4,445.00
Furnace – Forced Air (electric)	2,265.00
Furnace – Forced Air (gas)	1,975.00
Furnace – Forced Air (oil)	2,170.00
Heater – Baseboard (electric)	240.00
Heater – Baseboard (hot water)	240.00
Heater – Wall (gas)	1,070.00
Heater – Wall (electric)	210.00
Heater – Wall (electric w/ fan)	315.00
Equipment – Cooling and Heating:	
Package Unit	$11,240.00
Heat Pump System	8,350.00
Air Distribution/Ventilation:	
Air Duct (per linear foot)	$ 7.05
Air Duct – Insulated (per linear foot)	10.10
Air Exchanger (used w/ HVAC system)	460.00
Air Intake Grille	65.00
Air Register (return)	55.00
Air Register (supply)	75.00
Blower – Ventilation (used w/ HVAC system)	1,495.00
Exhaust Fan – Attic	340.00
Exhaust Fan – Attic w/ Shutter	980.00
Exhaust Fan – Kitchen/Bathroom	175.00
Exhaust Fan – Whole House	535.00
Fan – Window	145.00
Ventilator – Attic	120.00

UNIT METHOD

To replace individual items, use the costs below:

Component	
(Priced Each Unless Otherwise Shown)	
Heat Distribution:	
Pipe – Insulation (per linear foot)	$ 7.40
Pipe – Hot Water Branch (per linear foot)	34.00
Pipe – Hot Water Main (per linear foot)	51.00
Radiant Floor Heat – Hot Water (per square foot)	5.40
Radiant Ceiling Heat – Electric (per square foot)	1.20
Radiator – Fin Tube Hot Water (per linear foot)	70.00
Radiator – Hot Water (per section)	56.00
Miscellaneous:	
Air Conditioner – Window Unit	$1,525.00
Air Purifier – Electronic (used w/ HVAC system)	1,340.00
Air Purifier – Filtered (used w/ HVAC system)	660.00
Chimney – Metal	2,440.00
Dehumidifier (used w/ HVAC system)	605.00
Expansion Tank – Hot Water	475.00
Expansion Tank – Insulation	110.00
Humidifier (used w/ HVAC system)	640.00
Oil Tank	1,000.00
Oil Tank Supply Line – (per linear foot)	15.20
Thermostat	120.00
Thermostat – Programmable	195.00
Vent – Dryer	105.00
Vent Stack – Through Roof (per story)	470.00

SYSTEMS

ELECTRIC

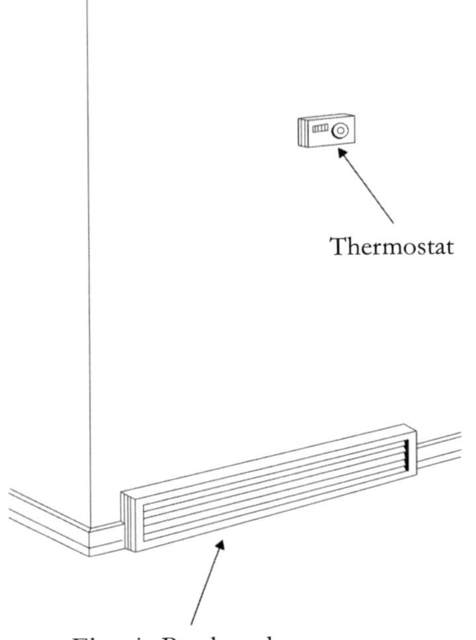

FORCED AIR FURNACE

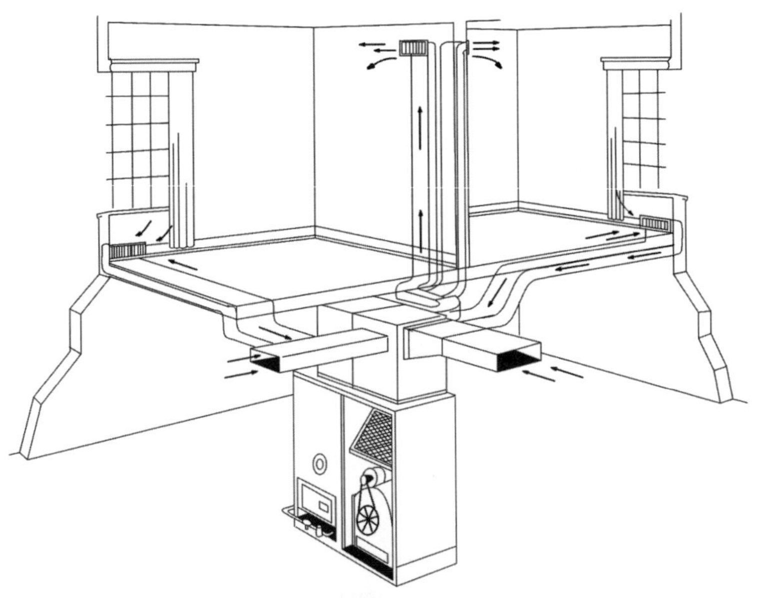

HEAT PUMP

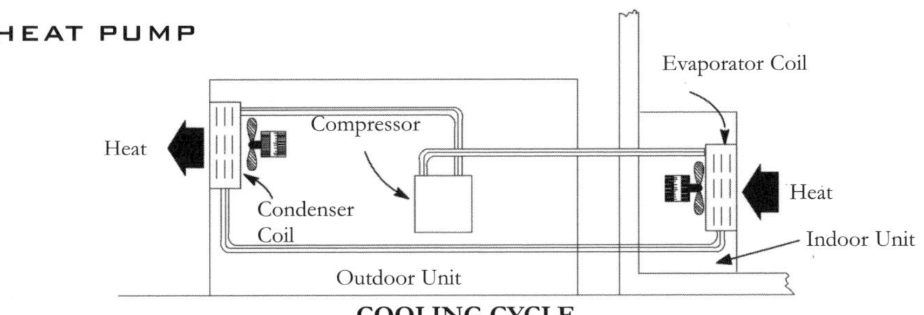

COOLING CYCLE

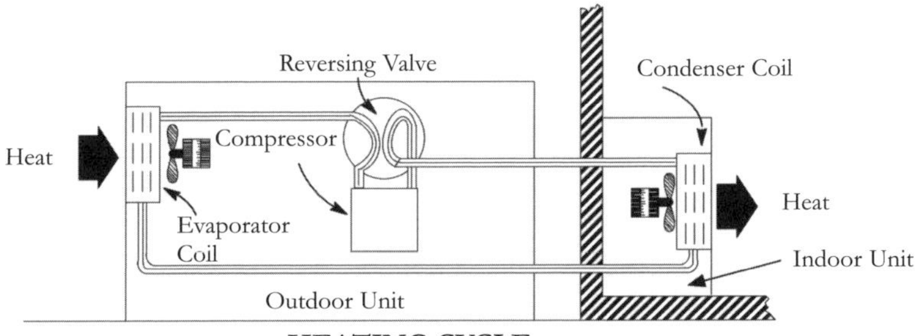

HEATING CYCLE

HOT WATER

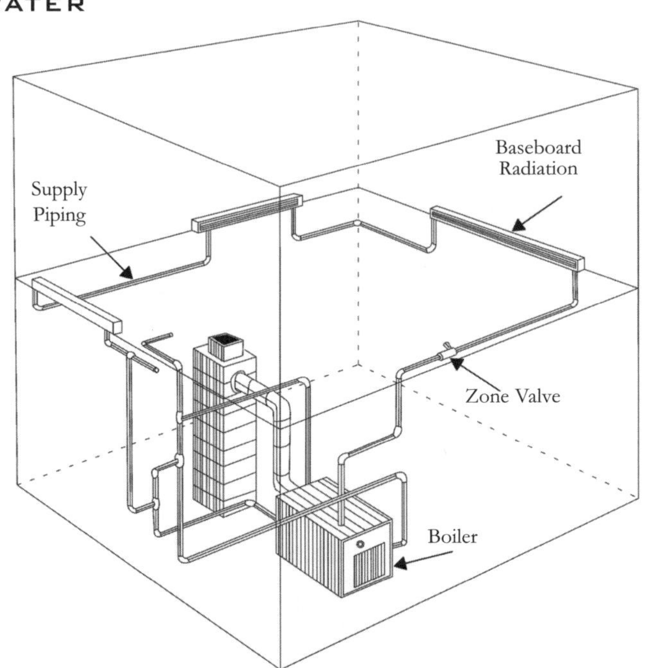

SOLAR HEATING

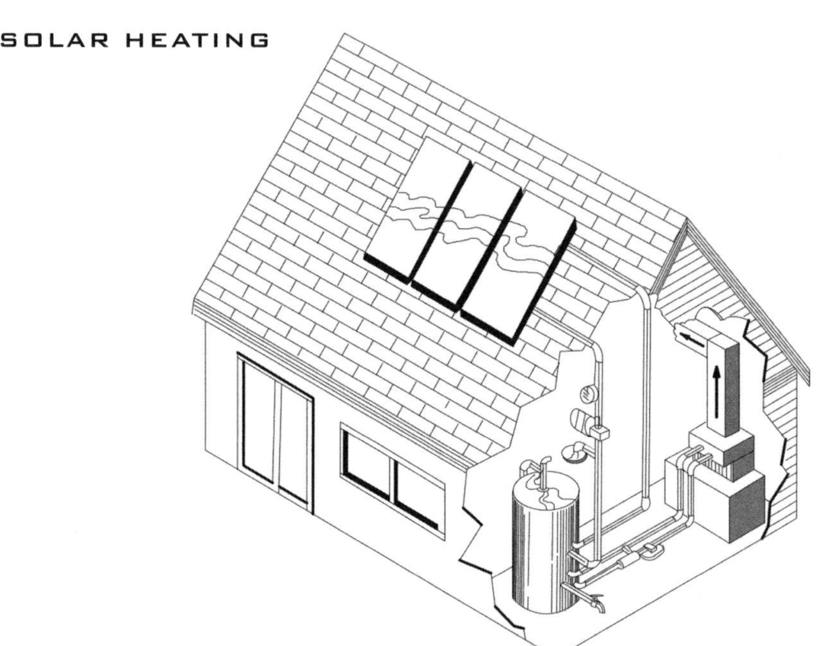

WALL FURNACE

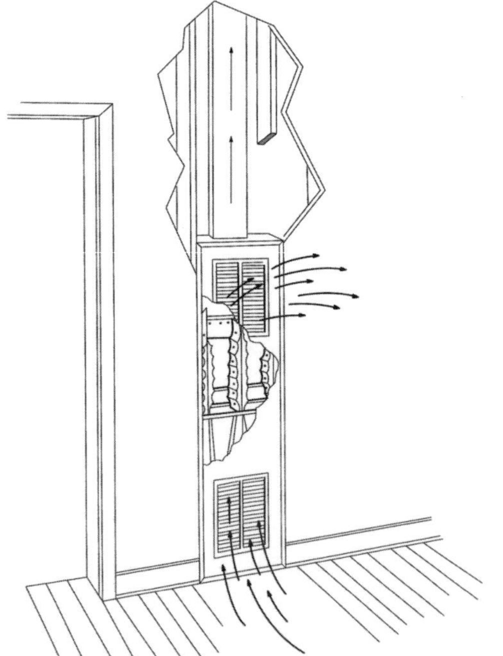

COMPONENT DESCRIPTIONS

Air Conditioner (Window)
A unit designed to be installed in a window opening or wall.

Air Duct
A duct, usually fabricated of sheet metal, fiberglass, or vinyl, sometimes wrapped in fiberglass for insulation.

Air Exchanger
A device located in air ducting. Used in conjunction with an HVAC system for transferring temperature from one air flow to another.

Air Intake Grille
The frame covering the opening of an air intake duct.

Air Purifier (Electronic)
An electronic device for cleansing air. Used in combination with an HVAC system.

Air Purifier (Filtered)
A filter device for cleansing air. Used in conjunction with an HVAC system.

Air Register (Supply)
A grille having a damper for the regulation of the air supply to a room from a heating/cooling unit.

Air Register (Return)
A grille covering a vent from a room into a return air duct leading to a heating/cooling unit.

Blower (Ventilation)
A fan used for the movement of air through a duct system. Used in conjunction with HVAC systems.

Boiler (Hot Water)
A central unit in which hot water is heated by gas, oil or electricity, and circulated by piping through the building.

Chimney (Metal)
A preconstructed metal flue used to vent a fireplace or furnace.

Dehumidifier
A device for removing moisture from the air. Used in conjunction with an HVAC system.

Exhaust Fan (Attic)
A fan used to withdraw and discharge hot air from an attic.

Exhaust Fan With Shutter (Attic)
An attic exhaust fan with an adjustable cover.

Exhaust Fan (Kitchen/Bathroom)
A device to remove air from a kitchen or bathroom.

Exhaust Fan (Whole House)
An attic fan designed to circulate air throughout a structure.

Expansion Tank (Hot Water)
A reservoir that holds the water overflow from heat expansion.

Expansion Tank Insulation
The insulating material encasing a hot water expansion tank.

Fan (Window)
A fan set into a window opening.

Furnace (Forced Air)
A warm-air central heating system equipped with a blower to circulate the air. Air can be heated by gas, oil or electricity.

Heat Pump System
An electrical refrigeration system that provides reverse cycle operations for cooling and heating.

Heater (Electric Baseboard)
An electrical heating system in which heating elements are installed in panels along the base of the wall.

Heater (Hot Water Baseboard)
A heating system in which centrally heated water is circulated through panels along the base of a wall.

Heater (Wall)
A self-contained hot air heater permanently attached to a wall. Air can be heated by either gas or electricity, sometimes fan forced.

Humidifier
A device used in combination with an HVAC system to add moisture to the air.

Oil Tank
A fuel oil storage container for a residential structure. Costs include the tank only.

Oil Tank Supply Line
A pipe that supplies fuel oil to a furnace from a central supply tank.

Package Unit
A combination heating/cooling package. Costs include the compressor but exclude the controls, ducting and piping.

Pipe (Hot Water Branch)
Distribution pipes of a hot water system that carry and return hot water throughout the system.

Pipe (Hot Water Main)
A large or main pipe that supplies a number of distribution pipes with hot water or return water from a central heating plant.

Radiant Ceiling Heat
A heating system using an electric grid in the ceiling plaster.

Radiant Floor Heat
A system of heating whereby hot water flows through piping installed within a floor.

Radiator
A unit that radiates heat by the use of hot water. The unit is usually exposed to view in the room.

Radiator (Fin Tube)
A heating system in which water that is centrally heated is circulated through finned tubes in an enclosure along a wall.

Thermostat
A device, activated by temperature changes, that controls the furnace and/or air-conditioning output limits.

Thermostat (Programmable)
A device that contains a clock system to determine the time periods in which heating/cooling controls are to be activated.

Vent (Dryer)
Ducting between a dryer and a vent.

Vent Stack
A vertical vent pipe installed through the roof, primarily for the purpose of conducting and discharging air.

Ventilator (Attic)
A mechanical fan, located in the attic space of a residence, that is used to vent attic air.

KITCHENS

- Base Cabinet
- Blender (Food Center)
- Countertop
- Dishwasher
- Faucet
- Freezer
- Garbage Disposal
- Microwave Oven
- Oven
- Range (Cooktop)
- Range Hood
- Range Combinations
- Refrigerator
- Sink (Kitchen)
- Trash Compactor
- Wall Cabinet

ROOM METHOD

NOTES

The costs for components described as "built-in" are for those appliances designed to be built into a cabinet, counter or other area where, under normal circumstances, the sides, back and top of the appliance do not have finished surfaces and are concealed. Freestanding appliances are finished on all exposed surfaces and are usually more expensive to replace.

The appliance installation cost includes the cost of direct connection to an existing electrical outlet or hardwiring to an existing electrical box and power source, and/or connection to existing gas, water and sewer services. If you need to run new service or replace or repair existing service connections, use the appropriate components from the Electrical and/or Plumbing sections in addition to the appliance.

The cost of plumbing installation includes the cost of direct connection to existing water and/or drain lines located in the immediate area of the installation location. If you need to run new service or replace or repair existing service connections, use appropriate components in addition to the item.

Costs include replacement of the complete kitchen.

Following is a list of appliances included in each quality level. If appliance adjustment is required, add or deduct costs from the Unit Method.

Economy
  refrigerator, range/oven, garbage disposal

Standard
  refrigerator, dishwasher, microwave, range hood, cooktop, oven (built-in single), garbage disposal

Custom
  refrigerator, dishwasher, oven (built-in double), range hood, cooktop, oven, trash compactor, microwave (built-in), garbage disposal

Room Size	Quality Levels		
(Square Foot Area)	Economy	Standard	Custom
80 Square Feet	$ 7,790.00	$16,020.00	$18,830.00
100 Square Feet	8,210.00	16,660.00	19,700.00
120 Square Feet	8,610.00	17,290.00	20,480.00
140 Square Feet	9,040.00	17,980.00	21,360.00
160 Square Feet	9,420.00	18,570.00	22,150.00
180 Square Feet	10,140.00	19,610.00	23,490.00
200 Square Feet	10,780.00	20,540.00	24,600.00
220 Square Feet	11,170.00	21,150.00	25,380.00
240 Square Feet	11,530.00	21,700.00	26,210.00
260 Square Feet	11,900.00	22,290.00	26,950.00

UNIT METHOD

To replace individual items, use the costs below:

Component	Quality Levels		
(Price Each)	**Economy**	**Standard**	**Custom**
Appliances – Built-in:			
Blender – Food Center	$ 255.00	$ 285.00	$ 340.00
Dishwasher	790.00	985.00	1,145.00
Oven – Double	1,235.00	1,380.00	1,550.00
Oven – Microwave	930.00	1,185.00	1,515.00
Oven – Single	810.00	925.00	1,040.00
Range – Cooktop	510.00	680.00	940.00
Range and Oven (double)	1,375.00	1,580.00	1,785.00
Range/Microwave/Oven Combination	2,290.00	2,640.00	3,040.00
Range and Oven (single)	850.00	1,075.00	1,345.00
Range Hood	320.00	460.00	635.00
Refrigerator – Undercounter	565.00	705.00	885.00
Trash Compactor	715.00	815.00	955.00
Appliances – Freestanding:			
Dishwasher	$ 855.00	$1,060.00	$1,285.00
Freezer	660.00	970.00	1,400.00
Microwave Oven	740.00	1,190.00	1,915.00
Range and Oven (double)	1,475.00	1,670.00	1,925.00
Range and Oven (single)	980.00	1,130.00	1,300.00
Range/Microwave Combination	2,335.00	2,665.00	3,065.00
Refrigerator	1,095.00	1,410.00	1,790.00

UNIT METHOD

To replace individual items, use the costs below:

Component	Quality Levels		
(Priced per Linear Foot Unless Otherwise Shown)	Economy	Standard	Custom
Cabinets/Counters:			
Base Cabinet – Metal	$135.00	$160.00	$190.00
Base Cabinet – Wood	150.00	175.00	210.00
Countertop – Butcher Block	80.00	95.00	120.00
Countertop – Laminated Plastic	55.00	60.00	65.00
Countertop – Simulated Marble	85.00	110.00	120.00
Countertop – Stainless Steel	125.00	135.00	150.00
Countertop – Tile	60.00	65.00	75.00
Wall Cabinet – Metal	130.00	155.00	185.00
Wall Cabinet – Wood	110.00	120.00	130.00
Miscellaneous:			
Garbage Disposal (each)	$340.00	$435.00	$590.00
Faucet (each)	125.00	180.00	275.00
Faucet – Combination (each)	170.00	230.00	320.00
Refinish Base Cabinet – Paint	9.75	14.15	20.40
Refinish Base Cabinet – Stain	33.25	36.50	46.30
Refinish Wall Cabinet – Paint	9.75	14.15	20.40
Refinish Wall Cabinet – Stain	24.90	27.55	34.60
Replace Cabinet Doors (each)	120.00	130.00	145.00
Sink – Kitchen, Double (each)	460.00	635.00	855.00
Sink – Kitchen, Single (each)	355.00	470.00	650.00

TYPICAL LAYOUT

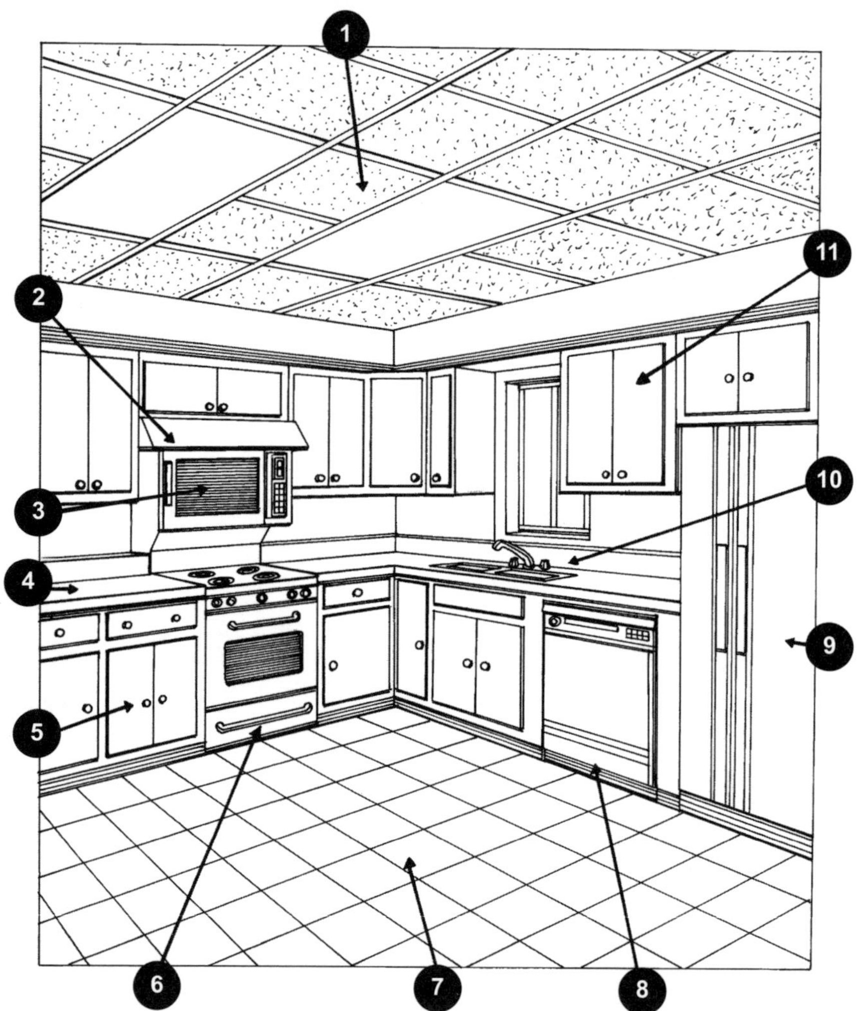

1. Drop Ceiling
2. Range Hood
3. Microwave Oven
4. Formica Countertop and Backsplash
5. Base Cabinets
6. Cooking Range/Oven
7. Vinyl Floor Tile
8. Dishwasher
9. Refrigerator
10. Sink with Faucet
11. Wall Cabinets

COMPONENT DESCRIPTIONS

Base Cabinet
A kitchen storage case usually made of wood or metal. Costs do not include the counter.

Blender (Food Center)
A food preparation device and control unit built into a kitchen counter.

Countertop
A top or working surface of a kitchen base cabinet, made from a variety of materials.

Dishwasher
A self-supporting appliance for cleaning dishware.

Dishwasher (Built-In)
An appliance for cleaning dishware that is built into a kitchen cabinet.

Faucet
A water outlet control device.

Faucet (Combination)
A plumbing valve that combines hot and cold water through one outlet.

Freezer
A self-supporting freezer.

Garbage Disposal
An electric device for grinding waste food prior to its entering the sewer pipe.

Microwave Oven
A self-supporting microwave oven.

Oven
A single or double oven that is built into a kitchen cabinet.

Oven (Microwave Built-In)
A microwave oven that is built into a kitchen cabinet.

Range (Cooktop)
A burner unit that is recessed into the surface of a kitchen counter.

Range Hood
An exhaust hood over a kitchen stove or range.

Range/Microwave Combination
A self-supporting stove and microwave attached as one common unit.

Range/Microwave/Oven Combination
A kitchen appliance consisting of range/oven and microwave as one total unit built into a kitchen cabinet.

Range/Oven
A self-supporting stove with either a single or double oven.

Range/Oven (Built-In)
A range/oven unit that is built into a kitchen cabinet. May contain either a single or double oven.

Refrigerator
A self-supporting refrigerator.

Refrigerator (Undercounter)
A refrigerator unit placed in or built into a kitchen cabinet, beneath the countertop.

Sink (Kitchen)
A kitchen sink fixture with either one or two basins. Costs include connection to a water supply and drain, but exclude faucets, shut-off valves, etc.

Trash Compactor
A trash compactor unit built into a kitchen cabinet.

Wall Cabinet
A wall-mounted, wood or metal case consisting of shelves and doors.

PLUMBING

- APPLIANCE HOOK-UP
- CLEAN SEWER PIPE
- DRAIN
- FAUCET
- FIXTURE CONNECTION
- FIXTURE ROUGH-IN
- FOUNTAIN (DECORATIVE)
- GARBAGE DISPOSAL
- HOSE BIB
- HOT-WATER HEATER
- PIPING
- PUMP (CIRCULATING)
- PUMP (SUMP)
- SERVICE SHUT-OFF VALVE
- SINK (LAUNDRY)
- SINK (WET BAR)
- TUBING (COPPER)
- WATER FILTER
- WATER SOFTENER
- WELL (DRILL AND CASE)
- WELL PUMP
- WELL WATER PRESSURE TANK

General Plumbing Installation:

The cost of plumbing installation includes the cost of direct connection to existing water and/or drain lines located in the immediate area of the installation location. If you need to run new service or replace or repair existing service connections, use appropriate components in addition to the item.

Fixture and Faucet Installation:

The cost of fixture and faucet installation includes the cost of direct connection to existing water and drain piping and assumes that the waterline connection lines, with shutoffs, and drain connection, with tailpipe and trap, are in the immediate area of the installation and will be reused. If you need to run new service or replace or repair existing water or drain service connections, use appropriate components in addition to the faucet or fixture.

The costs for built-in items such as sinks, consider a cabinet, counter or vanity is being reused and will not require changes or replacement. If changes or replacement are required, use appropriate components in addition to the fixture.

Hot-water Heater Installation:

The cost associated with the installation of a hot-water heater is limited to a direct connection to existing water and gas/electrical utilities located at the installation site. If you need to run new water, gas or electrical service or replace or repair existing service connections, use appropriate components in addition to the hot-water heater.

UNIT METHOD

To replace individual items, use the costs below:

Component (Priced Each Unless Otherwise Shown)	
Fixtures and Valves:	
Drain – Floor	$ 280.00
Drain – Roof	24.00
Faucet – Combination	230.00
Faucet – Double	150.00
Faucet – Single	130.00
Fountain – Decorative	565.00
Garbage Disposal	435.00
Hot-water Heater – Electric	730.00
Hot-water Heater – Gas	790.00
Hot-water Heater – Tankless	460.00
Hot-water Tank Insulation	125.00
Pump – Circulating	445.00
Pump – Sump	510.00
Sink – Laundry (double)	510.00
Sink – Laundry (single)	390.00
Sink – Wet Bar	415.00
Water Filter	180.00
Water Softener	1,230.00
Pipes and Fittings:	
Fixture Connection	$105.00
Fixture Rough-in	525.00
Hose Bib	75.00
Piping – Black Steel (per linear foot)	45.00
Piping – Cast Iron (per linear foot)	70.00
Piping – Copper (per linear foot)	14.05
Piping – Galvanized Steel (per linear foot)	11.15
Piping – Plastic (per linear foot)	9.05
Piping – Steel (per linear foot)	35.60
Tubing – Copper (per linear foot)	5.90
Service Shut-off Valve	160.00
Miscellaneous:	
Appliance Hook-up (gas)	$ 70.00
Appliance Hook-up (water)	60.00
Clean Sewer Pipe	290.00
Remove/reset toilet (labor only)	36.00
Well – Drill and Case (per linear foot)	40.00
Well Pump – Submersible	3,570.00
Well Water Pressure Tank	702.15

TYPICAL LAYOUT/PIPE SIZES

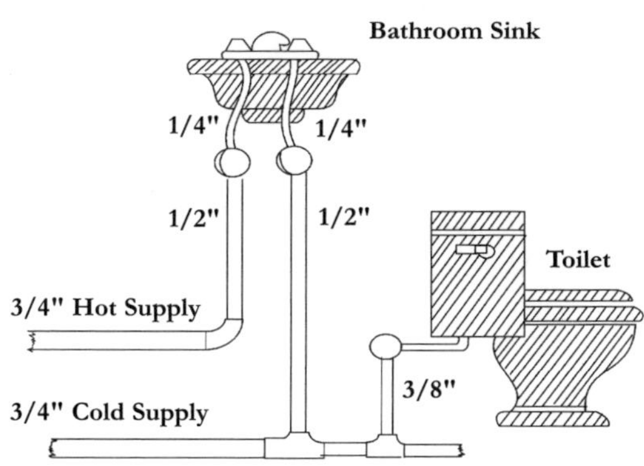

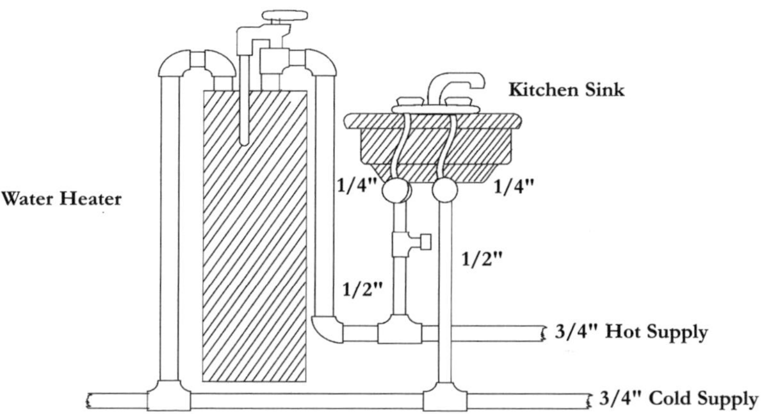

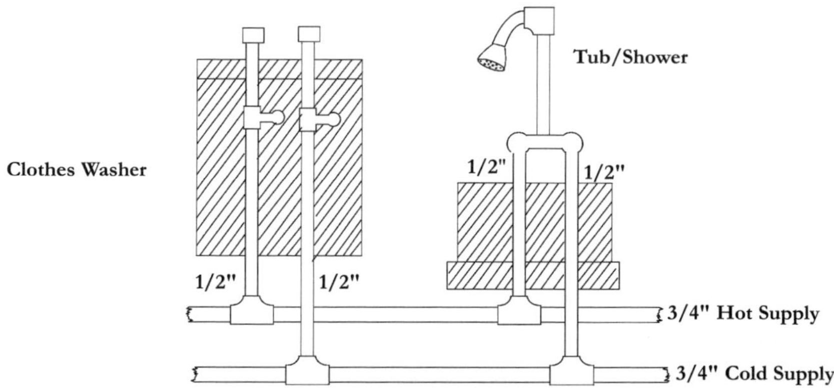

COMPONENT DESCRIPTIONS

Appliance Hook-Up

Piping connections necessary to provide gas or water to an appliance.

Clean Sewer Pipe

Cleaning of flow restrictions in a sewer pipe.

Drain (Floor)

An opening in a floor to drain water into a drain or sewer system.

Drain (Roof)

A drain used on a roof to collect water.

Faucet (Combination)

A plumbing valve that combines hot and cold water through one outlet.

Faucet (Double)

A plumbing valve with two water outlets.

Faucet (Single)

A plumbing valve with one water outlet.

Fixture Connection

A device for joining together a plumbing fixture with the plumbing system. Costs include flexible tubing, shut-off valves, drain, tailpipe and trap.

Fixture Rough-In

Installation of all parts of a plumbing connection that are completed prior to installation of a fixture. Costs include drainage, water supply, and vent piping.

Fountain (Decorative)

A pump system whose fountain is of typical residential quality, made of concrete, plastic or fiberglass.

Garbage Disposal

An electric device for grinding waste food prior to its entering the sewer pipe.

Hose Bib

An exterior water faucet that is threaded to provide a connection for a hose.

Hot-Water Heater

Package equipment for heating water that uses gas or electricity.

Hot-Water Heater (Tankless)

A water heater whereby water is heated as it passes over heating elements.

Hot-Water Tank Insulation

Insulating material surrounding a hot-water tank.

Piping (Cast Iron)

Piping made of cast iron. Costs include fittings but exclude excavation if required.

COMPONENT DESCRIPTIONS

Piping (Copper)

Lightweight rigid copper piping joined by soldering. Costs include fittings but exclude excavation if required.

Piping (Galvanized Steel)

Steel piping coated with zinc whose fittings are threaded. Costs include fittings, but exclude excavation if required.

Piping (Plastic)

Piping made of a synthetic material (PVC). Costs include fittings, but exclude excavation if required.

Pump (Circulating)

A pump used to provide a continuous flow of water within a closed circuit.

Pump (Sump)

A pump used to drain the accumulated liquid from a receptacle. Costs include connection to a nearby power supply and drain.

Service Shut-Off Valve

A valve for a primary service line.

Sink (Laundry)

A deep wide sink usually of porcelain or steel which can have either one or two basins. Costs include connection to a water supply and drain, but exclude the faucets, shut-off valves, tailpipe and trap.

Sink (Wet Bar)

A small basin usually used in a residential bar arrangement. Costs include connection to a water supply and drain, but exclude faucets, shut-off valves, tailpipe and trap.

Tubing (Copper)

Flexible copper piping joined by soldering, flaring, or compression fittings. The costs include fittings, but exclude excavation if required.

Water Filter

An in-line device used to trap sediment from the water supply.

Water Supply

An apparatus that chemically removes the calcium and magnesium minerals from a water supply.

Well (Drill And Case)

A complete well. Costs include engineering, setup, drilling, casing, sanitation and wellhead fixtures, but exclude excavation and piping to carry water from the well to the house.

Well Pump

A submersible pump used to pump water from a well to a storage tank.

Well Water Pressure Tank

A water tank designed to pressurize a well water system.

ROOFING

- Asphalt (Hot Mopped)
- Built-Up
- Clay Tile
- Concrete Tile
- Coping
- Copper
- Downspout
- Elastomeric (Single-Ply)
- Fascia
- Felt Paper
- Fiberglass
- Flashing
- Gravel Stop
- Gutter
- Insulation
- Metal
- Plastic Tile
- Roll Roofing (Composition)
- Sheathing
- Shingles (Composition)
- Skylight
- Slate Tile
- Soffit
- Wood Shakes
- Wood Shingles

UNIT·METHOD

NOTES

The unit of measure, "Square Feet of Roof Area," requires that the area of the roof, including consideration for roof slope and overhangs, be used. For buildings with sloping roofs, this area will be greater than the ground floor (i.e. footprint).

To replace individual items, use the costs below:

Component	Quality Levels		
(Priced per Square Foot)	Economy	Standard	Custom
Roof Covers:			
Asphalt – Hot Mopped	$ .30	$ .35	$ .45
Built-up	1.95	2.20	2.55
Clay Tile	9.70	10.20	10.80
Concrete Tile	7.05	7.85	9.20
Copper	13.65	17.25	21.55
Elastomeric, Single-ply	7.15	9.26	12.00
Felt Paper	.15	.20	.25
Fiberglass	1.10	1.40	2.00
Fiberglass – Corrugated	4.40	5.15	6.20
Metal	3.55	3.70	3.85
Plastic Tile	5.90	6.85	8.00
Roll Roofing – Composition	.75	.85	1.05
Slate Tile	12.30	13.60	15.10
Shingles – Composition	1.35	1.60	1.75
Wood Shakes	3.30	3.65	4.15
Wood Shingles	3.20	3.80	4.25

Component	
(Priced per Linear Foot Unless Otherwise Shown)	
Miscellaneous:	
Coping	$ 17.20
Downspout	6.25
Fascia – Aluminum	4.35
Fascia – Board	3.45
Flashing	4.50
Gravel Stop	3.55
Gutter	6.25
Insulation – Batt (per square foot)	1.45
Insulation – Rigid (per square foot)	1.40
Sheathing (per square foot)	2.10
Soffit – Aluminum	4.25
Soffit – Board	5.00
Skylight (each)	337.35

TYPICAL STYLES

FRAME

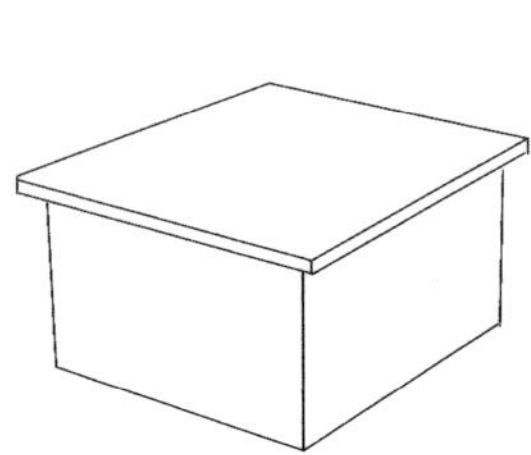

1. Flat

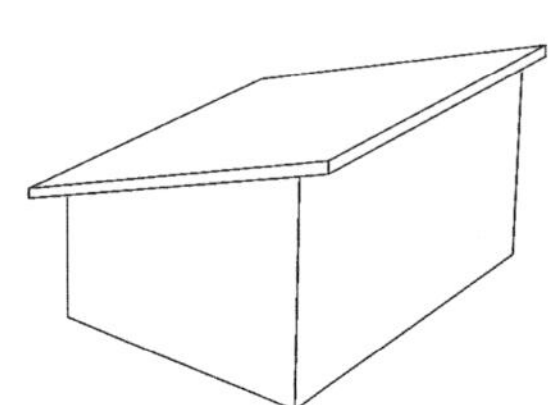

2. Shed

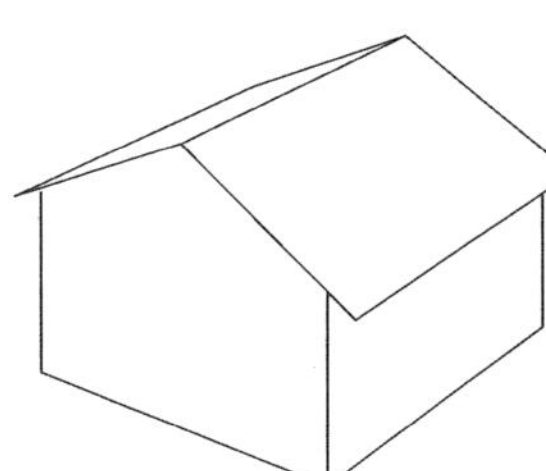

3. Gable

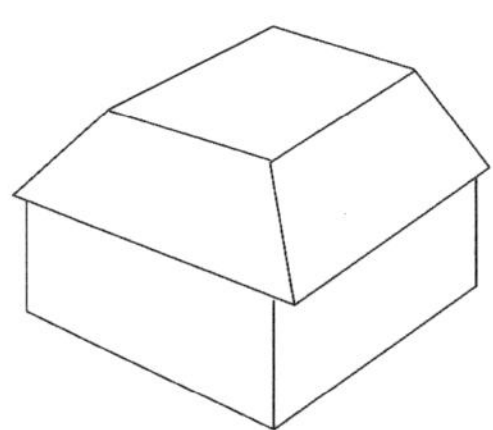

4. Mansard

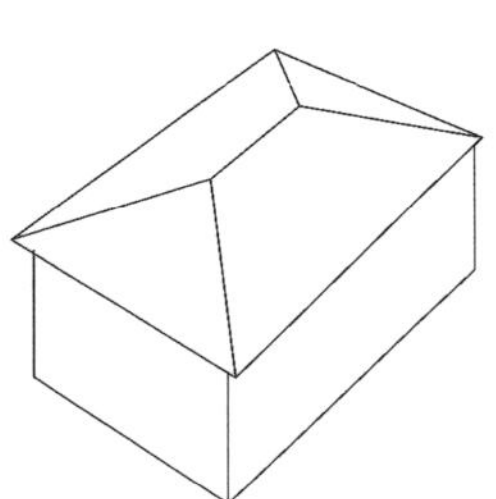

5. Hip

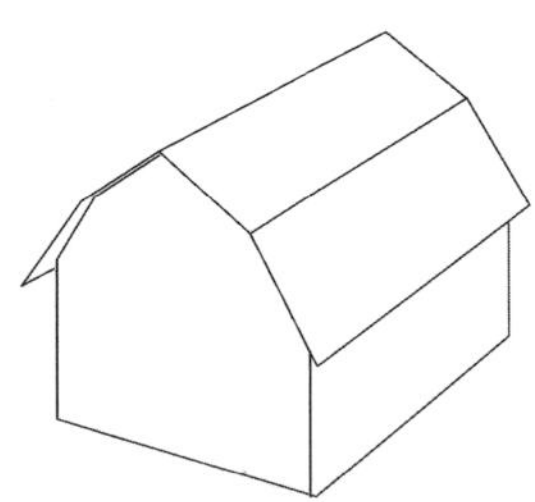

6. Gambrel

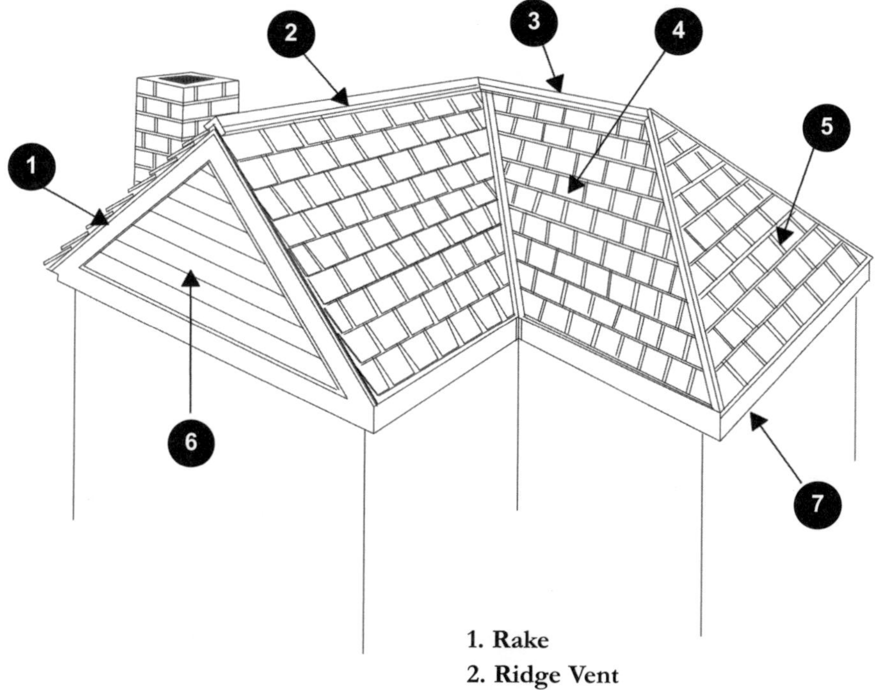

1. Rake
2. Ridge Vent
3. Ridge
4. Valley
5. Hip
6. Gable End
7. Eaves

TYPICAL MATERIALS

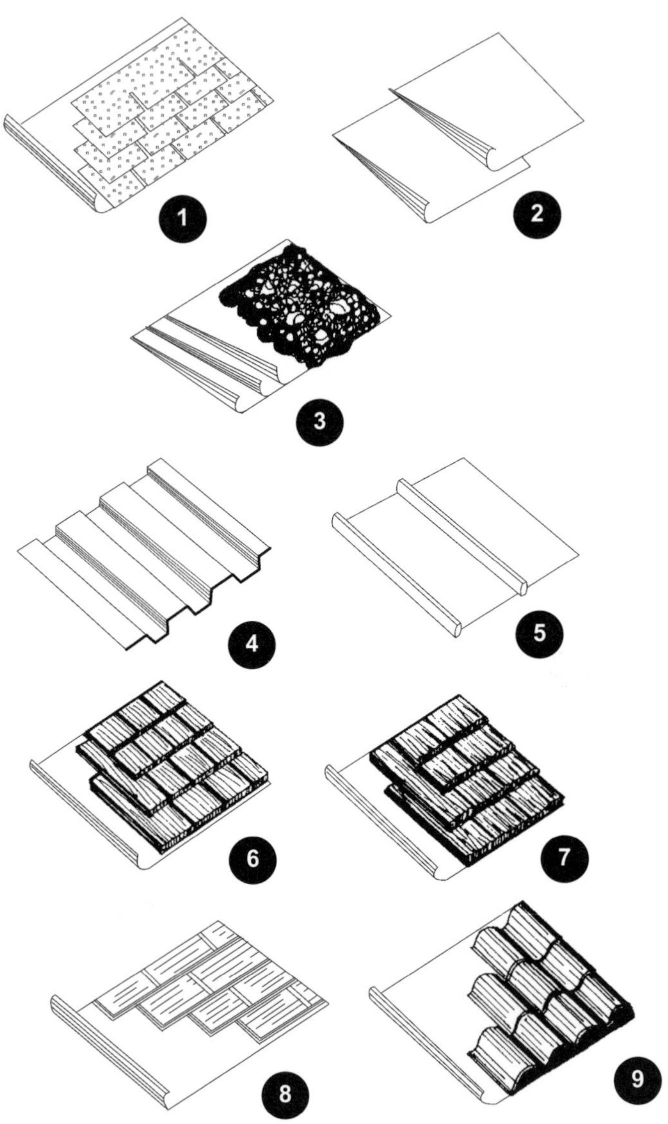

1. Asphalt Shingle (Low - $)
2. Roll (Low - $)
3. Built-up (Medium - $)
4. Preformed Metal (Low - $)
5. Standing Seam (Medium - $)
6. Wood Shingle (Medium - $)
7. Wood Shake (High - $)
8. Slate (High - $)
9. Spanish Tile (High - $)

COMPONENT DESCRIPTIONS

Asphalt (Hot Mopped)

A protective roof covering composed of a layer of hot asphalt.

Built-Up

A continuous roof covering of layers of saturated or coated felts that are alternated with layers of hot asphalt.

Clay Tile

A roof covering of clay tiles, commonly called Spanish or mission tiles, approximately 13¼" x 9¾".

Concrete Tile

A roof covering of tile made from concrete.

Coping

A cap placed on top of a parapet wall to act as waterproofing.

Copper

A roof covering of copper sheets with flat or standing seams.

Downspout

A vertical pipe, often of sheet metal, used to channel water from a roof or gutter to the ground.

Elastomeric (Single-Ply)

A roofing material having elastic properties that is capable of expanding or contracting with the surfaces to which the material is applied, without rupturing.

Fascia

An exterior piece of trim that is placed at the end of roof rafters.

Felt Paper

Asphalt-saturated or asphalt-coated felt applied over the roof deck or sheathing and under the roof cover.

Fiberglass

A protective roof covering composed of a synthetic material.

Fiberglass (Corrugated)

A roof cover of corrugated fiberglass sheets.

Flashing

A thin, continuous strip of metal, plastic, rubber or waterproofing membrane used to prevent the passage of water through a joint.

Gravel Stop

A metal piece placed along the edge of a gravel-covered roof to prevent the gravel from washing over the roof edge.

Gutter

A channel of metal, plastic, or wood to catch and carry off rainwater from a roof to the downspout.

Insulation (Batt)

A flexible blanket-type thermal insulation commonly used as insulation between rafters or joists in frame construction.

COMPONENT DESCRIPTIONS

Insulation (Rigid)

A rigid insulation; usually boards of polystyrene, mineral fiberglass, glass fiber, etc., applied on or below the roof sheathing.

Metal

A roof covering of either corrugated or shallow rib steel or aluminum.

Plastic Tile

A roof covering of tile made from plastic.

Roll Roofing (Composition)

A mineral-surfaced roof covering manufactured in rolls.

Sheathing

A covering of plywood sheets on roof rafters.

Shingles (Composition)

A roof covering of composition shingles of various weights. No felt underlayment is included.

Skylight

A glazed opening in a roof to allow in natural light.

Slate Tile

A roof covering of cut slate tiles.

Soffit

An exposed undersurface of a roof overhang.

Wood Shakes

A roof covering of thick wood shakes with an average exposure.

Wood Shingles

A roof covering of standard-size wood shingles with an average exposure.

SITEWORK

- Asphalt Paving
- Barbecue
- Block Walls
- Brick
- Chain-Links
- Concrete Paving
- Curbs
- Flagpole
- Flagstone/Tile Paving
- Hot Tub
- Landscaping
- Lawn Sprinkler
- Lighting
- Mailbox
- Ornamental Iron Gate
- Ramps

- Redwood Fence
- Refinish Swimming Pool
- Repair Wood Fence
- Replaster Swimming Pool
- Retaining Wall
- Septic Distribution Box
- Septic Leaching Lines
- Septic Tank
- Spa
- Split-Rail Fence
- Steps
- Stone Wall
- Swimming Pool
- Wood Decks
- Wrought Iron Fence

UNIT METHOD

To replace individual items, use the costs below:

Component	Quality Levels		
(Priced per Square Foot Unless Otherwise Shown)	Economy	Standard	Custom
Paving/Steps:			
Asphalt Paving	$ 2.40	$ 2.75	$ 3.10
Brick – Flat	6.65	7.95	9.05
Brick – on Edge	8.65	10.25	11.95
Concrete Paving	4.25	4.75	5.85
Curbs – Concrete (per linear foot)	14.00	15.20	16.60
Flagstone/Tile	13.85	15.70	17.80
Ramps – Concrete	8.90	9.85	10.95
Steps – Brick (per linear foot)	38.35	42.70	47.70
Steps – Concrete (per linear foot)	11.90	14.25	16.40
Wood Decks	18.30	22.90	28.50
Wood Paving – Flat	5.70	6.10	6.65
Wood Paving – on Edge	9.25	10.05	10.90

Component	Quality Levels		
(Priced per Linear Foot Unless Otherwise Shown)	Economy	Standard	Custom
Fences:			
Chain-link	$ 16.10	$ 17.45	$ 19.20
Chain-link Gate (each)	154.85	189.45	241.05
Ornamental Iron Gate (per square foot)	23.80	30.10	38.00
Repair Wood Fence	2.00	2.20	2.35
Redwood Fence	16.70	18.80	21.25
Split Rail (two rails)	10.50	11.95	13.60
Split Rail (three rails)	11.05	12.40	14.10
Split Rail (four rails)	12.50	13.95	15.45
Wood Board Fence	16.70	18.80	21.55
Wood Picket Fence	15.00	16.95	18.75
Wrought Iron (per square foot)	19.60	24.65	31.30

Component
(Priced per Square Foot)

Walls:	
Brick	$20.65
Block – Concrete	12.30
Block – Ornamental	10.30
Retaining Wall – Block	12.70
Retaining Wall – Concrete	19.00
Stone Wall	25.00

UNIT METHOD

To replace individual items, use the costs below:

Note: Swimming pool costs based on a standard 20' x 40'-size pool.

| Component | Quality Levels | | |
(Priced Each Unless Otherwise Shown)	**Economy**	**Standard**	**Custom**
Swimming Pools/Spas:			
Cover	$ 210.00	$ 265.00	$ 345.00
Diving Board	565.00	645.00	740.00
Filter	1,340.00	1,645.00	2,040.00
Heater	1,660.00	1,975.00	2,355.00
Hot Tub	7,100.00	8,245.00	9,605.00
Ladder	431.00	513.00	593.00
Repair Pool Cracks (per linear foot)	46.00	65.00	93.00
Repair Pool Tiles (per square foot)	25.00	35.00	40.00
Refinish Pool	1,145.00	1,590.00	2,145.00
Replaster Pool	1,430.00	1,865.00	2,440.00
Spa – Separate	7,660.00	9,710.00	12,275.00
Spa – Attached to Pool	4,800.00	5,800.00	7,500.00
Swimming Pool – Concrete	45,200.00	49,400.00	54,100.00
Swimming Pool – Fiberglass	26,400.00	28,600.00	31,400.00
Swimming Pool – Gunite	30,900.00	32,500.00	34,500.00
Swimming Pool (plastic lined)	13,435.00	15,171.65	16,946.85

| Component | |
(Priced Each Unless Otherwise Shown)	
Miscellaneous:	
Barbecue (built-in)	$ 745.00
Flagpole	2,145.60
Landscaping (per square foot)	5.95
Lawn Sprinkler – Head	35.20
Lawn Sprinkler – Control	330.80
Lawn Sprinkler – Piping (per linear foot)	10.00
Lighting	130.00
Mailbox – Post Type	85.00
Septic Distribution Box	211.60
Septic Leaching Lines (per linear foot)	20.00
Septic Tank	1,508.31

TYPICAL LAYOUT

WINDBREAK

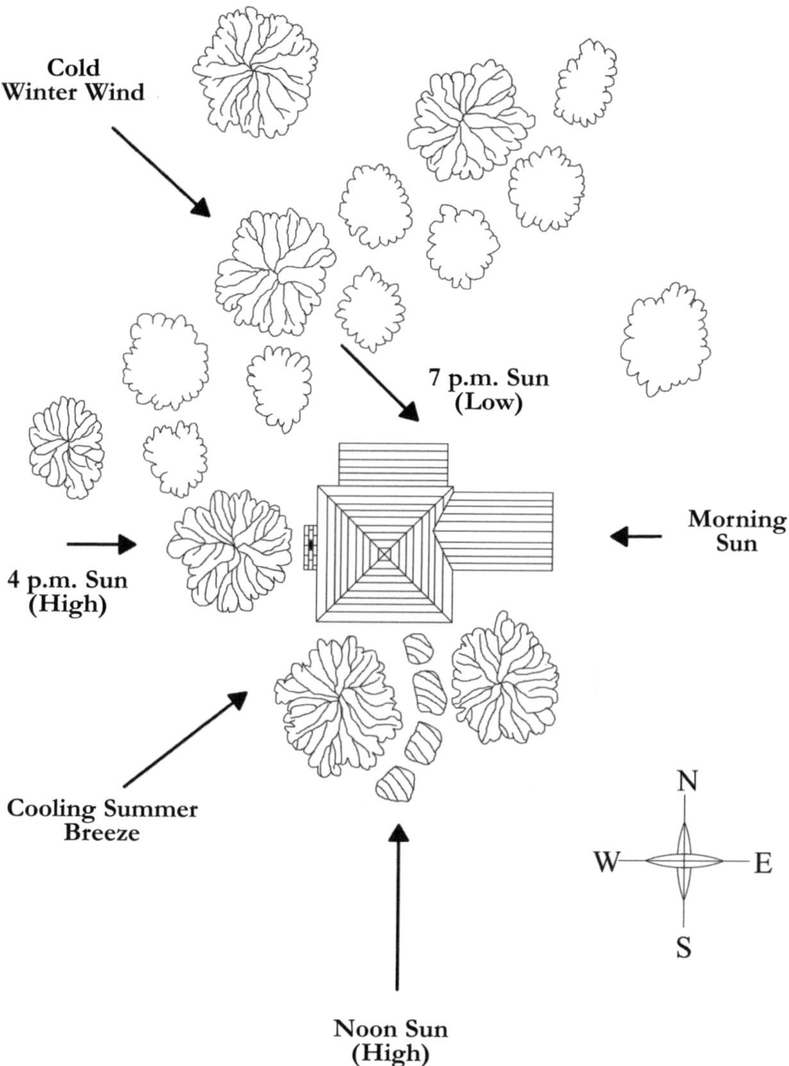

WIND DIRECTIONS

STANDARD WINTER WIND DIRECTIONS

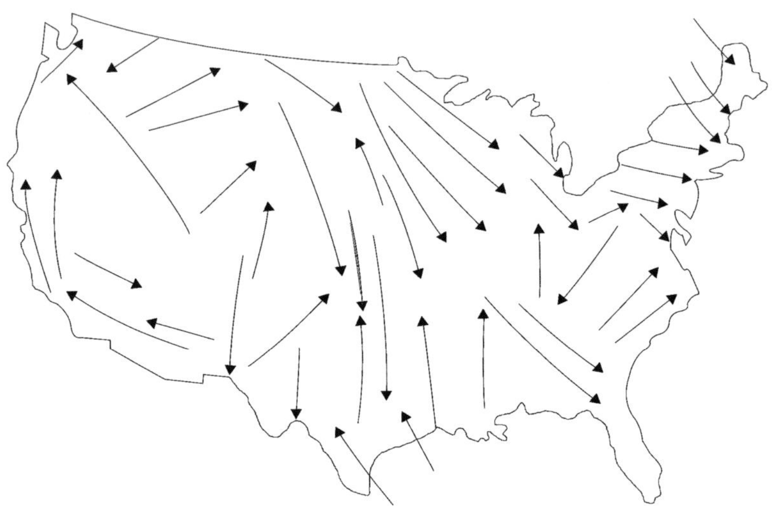

STANDARD SUMMER WIND DIRECTIONS

COMPONENT DESCRIPTIONS

Asphalt Paving
A paving consisting of asphalt cement.

Barbecue (Built-In)
A masonry-constructed box and chimney used for outdoor cooking.

Block Walls
A wall constructed of concrete block.

Brick Paving
A vitrified brick, laid flat or on edge, especially suitable for use in pavements.

Brick Walls
A wall constructed of brick.

Chain-Link Fence
Fencing consisting of tubular end, corner and pull posts, top and bottom rails or tension wires, and faced with a mesh fabric.

Chain-Link Gate
A chain-link gate including posts, rails and tension wires.

Concrete Paving
A paving consisting of concrete. Costs include reinforcing, framing and finishing.

Curbs (Concrete)
A raised rim of concrete forming the edge of a street.

Flagpole
A pole, base or setting, pulleys and rope that make up a flagpole.

Flagstone/Tile Paving
A surface of flat stone or tile units laid on a concrete base.

Hot Tub
A complete hot tub. Costs include all fittings.

Landscaping
Lawn, flowers, immature trees and bushes, and other flora constituting a landscape. Costs do not include unusual varieties.

Lawn Sprinkler Control
A lawn sprinkler control device with an automatic clock timer.

Lawn Sprinkler Head
That portion of piping connecting a water supply to a sprinkler system. Costs include the vertical pipe and nozzle.

Lighting
A yard-lighting fixture installed either on a post or on the ground.

Mailbox (Post Type)
A standard mailbox mounted on a post.

Ornamental Iron Gate
A gate constructed of decorative iron.

Ramps (Concrete)
A slope constructed of reinforced concrete, joining two levels.

Redwood Fence
A fence consisting of pieces of soft redwood.

Refinish Swimming Pool
Removal of a damaged swimming pool surface finish, and the application of a new finish.

Repair Swimming Pool Cracks
Filling in and surfacing over the cracks.

Repair Swimming Pool Tiles
Replacement of damaged tiles with new tiles.

Repair Wood Fence
The repair operation of re-aligning and bracing a wood fence that has fallen or been pushed down.

Replaster Swimming Pool
Replastering of a damaged swimming pool surface.

Retaining Wall
A freestanding or laterally braced wall that bears against an earth or other fill surface.

Septic Distribution Box
A box in which the effluent from a septic tank ensures equal distribution to each individual line of the disposal field.

Septic Leaching Lines
Lines used to distribute sewage effluent throughout a leach field.

Septic Tank
A watertight, covered receptacle designed and constructed to receive the discharge of sewage, separate solids from liquids, digest organic matter, store digested solids through a period of detention and allow the clarified liquids to discharge for final disposal.

Spa
A spa adjoined to or separate from a swimming pool. Costs include benches and aerators.

Split-Rail Fence
A fence made by connecting horizontal rails of split wood to posts.

Steps
Steps built with concrete or clay bricks. The costs include the necessary supporting structure but exclude the railing.

Stone Wall
A wall made of stone found in the local area.

Swimming Pool
A swimming pool constructed of either concrete, sprayed gunite, fiberglass or plastic-lined frame. Costs include the excavation, backfill, connection to existing electric, water and drain lines.

Swimming Pool Cover
A cover for the swimming pool that is placed over the pool by hand.

Swimming Pool Diving Board
Board, springs and other hardware associated with a diving board.

Swimming Pool Filter
An apparatus for clarifying pool water.

Swimming Pool Heater
A device designed to heat pools.

Swimming Pool Ladder
A stainless steel pool ladder.

Wood Board Fence
A fence of continuous wood boards that are butted together.

Wood Decks
A flat, open platform constructed of wood. Costs include piers and posts, but exclude railings.

Wood Paving
A durable flat surface of wood, 2" x 4", laid flat or on edge and set on a foundation of subgrade soil.

Wood Picket Fence
A fence formed of a series of wood pickets.

Wrought Iron Fence
A fence made of decorative iron.

SPECIALTIES/EQUIPMENT

- BLINDS
- BROOM CLOSET
- CLOSET POLE
- CLOTHES DRYER
- CLOTHES WASHER
- DESK (BUILT-IN)
- DRAPERIES
- DRAPERY ROD
- DRAPERY TRACK
- FIREPLACE CHIMNEY (MASONRY)
- FIREPLACE HEARTH (RAISED)
- FIREPLACE LOG LIGHTER
- FIREPLACE
- GREENHOUSE
- HOT TUB/SPA
- MAILBOX (WALL TYPE)
- PATIO ENCLOSURE
- RAILINGS
- SAUNA HEATING UNIT
- SAUNA ROOM
- SHADES
- SHAMPOO CARPET
- SHELVING
- SHUTTERS (INTERIOR)
- SPIRAL STAIRS
- STOVE (WOOD/COAL BURNING)
- WARDROBE
- WASH CEILING
- WASH FLOOR
- WASH WALLS
- WORKBENCH

UNIT METHOD

To replace individual items, use the costs below:

Component	
(Priced per Square Foot)	
Cleaning:	
Shampoo Carpet	$ .37
Wash Ceiling	.30
Wash Floor	.17
Wash Walls	.25

Component	Quality Levels		
(Price Each Unless Otherwise Shown)	**Economy**	**Standard**	**Custom**
Fireplace:			
Chimney – Masonry (per linear foot)	$ 90.00	$ 125.00	$ 145.00
Hearth (raised)	320.00	440.00	650.00
Log Lighter	160.00	200.00	285.00
Masonry Fireplace	2,645.00	3,490.00	4,625.00
Masonry Fireplace w/Heatilator	3,260.00	4,285.00	5,630.00
Prefabricated Fireplace	1,185.00	1,660.00	2,265.00
Stove (wood/coal)	1,015.00	1,425.00	2,045.00

Component	Quality Levels		
(Priced per Linear Foot)	**Economy**	**Standard**	**Custom**
Casework:			
Broom Closet (metal)	$160.00	$190.00	$240.00
Broom Closet (wood)	279.30	322.80	372.50
Closet Pole	3.20	3.85	5.30
Desk – Built-in (metal)	105.00	110.00	125.00
Desk – Built-in (wood)	123.45	142.90	162.45
Shelving (metal)	6.35	7.30	8.70
Shelving (wood)	6.35	6.50	7.40
Wardrobe (metal)	155.00	165.00	175.00
Wardrobe (wood)	150.00	160.00	180.00
Workbench (metal)	70.00	80.00	85.00
Workbench (wood)	72.75	79.35	86.00

UNIT METHOD

To replace individual items, use the costs below:

Component	Quality Levels		
(Priced per Linear Foot Unless Otherwise Shown)	Economy	Standard	Custom
Stair/Railings:			
Paint/Stain Railings	$ 1.75	$ 2.10	$ 2.50
Railing – Metal	37.00	43.00	49.00
Railing – Metal (wall-mounted)	25.00	35.00	40.00
Railing – Ornamental Iron	63.80	69.65	75.45
Railing – Wood	15.85	20.05	25.65
Railing – Wood (wall-mounted)	12.45	13.15	15.50
Spiral Stairs – Aluminum (per flight)	3,210.00	4,090.00	5,225.00
Spiral Stairs – Steel (per flight)	3,045.00	4,980.00	5,760.00
Spiral Stairs – Wood (per flight)	6,095.00	6,865.00	7,735.00

Component	Quality Levels		
(Priced as Shown)	Economy	Standard	Custom
Miscellaneous:			
Clothes Dryer (each)	$ 605.00	$ 790.00	$1,055.00
Clothes Washer (each)	741.00	979.00	1,289.00
Greenhouse (per square foot)	35.00	40.00	50.00
Hot Tub/Spa (each)	7,100.00	8,255.00	9,610.00
Mailbox – Wall Type (each)	59.50	92.65	132.30
Patio Enclosure Walls – Glass (per square foot)	11.45	14.55	18.25
Patio Enclosure Walls – Screen (per square foot)	3.85	5.65	8.50
Sauna Room (per square foot)	175.00	195.00	240.00
Sauna – Heating Unit (each)	1,740.90	2,085.00	2,516.75

Component	Quality Levels		
(Priced per Square Foot Unless Otherwise Shown)	Economy	Standard	Custom
Window Treatment:			
Blinds – Vertical	$11.45	$13.05	$14.75
Blinds – Horizontal	3.50	4.45	5.90
Draperies	5.40	6.75	8.40
Drapery Rod (per linear foot)	14.60	17.60	21.00
Drapery Track (per linear foot)	7.55	9.50	11.80
Shades (each)	28.50	34.15	45.60
Shutters – Interior	11.00	12.55	17.95

COMPONENT DESCRIPTIONS

Blinds

Blinds made of thin horizontal or vertical slats.

Broom Closet

A metal or wood case, for broom storage.

Closet Pole

A long rod of wood or metal, used to hang garments in a closet.

Clothes Dryer

A self-supporting clothes dryer.

Clothes Washer

A self-supporting clothes washer.

Desk (Built-In)

A wood or metal desk, permanently affixed to a structure.

Draperies

Material used to cover or decorate windows.

Drapery Rod

An ornamental horizontal pole on which to hang drapery.

Drapery Track

A horizontal device used to support and allow the opening and closing of window drapes.

Fireplace Chimney (Masonry)

A vertical masonry structure, containing one or more flues.

Fireplace Hearth (Raised)

The extra cost of a raised hearth.

Fireplace Log Lighter

A device for igniting wood logs in a fireplace.

Fireplace (Masonry)

A masonry box at the base of a chimney, usually an open recess in a wall. Costs do not include the chimney.

Fireplace (Masonry With Heatilator)

A masonry fireplace with the extra cost of a heatilator system.

Fireplace (Prefab)

A box at the base of a chimney, usually an open recess in a wall, constructed of metal. Costs do not include the chimney.

Greenhouse

A glass-enclosed, prefabricated greenhouse. Costs exclude foundation and floor slab.

Hot Tub/Spa

A complete hot tub or spa, including all fittings.

Mailbox (Wall Type)

A box recessed in, or attached to, the outer wall of a residence.

Patio Enclosure

An outside area enclosure, attached to a house, made of mesh/screened or glass/acrylic walls. Costs do not include the roofing or structure.

Railings

Wall-mounted, or freestanding, metal or wood railings.

Sauna Heating Unit

A unit that supplies heat for a sauna.

Sauna Room

A hot-air bath. Costs include paneling and benches.

Shades

A roller-type window shade.

Shampoo Carpet

Carpet cleaning by use of a shampooer.

Shelving

Metal or wood shelves, used for storage.

Shutters (Interior)

Interior window covers with movable slats.

Spiral Stairs

A flight of aluminum, steel, or wood steps, circular in design, whose treads wind around a central newel.

Stove (Wood/Coal Burning)

A self-contained, wood-burning stove. Costs include the damper and connection to a local vent or chimney.

Wardrobe

A built-in wood or metal storage unit, for clothing.

Wash Ceiling

Remove dirt from ceiling surfaces.

Wash Floor

Remove dirt from floor surfaces.

Wash Walls

Remove dirt from wall surfaces.

Workbench

Metal or wood worktable.

WALL FINISHES

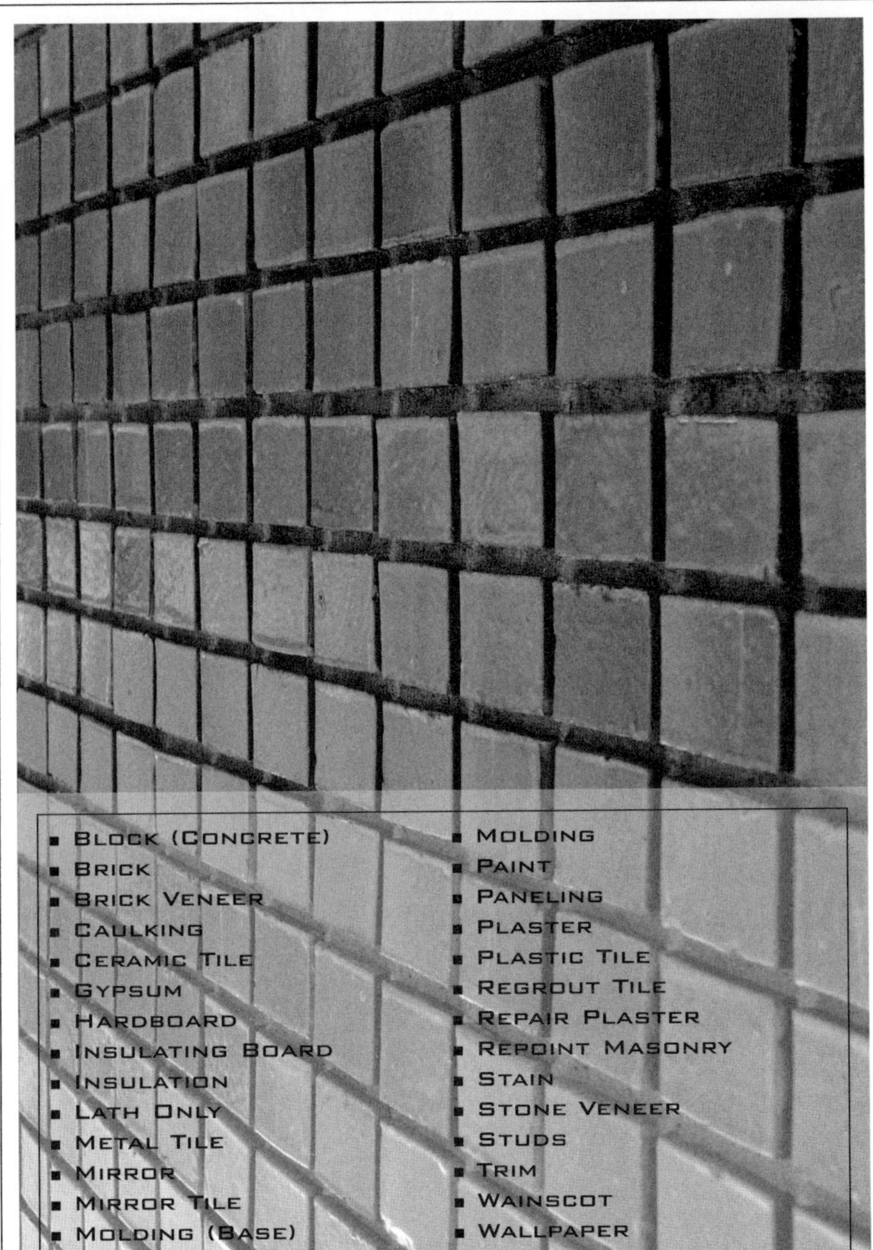

- Block (Concrete)
- Brick
- Brick Veneer
- Caulking
- Ceramic Tile
- Gypsum
- Hardboard
- Insulating Board
- Insulation
- Lath Only
- Metal Tile
- Mirror
- Mirror Tile
- Molding (Base)
- Molding
- Paint
- Paneling
- Plaster
- Plastic Tile
- Regrout Tile
- Repair Plaster
- Repoint Masonry
- Stain
- Stone Veneer
- Studs
- Trim
- Wainscot
- Wallpaper

ROOM METHOD

QUALITY LEVEL – ECONOMY

Costs are for replacing (and refinishing) walls completely.

Room size ranges:
Small — (48 Square Feet – 80 Square Feet)
Medium — (81 Square Feet – 144 Square Feet)
Large — (145 Square Feet – 200 Square Feet)
X-large — (201 Square Feet – 275 Square Feet)

Note: For unusually small or large rooms, use the Unit Method.

Component	Room Size			
(Priced per Room)	Small	Medium	Large	X-Large
Finishes/Covers:				
Gypsum Board	$ 565.00	$ 750.00	$ 895.00	$1,030.00
Paint	245.00	320.00	385.00	430.00
Paneling – Plywood (hardwood)	1,205.00	1,600.00	1,930.00	2,225.00
Paneling – Plywood (softwood)	625.00	825.00	1,000.00	1,150.00
Paneling – Solid (hardwood)	1,530.00	2,020.00	2,450.00	2,815.00
Paneling – Solid (softwood)	1,165.00	1,560.00	1,930.00	2,200.00
Plaster and Lath	1,255.00	1,685.00	2,030.00	2,295.00
Plaster – Thincoat	250.00	325.00	385.00	435.00
Stain	195.00	265.00	335.00	375.00
Wallpaper	445.00	600.00	740.00	850.00
Wainscot	415.00	555.00	690.00	790.00
Miscellaneous:				
Molding – Base	$ 70.00	$ 80.00	$ 95.00	$105.00
Molding – Ceiling	105.00	140.00	160.00	190.00
Repair Plaster	190.00	260.00	320.00	350.00
Paint Molding	50.00	60.00	65.00	70.00
Stain Molding	40.00	50.00	55.00	65.00

ROOM METHOD

QUALITY LEVEL – STANDARD

Costs are for replacing (and refinishing) walls completely.

Room size ranges:
- Small — (48 Square Feet – 80 Square Feet)
- Medium — (81 Square Feet – 144 Square Feet)
- Large — (145 Square Feet – 200 Square Feet)
- X-large — (201 Square Feet – 275 Square Feet)

Note: For unusually small or large rooms, use the Unit Method.

Component	Room Size			
(Priced per Room)	Small	Medium	Large	X-Large
Finishes/Covers:				
Gypsum Board	$ 610.00	$ 785.00	$ 955.00	$1,120.00
Paint	260.00	345.00	415.00	465.00
Paneling – Plywood (hardwood)	1,420.00	1,895.00	2,295.00	2,635.00
Paneling – Plywood (softwood)	810.00	1,075.00	1,300.00	1,505.00
Paneling – Solid (hardwood)	1,760.00	2,345.00	2,820.00	3,260.00
Paneling – Solid (softwood)	1,440.00	1,950.00	2,400.00	2,775.00
Plaster and Lath	1,455.00	1,925.00	2,330.00	2,650.00
Plaster – Thincoat	265.00	355.00	425.00	470.00
Stain	200.00	280.00	345.00	395.00
Wallpaper	605.00	810.00	1,010.00	1,170.00
Wainscot	555.00	760.00	945.00	1,090.00
Miscellaneous:				
Molding – Base	$ 75.00	$ 95.00	$115.00	$125.00
Molding – Ceiling	140.00	180.00	210.00	245.00
Repair Plaster	250.00	340.00	405.00	445.00
Paint Molding	55.00	60.00	70.00	75.00
Stain Molding	40.00	55.00	65.00	70.00

ROOM METHOD

QUALITY LEVEL – CUSTOM

Costs are for replacing (and refinishing) walls completely.

Room size ranges:
Small	(48 Square Feet – 80 Square Feet)
Medium	(81 Square Feet – 144 Square Feet)
Large	(145 Square Feet – 200 Square Feet)
X-large	(201 Square Feet – 275 Square Feet)

Note: For unusually small or large rooms, use the Unit Method.

Component	Room Size			
(Priced per Room)	Small	Medium	Large	X-Large
Finishes/Covers:				
Gypsum Board	$ 650.00	$ 870.00	$1,040.00	$1,190.00
Paint	280.00	385.00	465.00	525.00
Paneling – Plywood (hardwood)	1,640.00	2,190.00	2,615.00	3,035.00
Paneling – Plywood (softwood)	930.00	1,230.00	1,510.00	1,705.00
Paneling – Solid (hardwood)	1,985.00	2,660.00	3,215.00	3,690.00
Paneling – Solid (softwood)	1,585.00	2,140.00	2,635.00	3,040.00
Plaster and Lath	1,600.00	2,135.00	2,565.00	2,930.00
Plaster – Thincoat	280.00	375.00	455.00	520.00
Stain	230.00	320.00	380.00	440.00
Wallpaper	810.00	1,095.00	1,365.00	1,575.00
Wainscot	770.00	1,045.00	1,275.00	1,485.00
Miscellaneous:				
Molding – Base	$ 85.00	$115.00	$130.00	$160.00
Molding – Ceiling	160.00	220.00	275.00	305.00
Repair Plaster	325.00	415.00	510.00	575.00
Paint Molding	55.00	65.00	70.00	80.00
Stain Molding	31.05	42.70	48.75	50.00

UNIT METHOD

To replace (and refinish) individual items, use the costs below:

Notes: 1) Normal waste is built into costs.
2) Costs are based on square feet of wall area.

| Component | Quality Levels | | |
(Priced per Square Foot)	Economy	Standard	Custom
Interior Finishes:			
Brick Veneer	$16.90	$17.40	$17.95
Brick (simulated)	7.40	9.65	12.45
Ceramic Tile	9.50	10.65	12.40
Metal Tile	9.30	9.95	10.75
Mirror	20.40	26.65	35.15
Mirror Tile	7.55	8.75	10.00
Paint	.95	1.05	1.10
Paneling – Plywood (hardwood)	4.80	5.70	6.45
Paneling – Plywood (softwood)	2.50	3.35	3.75
Paneling – Solid (hardwood)	5.95	6.95	7.85
Paneling – Solid (softwood)	5.05	5.80	6.55
Plaster – Thincoat	.90	1.05	1.20
Plastic Tile	7.45	8.05	8.55
Stain	.60	.75	.95
Stone Veneer (imitation)	10.45	11.30	12.10
Wallpaper	1.95	2.60	3.50
Wallpaper – Grass Cloth	4.10	4.35	4.60
Wallpaper – Mural	4.60	5.10	5.35
Wainscot	3.90	5.40	7.35

UNIT METHOD

To replace (and refinish) individual items, use the costs below:

Component	Quality Levels		
(Priced per Linear Foot Unless Otherwise Shown)	Economy	Standard	Custom
Miscellaneous:			
Caulking	$ 3.50	$ 4.35	$ 5.65
Insulation – Batt (per square foot)	.70	1.05	1.25
Insulation – Rigid (per square foot)	1.50	1.70	2.10
Molding – Base	1.70	2.10	2.60
Molding – Base (two-member)	3.60	4.30	5.10
Molding – Base (three-member)	5.25	6.45	8.35
Molding – Base (ceramic tile)	12.20	13.25	14.50
Molding – Base (rubber)	1.95	2.20	2.40
Molding – Ceiling	2.90	3.75	4.85
Molding – Ceiling (crown)	3.15	4.10	5.20
Molding – Chair Rail	2.70	3.60	4.70
Molding – Corner	2.55	2.80	3.10
Molding – Panel Edge	1.85	2.15	2.50
Paint Molding	1.10	1.25	1.30
Regrout Tile (per square foot)	1.90	2.10	2.75
Repair Plaster (per square foot)	.75	1.10	1.30
Repoint Masonry (per square foot)	3.50	4.15	4.75
Stain Molding	.80	.95	1.05
Trim	3.25	3.60	3.85

Component	
(Priced per Square Foot)	
Interior Wall Covers:	
Gypsum Board	$2.50
Gypsum Board – Water Resistant	2.45
Hardboard	3.55
Insulating Board	2.25
Lath Only	1.85
Plaster Only	4.75
Plaster and Lath	5.05
Interior Structural Walls:	
Block – Concrete	$ 8.50
Brick	24.85
Studs	2.70

DRYWALL FINISH SYSTEM

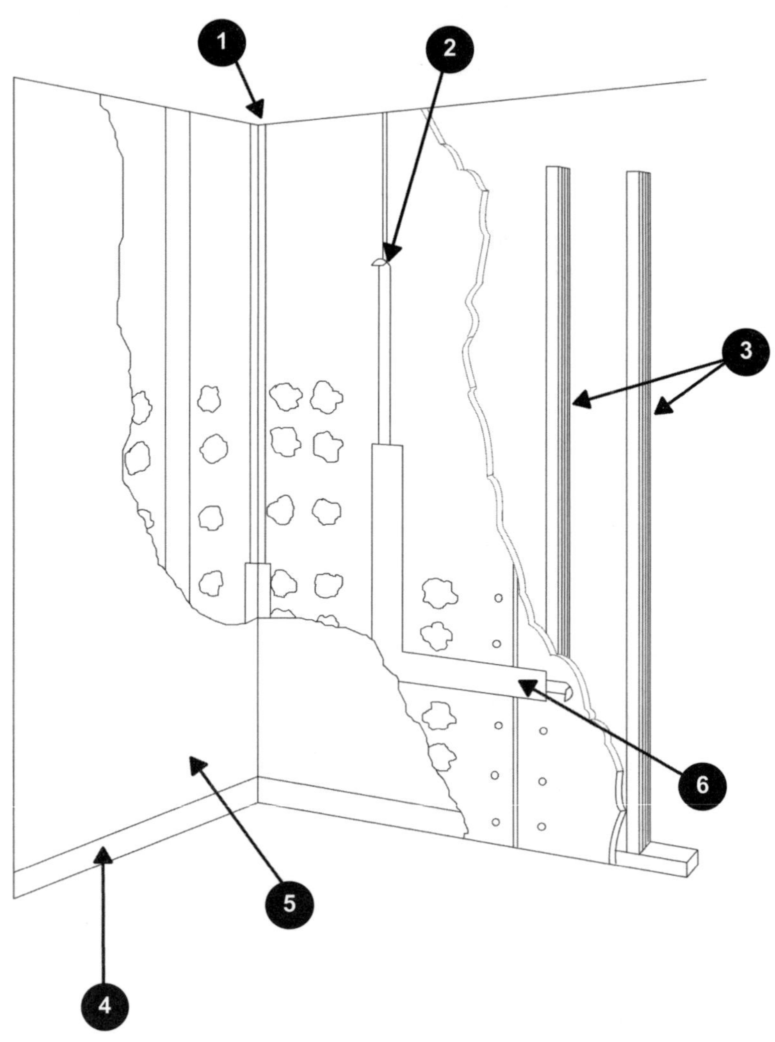

1. Corners

2. Tape Seams

3. Studs

4. Trim

5. Paint

6. Finish

COMPONENT DESCRIPTIONS

Block (Concrete)
An interior concrete, or masonry block, nonload-bearing wall. Normal thickness 4" to 6".

Brick (Solid)
An interior brick wall. May be load or nonload bearing.

Brick Veneer
An interior wall covering of face brick, laid against a frame or masonry wall.

Brick Veneer (Simulated)
An interior wall covering that has the appearance of brick veneer.

Caulking
Installation of a resilient mastic compound used to seal cracks, fill joints, prevent leakage and/or provide waterproofing.

Ceramic Tile
An interior wall covering of ceramic tile units.

Gypsum Board
$\frac{1}{2}$" to $\frac{5}{8}$" wallboards, also known as sheetrock or drywall. Costs include fill, sand, and finishing of joints and fastening spots.

Gypsum Board (Water Resistant)
A wallboard treated to resist the passage of water and moisture.

Hardboard
An interior wall covering of flush hardboard panels.

Insulating Board
An interior wall covering of prefinished insulating boards.

Insulation (Batt)
A flexible blanket or roll-type thermal insulation placed between studs in frame construction.

Insulation (Rigid)
A structural building board, applied to walls to resist heat transmission.

Lath Only
A thin metal mesh, or strips of narrow wood, fastened to framing in order to provide a base for plaster.

Metal Tile
An interior wall covering of metal tile units.

Mirror
An interior wall covering of reflective glass wall panels.

Mirror Tile
An interior wall covering of reflective glass tile units.

Molding (Base)
A horizontal strip, typically affixed to the bottom of the wall, to cover the flooring to wall material transition joint.

Molding (Ceiling)
A horizontal strip, typically affixed to the top of the wall, to cover the ceiling to wall material transition joint.

Molding (Corner)
A horizontal strip, usually of wood, affixed to the wall at a height that prevents backs of chairs from damaging the wall surface.

Molding (Corner)

A vertical strip, used to protect and trim an external angle, or two intersecting surfaces.

Molding (Panel Edge)

A metal or wood vertical piece, installed over the butt joint of two panels.

Paint

Costs include primer and finish coats applied to the walls.

Paneling (Plywood)

An interior wall covering of plywood paneling, with a softwood or hardwood surface.

Paneling (Solid)

An interior wall covering of hardwood or softwood panels.

Plaster (Only)

Three coats of gypsum plaster, applied to a wall surface.

Plaster And Lath

An interior wall covering of plaster, with a metal lath backing.

Plaster (Thincoat)

An interior wall finish covering, composed of a thin application of plaster.

Plastic Tile

An interior wall covering of plastic tile units.

Regrout Tile

Reapplying cement mortar between tile joints on a wall surface.

Repair Plaster

The repair of a plaster wall, such as repairing minor cracks, peeling, etc.

Repoint Masonry

Removing of mortar from between the joints of masonry units and replacing it with new mortar.

Stain

A wax-based stain, applied as a protective coating or polish on interior wood.

Stone Veneer (Imitation)

An interior wall covering that has the appearance of stone.

Studs

An interior wall, constructed using wood studs.

Trim

Visible woodwork or moldings of a room (baseboards, cornices, casings, etc.).

Wainscot

A decorative or protective facing, applied to the lower portion of an interior partition or wall, such as panels, usually reaching a height of four feet.

Wallpaper

A wall covering of quality paper or vinyl.

Wallpaper (Grass Cloth)

A wall covering of woven grass cloth.

Wallpaper (Mural)

A wall covering of paper or vinyl on which a painting has been rendered.

WINDOWS

- Acrylic/Plexiglas
- Awnings
- Awning Windows
- Casement Windows
- Combination Windows
- Double-Hung Windows
- Fixed Windows
- Greenhouse Windows
- Hardware
- Insulating Glass
- Jalousie
- Opaque Glass
- Paint
- Plate Glass
- Screens
- Security Grilles
- Security Mesh
- Shutters
- Single Glass
- Single-Hung Windows
- Skylight Glazing
- Sliding Windows
- Storm Windows
- Tempered Glass
- Trim
- Wired Glass

UNIT METHOD

To replace individual items, use the costs below:

Component (Priced per Square Foot)	Quality Levels		
	Economy	Standard	Custom
Glazed Windows (with insulating glass):			
Awning – Aluminum/Vinyl	$39.00	$43.00	$51.00
Casement – Aluminum/Vinyl	35.00	40.00	46.00
Casement – Wood	43.00	48.00	55.00
Combination – Aluminum/Vinyl	34.00	40.00	46.00
Combination – Wood	51.00	59.00	63.00
Double-Hung – Wood	36.00	40.00	44.00
Fixed – Aluminum/Vinyl	24.00	27.00	30.00
Fixed – Wood	26.00	28.00	37.00
Single-Hung – Wood	42.00	46.00	51.00
Sliding – Aluminum/Vinyl	29.00	32.00	36.00
Miscellaneous:			
Greenhouse Window	$32.40	$39.20	$47.15
Jalousie	20.55	23.80	27.45
Storm Windows	13.45	14.10	14.65

Component (Priced per Square Foot)	
Glazing Only:	
Acrylic/Plexiglas	$16.10
Insulating – Clear	33.65
Insulating – Tinted	38.20
Jalousie (louvered)	11.45
Opaque	16.65
Plate – Clear	17.80
Plate – Tinted	19.50
Single – Clear	9.40
Single – Tinted	10.70
Skylight Glazing	64.30
Tempered – Clear	21.00
Tempered – Tinted	22.90
Wired Glass	14.50

UNIT METHOD

To replace individual items, use the costs below:

Note: Costs based on square footage of window.

Component	Quality Levels		
(Priced per Square Foot Unless Otherwise Shown)	Economy	Standard	Custom
Miscellaneous:			
Awning – Aluminum (per linear foot)	$79.55	$82.45	$86.90
Awning – Canvas (per linear foot)	73.45	77.90	81.00
Hardware (each)	50.35	54.90	59.55
Paint Shutters	4.60	5.20	6.15
Paint Trim (per linear foot)	.45	.50	.65
Paint Windows	4.65	4.80	5.50
Screen – Aluminum Frame	2.80	3.45	3.90
Screen – Wood Frame	7.90	9.15	10.70
Security Grille	15.75	22.95	30.20
Security Mesh	14.80	17.05	19.95
Shutters – Louvered	10.80	11.70	13.10
Shutters – Plain	14.35	15.30	16.40
Trim – Exterior (per linear foot)	2.85	3.55	4.30
Trim – Interior (per linear foot)	3.70	4.00	4.45

UNIT TYPES

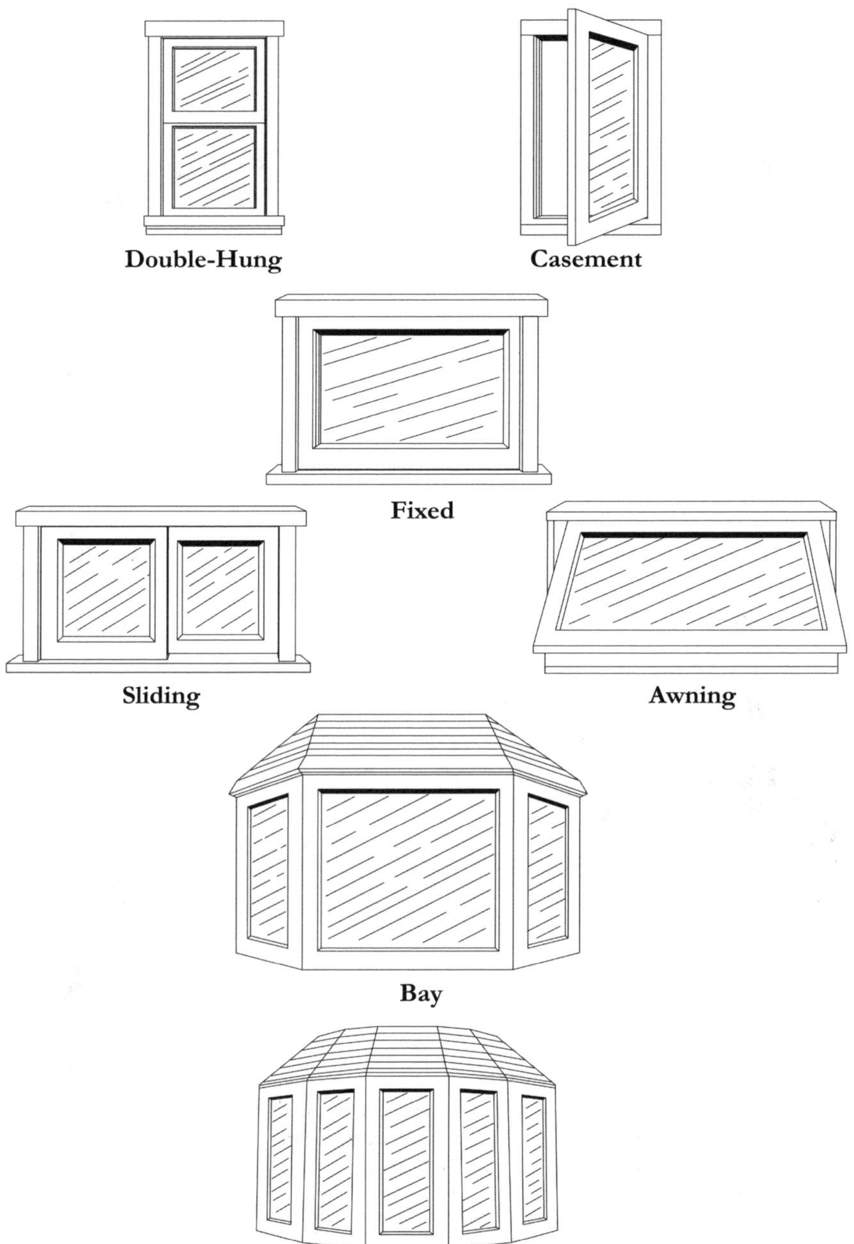

TERMINOLOGY

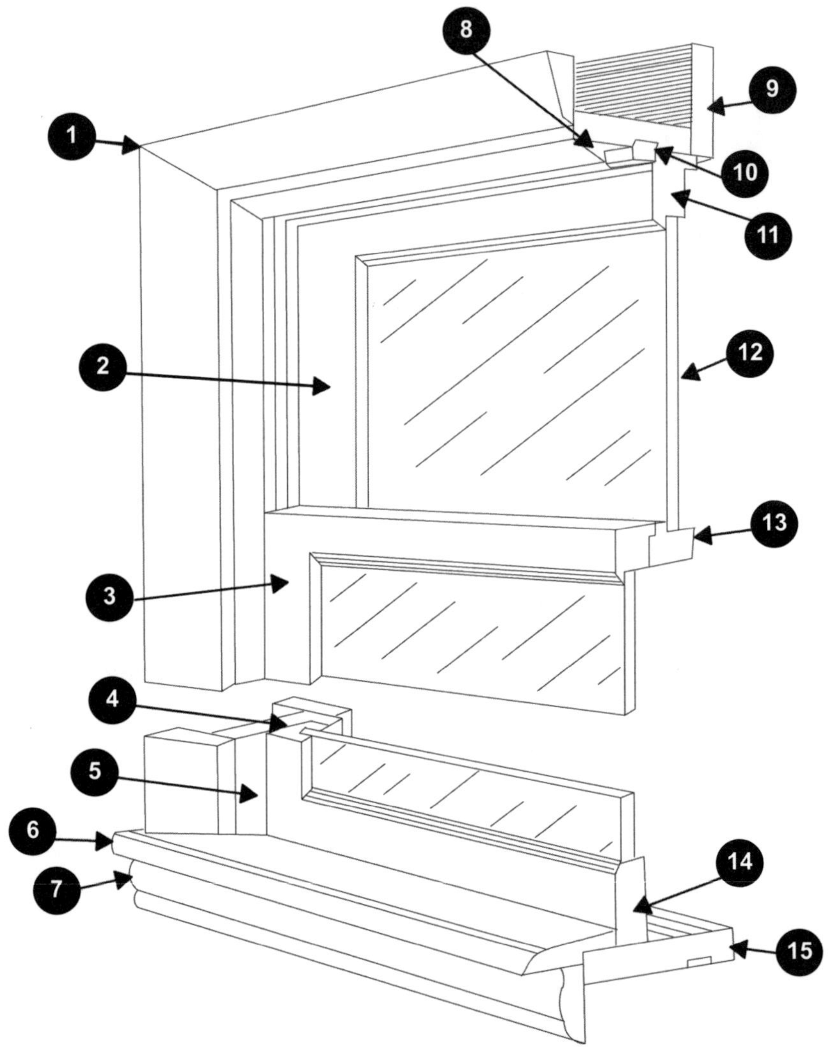

1. Inside Casing
2. Upper Sash
3. Lower Sash
4. Jamb
5. Stop
6. Stool
7. Apron
8. Stop
9. Outside Casing
10. Parting Stop
11. Rail
12. Glazing
13. Check Rail or Meeting Rail
14. Rail
15. Sill

COMPONENT DESCRIPTIONS

Acrylic/Plexiglas
The material and installation of acrylic/Plexiglas in a single frame.

Awnings
A rooflike covering of canvas or aluminum over a window.

Awning Windows
A sashed window that can be tilted outward. Costs do not include the window trim.

Casement Windows
A sashed window that swings open from the side. Costs exclude the window trim.

Combination Windows
A framed window that is equipped with removable or interchangeable screen and storm glass sections.

Double-Hung Windows
A sashed window having two vertically sliding sashes. Window trim is not included.

Fixed Windows
A window which does not open. Costs do not include the window trim.

Greenhouse Windows
A metal-framed window extending approximately one to two feet outside a window opening. Costs include standard glass.

Hardware
Items included in window hardware range from a variety of window locks to window handles.

Insulating Glass
The material and installation of insulation glass in a single frame.

Jalousie
A window consisting of glass louvers which pivot simultaneously in a common frame. Costs include hardware but exclude window trim.

Jalousie Glass (Only)
The material and installation of a series of overlapping, horizontal glass louvers which pivot simultaneously in a common frame.

Opaque Glass
The material and installation of a glass that transmits light but cannot be seen through.

Paint
Costs include primer and finish coats applied to the windows, trim, etc.

Plate Glass
The material and installation of $1/4$" plate glass in a single frame.

Screens
A window screen whose frame is of wood or metal.

Security Grilles
A grating or openwork barrier of strong metal to protect an opening.

Security Mesh
Heavy mesh screening placed on the exterior of a window for added security.

Shutters (Louver)
Exterior shutters with movable louvers.

Shutters (Plain)
Exterior plain shutters, with or without fixed louvers.

COMPONENT DESCRIPTIONS

Single Glass

The material and installation of one $^1/_8$" window pane in a single frame.

Single-Hung Windows

A framed window that is hung and balanced so that only the lower sash opens. Costs exclude the window trim.

Skylight Glazing

A glazed opening in a roof.

Sliding Windows

A sashed window that opens or closes horizontally along a fixed track.

Storm Windows

An auxiliary window, usually placed on the outside of an existing window. Costs include hardware.

Tempered Glass

The material and installation of tempered glass in a single frame.

Trim

Any visible member, usually of wood, around the exterior perimeter of the window frame.

Wired Glass

The material and installation of wired glass in a single frame.

USEFUL INFORMATION

TYPICAL HOUSE STYLES

One Story:
One-story residences have one level of living area. The roof structure has a medium slope. The attic space is limited and is not intended for living area.

One And One Half Story:
One-and-one-half-story residences have two levels of living area. Characterized by a steep roof slope and dormers, the area of the upper level, whether finished or unfinished, is usually 40% to 60% of the lower level.

Two Story:
Two-story residences have two levels of finished living area. The area of each floor is approximately the same. The roof structure has a medium slope. The attic space is limited and is not designed for usable living area.

Two Story Bi-Level:
Two-story Bi-level residences have two levels of living area, but unlike a conventional Two Story, the lower level, which may be partially below grade, is partially unfinished. A distinguishing characteristic is its split-foyer entry.

Two And One Half Story:
Two-and-one-half-story residences have three levels of living area. Also having a steep roof slope with dormers, the area of the third floor, whether finished or unfinished, is usually 40% to 60% of the second floor.

Split Level:
Split-level residences have three levels of finished living area: lower level, intermediate level and upper level. The lower level is immediately below the upper level as in a Two-Story. The intermediate level, adjacent to the other levels, is built on a grade approximately four feet higher than that of the lower level.

TYPICAL HOUSE STYLES

Mobile/Manufactured Housing:

Often referred to as mobile homes, these structures, whether on a permanent or semipermanent foundation, have a steel undercarriage as a necessary structural component.

Multiples:

Multiples, often referred to as apartments, are multifamily residences, intended for permanent habitation, and are three stories or less.

Town Houses And Duplexes:

Both Town Houses and Duplexes are single family, attached residences. They do not have other units above or below, do not have more than two walls that are common with adjacent units and always have individual exterior entries.

Urban Row Houses:

Urban Row Houses are single-family residences and can be either attached or detached. Unlike Town Houses, Urban Row Houses are usually individually built, with adjacent units not sharing common structural systems (i.e., roof, foundation, etc.). A distinguishing characteristic is that the living area is entirely on the second level. The ground floor, sometimes referred to as the basement level, usually contains the garage and utility area.

TYPICAL GARAGE & CARPORT STYLES

Detached Garages:
Detached Garages are freestanding buildings with independent structural systems (i.e. foundation, roof, etc.).

Garages:
Attached Garages share a common wall with the residence.

Built-In Garages:
Built-in Garages have living area both adjacent to and above.

Basement Garages:
Basement Garages have living area above and have two to three walls below grade.

Carports
Sheds or Flat Roofs have a two-dimensional roof structure.

Gable Roofs have a three-dimensional, trussed roof system and are usually an extension of the residence roof structure.

HEIGHT MEASUREMENT TECHNIQUE

The total height of a building may be measured by dropping a tape from the roof of the building, measuring down through a stairwell or similar vertical opening, or measuring ceiling heights and allowing for the thickness of the floors. Sometimes the height is more easily estimated by standing back from the building and sighting using the following formula:

$$H = A \times \frac{h}{a}$$

A = Distance from eye to wall
a = Distance from eye to ruler
h = Distance on ruler

H = Height of wall

For example, substituting in the aforementioned formula:

$$H = 90' \times \frac{21''}{27''}$$

$$H = 70'$$

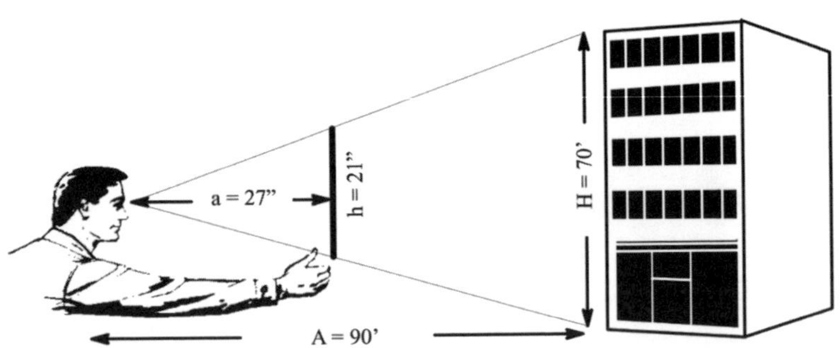

DETERMINING AVERAGE STORY HEIGHT

When figuring the average story height of a building with a balcony or mezzanine, these added interior items should be disregarded.

In the case of high-pitched roofs, some adjustment should be made for the gable ends and the large roof area. Usually it is sufficiently accurate to add one-half the vertical distance from the eave line to the ridge to obtain an effective wall height for adjustment. This can also be used with an A-frame, where the effective wall height would be one-half the distance from the floor to the ridge.

Normally, the average story height of the building is the distance from the ground or top of the basement wall to the eaves, divided by the number of stories.

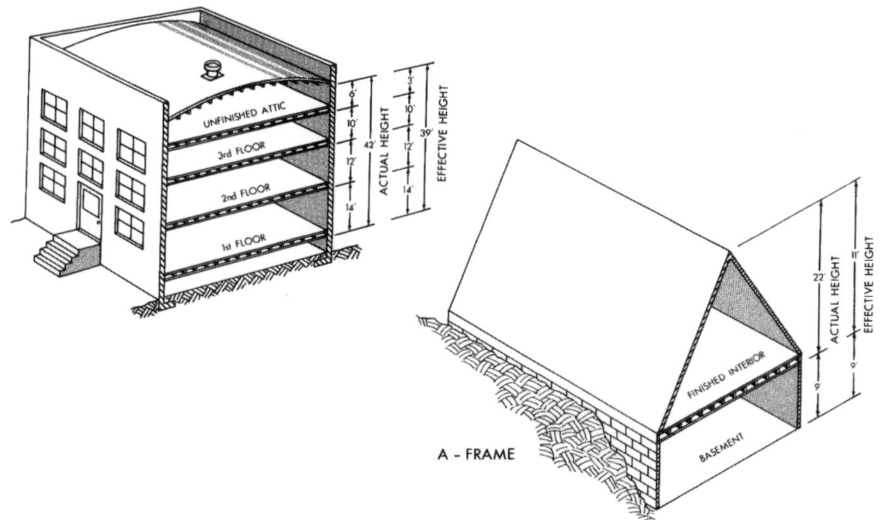

MEASURING FLOOR AREAS

Use a steel or metallic tape with a hook on one end for your measuring. Metallic tapes are cloth tapes with wire in them to keep their length uniform. Plain cloth tapes are unreliable as they tend to shrink or stretch. Caution should be used with both metallic and steel tape around electricity. If a wheel device is used, it should be closely checked and calibrated.

Draw each line to scale and go completely around the building, bringing your lines back to the starting point. Errors in scale or measurement will then show up while you are in the field.

COMPUTING AREAS

Floor areas are based on the outside dimensions of the building. Most buildings can be broken down into rectangles and the area of each rectangle computed with no difficulty. Other shapes can be computed as shown below.

PARALLELOGRAM
A quadrilateral having its opposite side parallel.

AREA = b x h

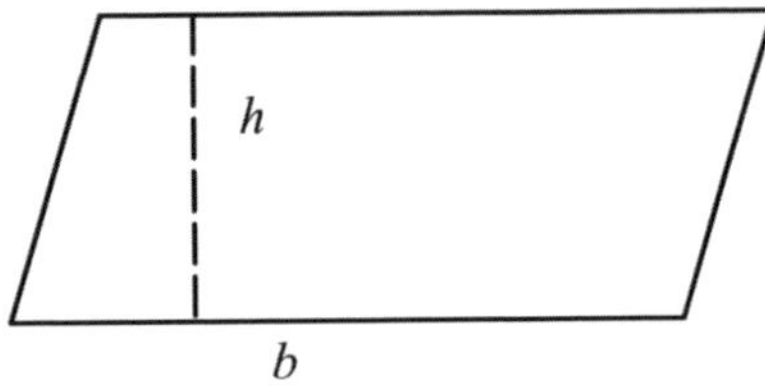

The altitude (h) of a parallelogram or trapezoid is the perpendicular distance between the parallel sides.

TRAPEZOID
A quadrilateral having two and only two sides parallel.

AREA = h x 1/2 (b + c)

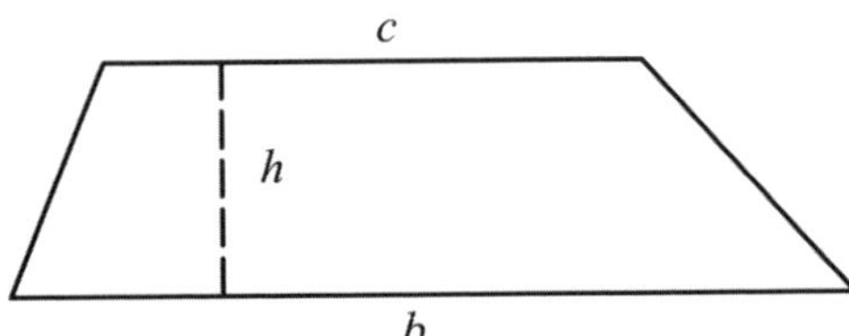

TRIANGLE
A three-sided polygon.

AREA = 1/2 b x h

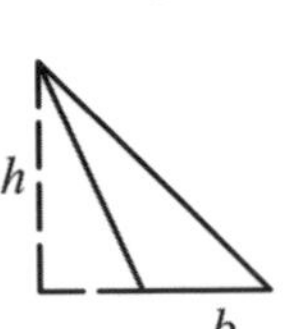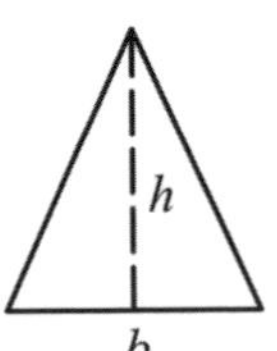

The altitude (h) of a triangle is the perpendicular distance from any vertex to the opposite side or its extension.

COMPUTING AREAS

IRREGULAR POLYGONS

The area of irregular polygons can be determined by dividing the area into the shapes on the previous page and adding the area of the parts.

AREA $= \frac{1}{2}$ a x b

$\qquad + \, c \times \frac{1}{2}$ (b + d)

$\qquad + \, \frac{1}{2}$ e x d

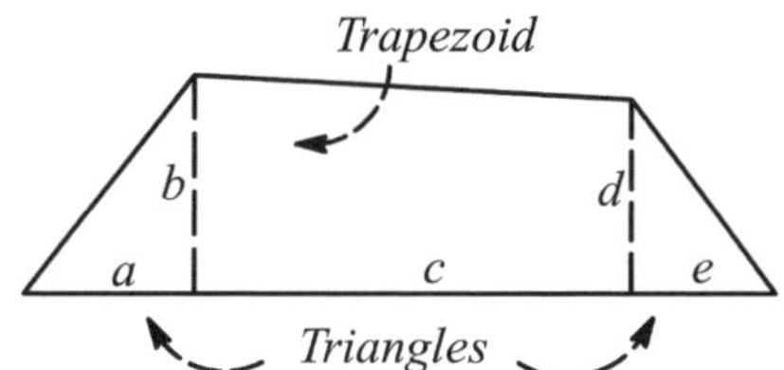

TRAPEZIUM

A quadrilateral having no two sides parallel. The area of a trapezium can only be determined by dividing the figure into triangles, parallelograms and/or trapezoids and totalling the individual areas.

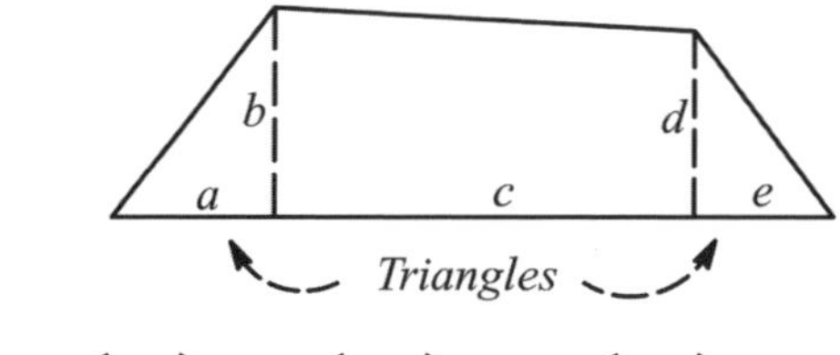

$$\text{AREA} = \left(\frac{a \times b}{2}\right) + \left(\frac{b + d}{2}\right)c + \left(\frac{e \times d}{2}\right)$$

PROPERTIES OF A CIRCLE

$$\begin{aligned}
\text{Area} &= D^2 \times .7854 \\
&= R^2 \times 3.1416 \\
&= C^2 \times .07958 \\
\text{Diameter} &= R \times 2 \\
&= C \times .3183 \\
\text{Circumference} &= D \times 3.1416 \\
&= R \times 6.283185 \\
\text{Radius} &= D \div 2 \\
&= C \times .159155
\end{aligned}$$

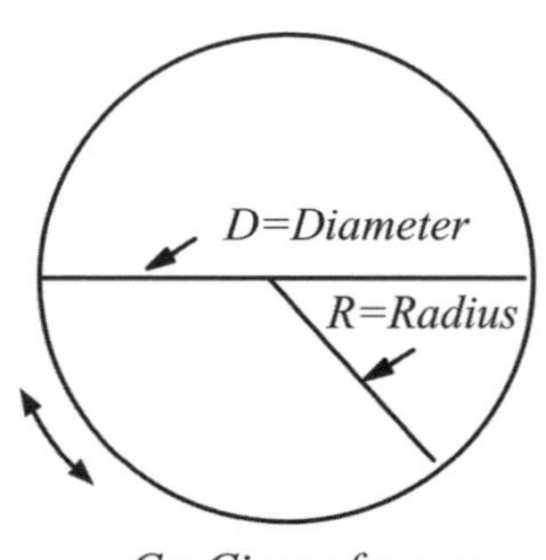

WEIGHTS & MEASURES

Decimal and Fractional Equivalent of Feet (In./Ft. Equivalents)

Inch	Decimal	Fraction	Inch	Decimal	Fraction	Inch	Decimal	Fraction
1"	.08	1/12	5"	.42	5/12	9"	.75	3/4
2"	.17	1/6	6"	.50	1/2	10"	.83	5/6
3"	.25	1/4	7"	.58	7/12	11"	.92	11/12
4"	.33	1/3	8"	.67	2/3	12"	1.00	1

Weights

1 ounce . . . . 16 drams (dr.)	4 quarters . . . one-hundred wt. (cwt)
1 pound . . . . 16 ounces (oz.)	1 short ton (s.t.) . . 2,000 pounds
1 quarter . . . . 25 pounds (lbs.)	1 long ton (l.t.) . . . 2,240 pounds

Measures

Linear Measure

1 inch: .0833 ft. 1 link: 7.92 in. 1 foot: 12 in. 1 yard: 3 ft. 1 rod: 16.5 ft. 25 links	1 chain: 66 ft. 4 rods 100 links 1 mile: 5,280 ft. 1,760 yards 80 chains 320 rods	1 acre: 208.71033 sq.ft. 132 ft x 330 ft. 110 ft x 396 ft. 145.2 ft x 300 ft. 198 ft x 220 ft. or any rectangle tract, the area of which is 43,560 sq. ft.

Square Measure / Cubic Measure

Square Measure		Cubic Measure
1 sq. ft.: 144 sq. in. 1 sq. yd.: 9 sq. ft. 1 sq. rod: 272.25 sq. ft. 30.25 sq. yds. 1 sq. chain: 4,356 sq. ft. 16 sq. yds.	1 acre: 43,560 sq. ft. 4,840 sq. yds. 160 sq. rods 10 sq. chains 1 sq. mile: 640 acres 1 full section: 1 sq. mile 1 township: 36 sections	1 board ft.: 144 cu. in. 1 cu. ft.: 1,728 cu. in. 7,481 gal. 1 cu. yd.: 27 cu. ft.

Metric Conversion Table

Linear Measure	Square Measure	Cubic Measure
inches x 2.54 = cm feet x .305 = m yards x .914 = m	sq. in. x 6.452 = sq. cm sq. ft. x .093 = sq. m sq. yd. x .836 = sq. m	cu. in. x 16.387 = cu. cm cu. ft. x .0283 = cu. m cu. yd. x .7645 = cu. m

ARCHITECTS' FEES

The architects' fees listed on the next page are based on averages of fees actually charged or recommended. Actual fees, since they are based on the size of the project, technical difficulty, artistic requirements, reputation of the architect and his/her willingness to accept the assignment, vary greatly. The estimate of the fee is a matter for the valuator's judgment. In cases where superior quality and detail are required, the fee may be higher than the average, while very low-quality and standardized buildings may call for a lower fee.

The fee schedules contain approximately 30% for contract administration and supervision. In many cases, this function may be performed by the contractor, an employee of the owner or an outside consultant. In any case, this is a proper charge against the building, and the total fee should be added to building costs.

Architects' fees normally include part or all of the following:

1. Plans and specifications including consultations, estimates and engineering studies.

2. General administration and overall supervision of construction, not including superintending construction.

3. Approving payment vouchers to the contractor.

4. Approval and acceptance of completed construction.

Regardless of the size and type of construction, all of these services must be performed by someone. On some projects the owner or the general contractor may do the supervision.

The architects' fee percentages given here are only a guide. On a simple residence, stock plans and specifications may be purchased for around $200, while on a large housing development, the architect may get full fees for each individual design and payments as low as $150 per unit for additional uses of the plans, or he may work as a corporate employee.

In actual practice, architects' fees are normally based, by contract, on a percentage of the entire cost, a multiplier of the technical payroll plus incidental expenses or a fixed sum plus listed expenses.

ARCHITECTS' FEES

In the final analysis, the architect's function, when fully performed, is a proper cost of construction. A well-considered matching of structure to land may enhance the end value by more than the fees involved. However, when poorly performed, the cost of design and drafting work may be wasted and result in functional obsolescence in a new structure. This determination is a matter of judgment.

The average fees listed for buildings do not include fees for design or furniture, built-in equipment, off-site layout or other detailed special items designed for specific trade or personal use.

Table I

Luxury Residences

Table II

Residences, Individually Designed

Table III

Multiple Residences, Town and Row Houses

Project Cost Up To	Table		
	I	II	III
$ 50,000	10.7%	7.9%	7.1%
100,000	10.3	7.6	6.9
200,000	10.0	7.4	6.7
500,000	9.5	7.1	6.4
1,000,000	9.2	6.9	6.2
2,000,000	8.9	6.6	6.0
3,000,000	8.7	6.5	5.9
5,000,000	8.4	6.4	5.8
10,000,000	8.1	6.2	5.6

CONSTRUCTION TIME

The following table of average periods of construction lists points on empirical curves that have been developed from figures for actual construction jobs. The data was adjusted for time lost due to labor shutdowns, and extreme cases were discarded. No adjustments were made for holidays, inspection delays or other minor shutdowns. Figures are the number of contract days from groundbreaking to completion of project.

Designed Occupancy	Total Cost of Project (in thousands of $)								
	50	100	200	500	1,000	2,000	3,000	5,000	10,000
Multiple residence	-----	100	145	205	250	295	320	350	395
Residential, single-family, town houses	90	105	135	190	245	315	-----	-----	-----

PERCENT OF COMPLETION

The following is a guideline for estimating percent of completion for a typical Average-quality, single-family, detached residence:

		Percent of Total	Cumulative Percent of Total
1.	Plans, permits and survey	2	2
2.	Excavation, forms, water/sewage hookup	4	6
3.	Concrete	8	14
4.	Rough framing	21	35
5.	Windows and exterior doors	2	37
6.	Roof cove	3	40
7.	Rough-in plumbing	4	44
8.	Insulation	1	45
9.	Rough-in electrical and mechanical	11	56
10.	Exterior cover	6	62
11.	Interior drywall and ceiling finish	8	70
12.	Built-in cabinets, interior doors, trim, etc.	13	83
13.	Plumbing fixtures	5	88
14.	Floor covers	3	91
15.	Built-in appliances	3	94
16.	Light fixtures and finish hardware	2	96
17.	Painting and decorating	4	100
	TOTAL =	**100%**	

MECHANICAL AND ELECTRICAL

The following table records the results of studies of many completed buildings by occupancy, giving the percentage of total contract cost spent on the mechanical and electrical items. The average used is the median; the high and low percentages that are given do not include extremes but are computed to include approximately 90% of all cases within the given range (45% each side of the median).

Occupancy		Heating Only	Heating & Cooling	Plumbing	Electrical
Multiple Residences	Low	2.6	6.8	7.9	5.3
	Median	4.0	8.5	10.9	6.9
	High	7.7	12.0	15.2	10.1
Single-family Residences	Low	2.4	6.9	7.1	4.3
	Median	3.8	8.4	8.8	5.3
	High	6.2	10.3	10.8	7.8

AIR-CONDITIONING REQUIREMENTS

Air-conditioning requirements are greatly dependent on the occupancy of the structure. The following figure gives typical quantities by occupancy in square feet per ton of cooling capacity, except as otherwise stated. The range of areas includes approximately 80% of all cases.

Occupancy	Square Feet/Ton
Residential occupancies	400 – 750

CLIMATE CLASSIFICATION KEY

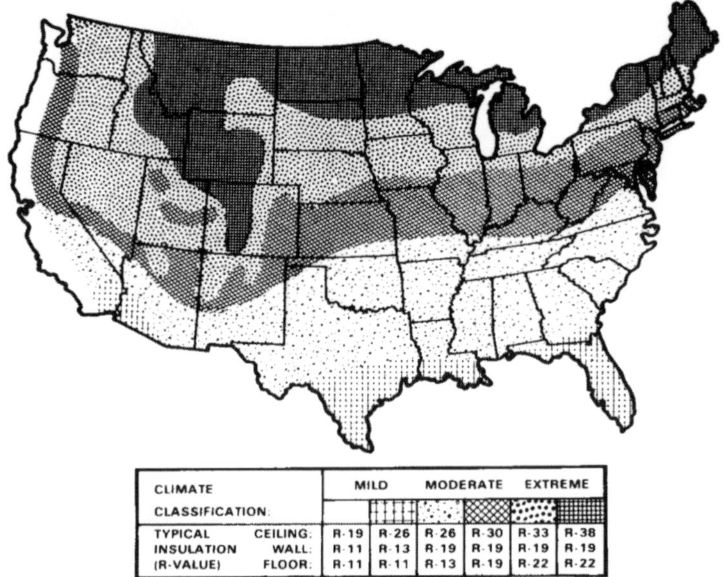

CLIMATE CLASSIFICATION:	MILD		MODERATE		EXTREME	
TYPICAL INSULATION (R-VALUE) CEILING:	R-19	R-26	R-26	R-30	R-33	R-38
WALL:	R-11	R-13	R-19	R-19	R-19	R-19
FLOOR:	R-11	R-11	R-13	R-19	R-22	R-22

INSULATION REQUIREMENTS

The following table lists the typical thickness required: ½" at a designated value for fiberglass or mineral wool insulation which is used in residential construction for the ceiling, wall and floor areas. Rockwool is typically ½" thinner than fiberglass at the same R-value. R-values are averages of unfaced, foil-faced and kraft paper-faced insulation when available.

Ceilings

Fiberglass batt or blanket insulation:
R-13   One 3 ⅝" batt
R-19   One 6 ½" batt
R-26   Two 3 ⅝" batts
R-30   One 6 ½" batt
       & one 3 ½" batt
R-35   One 7" batt & one 3 ⅝" batt
R-38   Two 6 ½" batts
Loose fill wool & fiberglass batts/blankets:
R-19   7 ½" wool fill or 6 ½" batt
R-26   2 ½" wool fill & 6 ½" batt
R-30   4 ½" wool fill & 6 ½" batt
R-38   7 ½" wool fill & 6 ½" batt

Walls

R-5.5   ⅝" rigid insulation board
R-7   2 ½" fiberglass batt
R-11   3 ½" fiberglass batt
R-19   3 ⅝" fiberglass batt
      & 1" polystyrene sheathing,
      or one 6 ½" batt

Floors

R-11   3 ½" fiberglass batt/blanket
R-13   3 ⅝" fiberglass batt/blanket
R-19   6 ½" fiberglass batt/blanket
R-22   7" fiberglass batt/blanket

PRECENTAGE BREAKDOWN OF BASE COSTS

The following percentages indicate the approximate portion of the total cost of average-quality wood frame houses attributable to each component listed, as derived from an analysis of several groups of residences. Costs of plans and other components are based on several developments containing between five and fifty houses each.

AVERAGE-QUALITY HOUSE

Plans	.6%
Plan check and permit	.6%
Survey	.3%
Water meter and temporary facilities	.4%
Excavation, forms, concrete and backfill	5.5%
Lumber, rough	11.0%
Carpenter labor, rough	9.5%
Roofing	4.7%
Insulation and weather stripping	1.6%
Exterior Finish: siding, stucco, masonry veneer	4.8%
Interior Finish: plaster and drywall	5.5%
Sash, doors and shutters	4.0%
Lumber, finish	1.0%
Carpenter labor, finish	1.7%
Hardware, rough	.4%
Hardware, finish	.7%
Cabinets	3.1%
Tile	2.0%
Floor covering: hardwood or carpeting	2.7%
resilient	1.2%
Plumbing	8.8%
Shower doors/mirrors/tub enclosure	.4%
Electrical	4.5%
Light fixtures	.6%
Built-in appliances	1.7%
Heating	3.2%
Sheet metal	.6%
Ornamental iron	.3%
Painting	3.6%
Sewer connection	.8%
Miscellaneous	.9%
Cleanup	.6%
General contractors' overhead and profit	12.7%
TOTAL	**100.0%**

The 12.7% listed for general contractors' overhead and profit is the percentage of the total cost. This is the equivalent of 14.8% of the labor, material and subcontract cost, excluding costs of plans, survey, plan check and permit, with a range from 11.9% to 17.0%.

PRECENTAGE BREAKDOWN OF BASE COSTS

The following percentages indicate the approximate portion of the total cost of average-quality multiple residences attributable to each component listed, as derived from an analysis of several 20- to 40-unit, 2-story, wood frame buildings. Costs of plans are normally on a flat fee basis and include simple details with supervision by architect.

AVERAGE-QUALITY MULTIPLE

Plans and engineering	2.0%
Plan check and permit	.7%
Survey	.3%
Water meter and temporary facilities	.4%
Excavation, forms, concrete and backfill	4.5%
Lightweight concrete	.8%
Rough carpentry (material)	10.6%
Rough carpentry (labor)	8.8%
Roofing	1.5%
Insulation and weather stripping	1.2%
Siding, stucco, masonry veneer	5.3%
Plaster and drywall	6.0%
Sash and doors	3.0%
Finish carpentry (material)	1.0%
Finish carpentry (labor)	1.8%
Hardware, rough	.4%
Hardware, finish	1.2%
Cabinets	4.2%
Tile/countertops	1.9%
Floor covering: carpeting	3.1%
resilient	1.0%
Plumbing and sewer connection	10.5%
Tub enclosures and toilet accessories	.4%
Electrical	6.1%
Light fixtures	.6%
Built-in appliances	3.3%
Heating	2.7%
Sheet metal	.8%
Ornamental iron	.7%
Painting	2.4%
Miscellaneous	.5%
Cleanup	.4%
General contractors' overhead and profit	11.9%
TOTAL	**100.0%**

The 11.9% listed for general contractors' overhead and profit is the percentage of the total cost. This is the equivalent of 14.0% of the labor, material and subcontract cost, excluding costs of plans, survey, plan check, permit and engineering, with a range from 10.8% to 16.8%.

FINANCING

- TYPES OF HOME MORTGAGES

- HOME IMPROVEMENT LOAN TABLE

- MORTGAGE PAYMENT TABLE

TYPES OF HOME MORTGAGES

Adjustable-rate (ARM)
Interest rate tied to published financial index such as prime lending rate. Most have annual and lifetime caps.

Assumable
Buyer takes over seller's mortgage.

Balloon
Payments based on long term, but principal due in short term.

Blanket
One mortgage covering several properties.

Buy-down
Seller pays part of interest for first years.

Construction
Finance construction of improvements.

Fixed-rate (FRM)
Interest rate and monthly payments constant for life of loan (usually 30 years).

Graduated-payment (GPM)
Payments increase for first few years, then remain constant. Interest rate may vary.

Growing-equity (GEM)
Payments increase annually, with increase applied to principal. Interest rate usually constant.

Interest-Only
Entire payment goes toward interest only. Principal remains at original amount.

Leasehold
Usually obtained to construct improvements.

Open-end
Additional funds with same agreement.

Owner-financed (seller takeback)
Seller holds either first or second mortgage.

Purchase-money
Purchase subject property.

Renegotiable (rollover)
Same as adjustable-rate mortgage, but interest rate adjusted less often.

Reverse-annuity
Lender makes monthly payments to borrower. Debt increases over time to maximum percentage of appraised value of property.

Shared-appreciation (SAM)
Lender charges less interest in exchange for share of appreciation when property sold.

Variable-rate
Interest rate varies with a standard rate.

Zero-interest (no-interest)
No interest charged. Fixed monthly payments usually over short term.

LOAN AND PAYMENT TABLES

HOW TO USE THE FOLLOWING TABLES

Monthly Payment

The following tables show monthly payments for each $1,000, borrowed for fixed interest rates, from 7 to 20¾ percent and for periods of 5 to 30 years.

Example:

What are the monthly payments on a 10-year, $20,000 loan at 12% interest? From the table, the monthly payment for each $1,000 is $14.35. Therefore the total monthly payment is:

$$20 \times \$14.35 = \$287.00$$

Total Interest Paid

Knowing the monthly payment, it's easy to find the total interest paid over the life of a loan. Total interest is the difference between the sum of the payments over life, and the original amount.

Example:

For a 25-year, 10½ percent, $100,000 mortgage, what is the total interest paid? From the table, the monthly payment for each $1,000 is $9.45. Therefore, the total lifetime payment is:

$$100 \times 12 \text{ months} \times 25 \text{ years} \times \$9.45 = \$283,500$$

Since the original loan is for $100,000, the total interest paid is the difference: $183,500.

HOME IMPROVEMENT LOAN
AND MORTGAGE PAYMENT TABLES
Monthly Payment, Fixed Term and Interest per $1,000

TERM RATE, %	5	10	15	20	25	30
7	19.81	11.62	8.99	7.76	7.07	6.66
7 ¼	19.92	11.75	9.13	7.91	7.23	6.83
7 ½	20.04	11.88	9.28	8.06	7.39	7.00
7 ¾	20.16	12.01	9.42	8.21	7.56	7.17
8	20.28	12.14	9.56	8.37	7.72	7.34
8 ¼	20.40	12.27	9.71	8.53	7.89	7.52
8 ½	20.52	12.40	9.85	8.68	8.06	7.69
8 ¾	20.64	12.54	10.00	8.84	8.23	7.87
9	20.76	12.67	10.15	9.00	8.40	8.05
9 ¼	20.88	12.81	10.30	9.16	8.57	8.23
9 ½	21.01	12.94	10.45	9.33	8.74	8.41
9 ¾	21.13	13.08	10.60	9.49	8.92	8.60
10	21.25	13.22	10.75	9.66	9.09	8.78
10 ¼	21.38	13.36	10.90	9.82	9.27	8.97
10 ½	21.50	13.50	11.06	9.99	9.45	9.15
10 ¾	21.62	13.64	11.21	10.16	9.63	9.34

LOAN AND PAYMENT TABLES

HOME IMPROVEMENT LOAN AND MORTGAGE PAYMENT TABLES
Monthly Payment, Fixed Term and Interest per $1,000

TERM RATE, %	5	10	15	20	25	30
11	21.75	13.78	11.37	10.33	9.81	9.53
11 $^{1}/_{4}$	21.87	13.92	11.53	10.50	9.99	9.72
11 $^{1}/_{2}$	22.00	14.06	11.69	10.67	10.17	9.91
11 $^{3}/_{4}$	22.12	14.21	11.85	10.84	10.35	10.10
12	22.25	14.35	12.01	11.02	10.54	10.29
12 $^{1}/_{4}$	22.38	14.50	12.17	11.19	10.72	10.48
12 $^{1}/_{2}$	22.50	14.64	12.33	11.37	10.91	10.68
12 $^{3}/_{4}$	22.63	14.79	12.49	11.54	11.10	10.87
13	22.76	14.94	12.66	11.72	11.28	11.07
13 $^{1}/_{4}$	22.89	15.08	12.82	11.90	11.47	11.26
13 $^{1}/_{2}$	23.01	15.23	12.99	12.08	11.66	11.46
13 $^{3}/_{4}$	23.14	15.38	13.15	12.26	11.85	11.66
14	23.27	15.53	13.32	12.44	12.04	11.85
14 $^{1}/_{4}$	23.40	15.68	13.49	12.62	12.23	12.05
14 $^{1}/_{2}$	23.53	15.83	13.66	12.80	12.43	12.25
14 $^{3}/_{4}$	23.66	15.99	13.83	12.99	12.62	12.45
15	23.79	16.14	14.00	13.17	12.81	12.65
15 $^{1}/_{4}$	23.93	16.29	14.17	13.36	13.01	12.85
15 $^{1}/_{2}$	24.06	16.45	14.34	13.54	13.20	13.05
15 $^{3}/_{4}$	24.19	16.60	14.52	13.73	13.40	13.25
16	24.32	16.76	14.69	13.92	13.59	13.45
16 $^{1}/_{4}$	24.46	16.91	14.87	14.11	13.79	13.65
16 $^{1}/_{2}$	24.59	17.07	15.04	14.29	13.99	13.86
16 $^{3}/_{4}$	24.72	17.23	15.22	14.48	14.18	14.06
17	24.86	17.38	15.40	14.67	14.38	14.26
17 $^{1}/_{4}$	24.99	17.54	15.57	14.86	14.58	14.46
17 $^{1}/_{2}$	25.13	17.70	15.75	15.05	14.78	14.67
17 $^{3}/_{4}$	25.26	17.86	15.93	15.25	14.98	14.87
18	25.40	18.02	16.11	15.44	15.18	15.08
18 $^{1}/_{4}$	25.53	18.18	16.29	15.63	15.38	15.28
18 $^{1}/_{2}$	25.67	18.35	16.47	15.82	15.58	15.48
18 $^{3}/_{4}$	25.81	18.51	16.65	16.02	15.78	15.69
19	25.95	18.67	16.83	16.21	15.98	15.89
19 $^{1}/_{4}$	26.08	18.84	17.02	16.41	16.18	16.10
19 $^{1}/_{2}$	26.22	19.00	17.20	16.60	16.39	16.30
19 $^{3}/_{4}$	26.36	19.17	17.38	16.80	16.59	16.51
20	26.50	19.33	17.57	16.99	16.79	16.72
20 $^{1}/_{4}$	26.64	19.50	17.75	17.19	16.99	16.92
20 $^{1}/_{2}$	26.78	19.66	17.94	17.39	17.20	17.13
20 $^{3}/_{4}$	26.92	19.83	18.12	17.58	17.40	17.33

DEPRECIATION

- TYPES OF DEPRECIATION
- DEFINITIONS AND EXAMPLES
- LIFE EXPECTANCY GUIDELINES
- BUILDING DEPRECIATION TABLE
- COMPONENT DEPRECIATION TABLE
- LIFE CYCLE CHART

DEFINITIONS AND EXAMPLES

DEFINITIONS

DEPRECIATION is loss in value due to any cause. It is the difference between the market value of a structural improvement or piece of equipment (HVAC, built-in appliances, etc.) and its reproduction or replacement cost as of the date of valuation. Depreciation is divided into three general categories:

PHYSICAL depreciation is loss in value due to physical deterioration.

FUNCTIONAL or technical obsolescence is loss in value due to lack of utility or desirability of part or all of the property, inherent to the improvement or equipment. Thus a new structure or piece of equipment may suffer obsolescence when built.

EXTERNAL, locational or economic obsolescence is loss in value due to causes outside the property and independent of it, and is not included in the tables.

EFFECTIVE AGE of a property is its age as compared with other properties performing like functions. It is the actual age less the age which has been taken off by face-lifting, structural reconstruction, removal of functional inadequacies, modernization of equipment, etc. It is an age which reflects a true remaining life for the property, taking into account the typical life expectancy of buildings or equipment and usage. It is a matter of judgment, taking all factors – current and those anticipated in the immediate future – into consideration. Determination of effective age on older structures may best be calculated by establishing a remaining life which, subtracted from a typical life expectancy, will result in an appropriate effective age with which to work. Effective age can fluctuate year by year or remain somewhat stable in the absence of any major renewals or excessive deterioration.

EXTENDED LIFE EXPECTANCY is the increased life expectancy due to seasoning and proven ability to exist. Just as a person will have a total normal life expectancy at birth which increases as he grows older, so it is with structures and equipment.

REMAINING LIFE is the normal remaining life expectation. It is the length of time the structure may be expected to continue to perform its function economically at the date of the appraisal. This does not imply a straight-line expiration, particularly for mortgage purposes, since normal recurring maintenance and renewal of replaceable items will continue to contribute toward an extended life expectancy. This extended life process is accomplished by use of effective age as the sliding scale and not by continually lengthening the typical life expectancy as the structure ages chronologically.

PERCENT GOOD equals 100% less the percentage of cost represented by depreciation. It is the present value of the structure or equipment at the time of appraisal, divided by its replacement cost.

APPROACHES TO DEPRECIATION

The simplest and in past years a widely used accounting-type concept of depreciation was the straight-line (age/life) approach. A life expectancy is estimated and a constant annual percentage is taken for depreciation so that at the end of that life the depreciation equals 100% of the initial cost. This approach is simple and easy to use but does not represent reality in most cases since time is not the only factor affecting depreciation, and it fails to recognize any value-in-use.

DEFINITIONS AND EXAMPLES

Although age is a critical factor, the best approach to the physical depreciation estimate is a combination of age and condition. The observed condition of each component subject to wear is estimated relative to new condition. A major replaceable component, such as an HVAC system, can wear out quite rapidly, shortening the life expectancy before replacement, while many other portions of a structure wear out slowly, if at all, such as excavations, foundations and concrete exterior walls. Such long-lived portions often represent a major portion of the total reproduction cost, and if still functional will contribute toward an extended life expectancy. Physical depreciation cannot be considered a straight-line deduction from reproduction cost, since necessary and normal maintenance can offset, retard, and even eliminate deterioration.

Another approach to depreciation is the mid-life theory. This takes into account that most buildings depreciate little during the first few years. When it becomes evident that the buildings are no longer new, even though they are adequately maintained, the maintenance expenses rise, rentals tend to decrease and the building depreciates faster. After a number of years, they reach the period called mid-life, at which time, if the buildings are structurally sound and properly maintained, the depreciation remains constant. The mid-life theory suffers from the fact that maintenance expenses on the average building continue to go up in order to maintain the same appearance and utility, and at any age, certain building features may suffer from obsolescence.

These concepts lead to a third theory, the extended life concept, which starts with the hypothesis that buildings age in much the same manner as people and that the older they get, the greater their total life expectancy. This concept recognizes that a building is in the prime of life before mid-life and that the road is downhill after that, but that correction of deficiencies may lower the effective age and lengthen the remaining life. This recurring revitalization process periodically reverses a continuous progression down the effective age scale, reducing the indicated depreciation percentage as components are renewed throughout the life span of the building.

OVERVIEW

DEPRECIATION is an opinion of a structure's loss in value in relation to its cost-new estimate. If you properly consider all the pertinent factors, you should be able to reliably estimate depreciation. The overall depreciation tables in this section consider the progression of normal deterioration and functional obsolescence based on age, condition and usage of the improvement. Any abnormal or excessive functional obsolescence and any or all external obsolescence are considered separately and are not included in the tables.

PHYSICAL DETERIORATION is the wearing out of the improvement through the combination of wear and tear of use, the effects of the aging process and physical decay, action of the elements, structural defects, etc. It is typically divided into two types: curable and incurable. These may be individually estimated by the component breakdown method using an age-life approach. Damage caused by accidents, vandalism, etc., may be further categorized as deferred maintenance, whether curable or incurable, and treated separately based on the cost to repair the item(s).

CURABLE physical deterioration is generally associated with individual short-lived items such as paint, floor and roof covers, hot-water heaters, etc., requiring periodic replacement, renewal or modification continuously over the normal life span of the improvement.

DEFINITIONS AND EXAMPLES

INCURABLE physical deterioration is generally associated with the residual group of long-lived items such as floor and roof structures, mechanical supply systems and foundations. Such basic structural items are not normally replaced in a typical maintenance program and are usually incurable except through major reconstruction. The distinction here is whether or not such corrections would be justified economically and/or practically in view of the cost, time and value gain involved. Exceptions might be historical or landmark buildings or a component that threatens the structural integrity of the structure itself.

In estimating the loss of value attributable to physical deterioration, you are attempting to set up the cost of restoring the building to new condition. A new improvement, suitable for its site, requires little study to establish a reasonable estimate of accrued depreciation. However, after weathering for a few years, a structure showing signs of age, deterioration and abuse requires a more detailed analysis to determine the extent of value loss. This seasoning can be prolonged with sound, well-maintained components or be accured rather rapidly, as in the case of a building shoddily or improperly constructed of inexpensive, short-lived components that have been inadequately or poorly maintained. A detailed building appraisal itemizes the component parts of a structure, and where total depreciation may be difficult to judge, the depreciation of individual components may be more logically estimated. This detailed component breakdown can then form the foundation from which the overall depreciation tables may be reasonably used once properly benchmarked.

PHYSICAL INDICATORS

When considering the extent of physical deterioration, pay particular attention to the following indicators:

- **Floors and Floor Coverings** – Cracks, unevenness, sagging, worn finish, rough or scarred finishes, creaking or springiness underfoot, cracks in slabs at column connections and separation at expansion joints in slabs, damaged insulation or drainage.

- **Interior Construction** – Cracks in plaster, open joints in millwork, sticking doors, peeling paper or paint, scars, missing or loose hardware, smoke stains, mildew stains or the effect of prolonged dampness, rodent, insect or termite infestation, damage or decay.

- **Mechanical Equipment** – Defective wiring, broken or tarnished light fixtures, loose switches, worn, broken or stained plumbing fixtures, leaking faucets or piping connections, odors indicative of faulty sewer piping, drip pans, escaping steam, noisy radiators, rusting pipes, battered or rusted ductwork, furnaces or boilers in poor repair, mold, mildew from defective filters, air cleaners and venting, excessive soot or dust stains.

- **Roof** – Evidence of leakage, oxidized roof metal, shingles or tiles missing or split, stained interior ceilings, sagging or decaying roof structure, cracking laminated trusses, tie rods to strengthen bottom chords of timber trusses, damaged truss bracing, plugged roof drains, evidence of standing water, vibration from mechanical equipment, damaged insulation.

- **Exterior Walls** – Peeling paint, cracked or loose mortar joints, oxidized sheet metal, frame lines out-of-plumb, loose or decaying wood siding, loose ornamentation, exposed reinforcing bar at joints or in footings, unprotected or deteriorating steel framing, brick that needs painting or pointing, inoperable windows or clerestory sashes, broken or rusted screens, sticking doors, inoperable hardware.

Some of the external factors affecting the extent and rate of physical deterioration are:

- **Temperature Extremes** – Extreme heat tends to dry out and warp lumber, damage roofing, cause cracks in stucco or plaster due to expansion and contraction, and oxidize paint coatings. Extreme cold with freezing down to frost line, expansion and contraction, etc., can cause similar problems.

- **Humidity Extremes** – High humidity tends to promote dry rot and insect infestation.

- **Weather Extremes** – Heavy snow, floods, hurricanes and tornadoes obviously cause damage. Torrential rains can undermine foundations and create ponding and leaks in roof structures, which in turn may damage interior finishes. Rainstorms accompanied by high winds can damage walls, doors, flooring and mechanical building equipment.

- **Earthquakes** – Earthquakes may not only cause damage which is apparent, but structural damage to substructures and bearing soils which may not become evident until years after the disturbance.

- **Airborne Corrosives** – Structures located near oceans are subjected to corrosive salt air, which attacks nearly every part of the structure. Buildings located in areas where large concentrations of corrosive industrial waste gases are vented into the atmosphere typically have relatively short physical lives also.

FUNCTIONAL OBSOLESCENCE is the perceived market reaction to under- or over-improvements in the utility or desirability of part of or all of the improvement. This is divided into two types: curable or incurable. These are further subdivided into inadequacies, also known as deficiencies, and superadequacies, also known as excesses. Again the test as to when an item is curable or incurable is whether the capitalized gain or value added by correcting the obsolescence by replacement, remodel, addition or removal, is equal to or greater than the cost to cure as indicated in the market.

INADEQUACIES are some kind of building deficiencies that does not meet current market expectations. Inadequate fixtures or ceiling insulation may be curable while a poor floor plan or tandem rooms may be incurable.

SUPERADEQUACIES are those unwanted items that do not add at least equal value to their cost — notably special- or singular-purpose features for a particular user. Many superadequacies are incurable except where excess maintenance costs might make it economical to remove or replace the item.

FUNCTIONAL INDICATORS

When considering the extent of functional obsolescence, pay particular attention to the following indicators:

- **Design Characteristics** – Appealing or poor or antiquated style or design, traffic and noise levels, maintenance or serviceability, security, evacuation, market acceptance or resistance, environmentally responsible or safe, eye appeal, symmetry, scale, orientation, interaction or appropriate blend of materials, glazing, durability, colors, etc., suitable for the designed use, distinctive motif of a singular or special-purpose use or architectural style.

- **Physical Layout** – Suitable room layout and orderly flow, overall or room size, net vs. gross space, volume, appropriate wall heights, lighting levels, natural light and ventilation, adequate support facilities, storage, counter, cabinet size and placement.

- **Mechanical Equipment** – Inadequate or excess number of poorly spaced or antiquated plumbing or electrical and lighting fixtures, HVAC, conveyance, appliances, intercom systems and other equipment, service or power requirements, energy consumption or efficiency, actual vs. rated capacity or performance, abnormal operating costs, proper emission controls, technological changes (e.g., electric vs. standing pilot ignition, etc.), appropriate air quality and changes.

- **Site Assessment** – Land use, size, shape, topography, access, easements or other encroachments, utilities, soil type, stability, drainage and percolation, water table and use, erosion, vegetation, land- or waterscape, view or other amenities, flood plain, wetlands, coastal, brush or fault areas, presence of hazardous contaminants (see Environmental below), etc.

Some of the external factors affecting the extent of functional obsolescence are:

- **Code Requirements** – Building codes or zoning for conforming use, height, stories, area, setback, building separation, size/mansionization, energy equivalency trade-offs, etc., Fire and Life Safety compliance (see below).

- **Fire Protection Requirements** – Proper rating, detection for life safety and security, signaling controls, communications, signage, standpipe, sprinklers, extinguishers, hydrants, door and smoke controls, appropriate exits, overhang, balcony and deck exposures, stairways, roofing classification, safety or double glazing.

- **Handicapped Requirements** – ADA compliance, barrier-free design, parking, ramps, automatic entry, door, hallway widths, markings, signage, alarms, service, cabinet and railing heights, drinking fountains, grab bars, exposed hot-water piping, handicap fixtures, turnaround space, elevator controls, cab size, lifts, etc.

- **Environmental** – EPA, wetlands and air quality compliance, water, soil, radon, asbestos, UREA formaldehyde foam insulation, PCBs, CFCs, high-voltage lines, halon, heavy metals or lead contamination, runoff, emissions or sediment containment, detection and testing, septic tanks, leach fields, demolition constraints, disposal or remediation. Evidence of leakage, absence of plants or animals, sick or stressed plants or animals, discolored soil or water, surface sheens and noxious odors, presence of discarded batteries, abandoned wells, sumps, tanks, barrels or other containers of fertilizer, pesticides and herbicides, paints and thinners, heating oil, petroleum or other hazardous chemical substances.

- **Weather Extremes** – Appropriate insulation levels, heat gain or loss, shading, passive or active alternatives, energy equivalency trade-offs, window treatment, glass strength, proper trusses, size, spacing, pitch and drainage for rain and snow loading, proper connections for hurricane wind forces, uplift exposure, operable shutters.

- **Earthquakes** – Appropriate bracing, connections to structural shell, shear walls, overhang exposure, irregular shape, framing stress, torsion, distance from other structures for pounding, etc.

EXTERNAL OBSOLESCENCE is a change in the value of a property, usually negative but can be an enhancement, caused by forces outside the property. For example, a property's proximity to a highway system might be a source of external obsolescence. External obsolescence can be measured by market abstraction and capitalization of the imputed loss or gain to the improvements and the land. External obsolescence is not included in the tables that follow.

EXTERNAL INDICATORS

When considering the extent of external obsolescence, pay particular attention to the following indicators in the immediate vicinity, marketing area or community as a whole:

- **Physical Factors** – Proximity of desirable or unattractive natural or artificial features or barriers, general neighborhood maturity, conformity, deterioration, rehabilitation or static character, known cleanup sites, nuisances, graffiti, waste dump, swamp, toxic industry, electromagnetic fields, brush area, lack of view or landscaping, floodplain, drainage, water table, sinkholes, fault zones, soil types, liquefaction, landslides, local ecosystem, endangered species, habitat areas.

- **Infrastructure** – Highest and best use, quality, availability and source of utilities, public services, fire stations, staffed or volunteer, distance from hydrants, street improvements, traffic patterns, public transportation, parking, retail, recreation, education facilities, etc.

- **Economic** – Demand/supply imbalance, saturation or monopoly, competition or alternatives, market share, industry or major plant relocation, employment development and growth patterns, utility and insurance rates, availability of funds or terms, labor and materials, interest rates, vacancy, building rates, general inflation or deflation rates, tenant ratings, length of time on market or lease up or absorption, income streams and returns, changing consumer habits, purchasing power, property association or government forces, zoning, land use, air rights, legal nonconformity, permit, taxing and assessment policies and bureaucracy or other limiting conditions or restrictions.

GENERAL CONDITION RATINGS can be assigned to the improvement to assist in the development of an appropriate effective age based on observed condition, utility and age. The better the overall condition, the younger or lower the effective age, which lowers the percentage and amount of depreciation. Condition is an integral part in measuring the degree at which items subject to depreciation have been maintained. Applying any additional condition modifier once the effective age has been established based on condition would be redundant.

Effective age will change as changes in condition fluctuate by the amount of observed deterioration and obsolescence at the date of the appraisal. Over the life of a structure, you could expect the condition rating and effective age to move up and back down the effective age scale many times over. During the mid-life cycles, the effective age will drift upward at a relatively slow pace, assuming normal maintenance, for longer periods of time than at any other period over the structure's entire life span. With each evaluation, the effective age choice must be reconsidered based on the actual conditions encountered at the current date, taking into account any changes that may have taken place since the last appraisal. Neglect or weather extremes could have accelerated the effective age, while major repairs will correct deficiencies to a like-new condition, lowering the effective age and starting the cycle all over again.

CONDITION RATING INDICATORS

Excellent Condition – All items that can normally be repaired or refinished have recently been corrected, such as new roofing, paint, furnace overhaul, and state-of-the-art components. With no functional inadequacies of any consequence and all major short-lived components in like-new condition, the overall effective age has been substantially reduced upon complete revitalization of the structure, regardless of the actual chronological age.

Very Good Condition – All items well maintained, many having been overhauled and repaired as they have shown signs of wear, increasing the life expectancy and lowering the effective age. Little deterioration or obsolescence evident with a high degree of utility.

Good Condition – No obvious maintenance required but neither is everything new. Appearance and utility are above the standard and the overall effective age will be lower than the typical property.

Average Condition – Some evidence of deferred maintenance and normal obsolescence with age in that a few minor repairs are needed, along with some refinishing. All major components still functional and contributing toward an extended life expectancy, effective age and utility that are standard for like properties of its usage.

Fair Condition (Badly Worn) – Much repair needed. Many items need refinishing or overhauling, deferred maintenance obvious, inadequate building utility and services all shortening the life expectancy and increasing the effective age.

Poor Condition (Worn Out) – Repair and overhaul needed on painted surfaces, roofing, plumbing, heating, numerous functional inadequacies, substandard utilities, etc. (found only in extraordinary circumstances). Excessive deferred maintenance and abuse, limited value-in-use, approaching abandonment or major reconstruction, reuse or change in occupancy is imminent. Effective age is near the end of the scale regardless of the actual chronological age.

EXPLANATION OF DEPRECIATION TABLES

The depreciation tables in this section were developed from actual case studies of sales and market value appraisals and are based on an extended life theory which encompasses a remaining life and effective age approach. From confirmed sales prices, the land value was deducted to obtain a building residual and the replacement cost of the building was computed. The difference between the replacement cost of the building and the residual sales price of the building was divided by the replacement cost, to give the market depreciation in percentage. A similar procedure was followed with the market value appraisals, always excluding those cases having excessive obsolescence.

USE OF THE TABLES

1. Determine the condition and chronological age of the residence.

2. Compare the subject residence with like properties and study the effect of, lack of or need for any modernization or major repair to determine Effective Age.

3. Determine Typical Life Expectancy from table below.

4. Enter the Depreciation Table (Page 143) in the column for the appropriate Life Expectancy and at the Effective Age estimated in Step 2. The corresponding number is a normal percentage of depreciation.

TYPICAL BUILDING LIVES

Typical life expectancies of single and multifamily residences are based on case studies of both actual mortality and ages at which major reconstruction had taken place. Typical life expectancies for modular structures assume conformity to site-built residences in both quality and design. All cases of abnormal or excessive obsolescence due to external causes outside of and not inherent to the subject properties were excluded.

QUALITY OF CONSTRUCTION	SINGLE-FAMILY (Detached) Site-built or modular: Frame/Masonry	MULTIFAMILY, SENIOR CITIZEN AND SINGLE-FAMILY (Attached) Site-built or modular: Frame/Masonry
Low	45 / 50	-----
Fair	50 / 55	45 / 50
Average	55 / 60	50 / 55
Good	55 / 60	50 / 55
Very Good	60 / 60	55 / 60
Excellent	60 / 65	55 / 60

REPLACEABLE COMPONENTS

When capitalizing the income of investment properties, it is necessary to include in the expenses an annual reserve for the replacement of various components which have a shorter life than the building as a whole. To estimate the annual reserve for replacement of a component, divide the estimated years of life into the total cost of the component. The following guide gives the most typical life cycle of such items and an estimated life expectancy under standard applications in years for each, subdivided by quality. Individual component lives can have a wide range depending on the loads and conditions placed on them, the method of installation and appropriate maintenance and warranties. Lives may be shortened under severe requirements due to heavy wear, corrosive contact and/or atmospheric conditions, etc., or lengthened under very light usage, mild circumstances, protective coatings, etc. Costs for the various components may be selected from appropriate tables throughout the guide. The allocation of a component cost over its expected service life can also be used in establishing reserves for condominium or owners' association budgets or sinking funds, etc., and in the evaluation of life-cycle costing for use in the component selection or design alternative process, for financial planning, energy analysis or audits, etc. For those items not listed, select the life for a component which has similar characteristics, modifying as necessary. For long-lived items use the typical life of the building or appropriate extended life.

COMPONENT	LOW	AVG	GOOD	EXCL
Appliances				
Major appliances, residential	10	12	15	18
Garage door openers	8	9	10	11
Garbage disposals, washing machines	6	8	10	12
Home electronics	5	7	9	12
Radio-intercoms, paging systems	12	15	19	24
Telephone systems	9	10	11	12
Vacuum-cleaning systems	12	13	15	17
Floor Covering				
Carpets and pads	4	5	7	10
Carpet tiles	5	6	8	10
Ceramic, quarry, precast terrazzo tile/pavers	25	30	34	40
Indoor-outdoor carpets	3	5	7	10
Linoleum	10	13	16	20
Rubber mats	3	4	5	6
Terrazzo, bonded or epoxy	25	32	40	50
Vinyl composition tiles or sheets	7	10	14	19
Vinyl or rubber tiles or sheets	12	15	19	24
Wood flooring	20	25	30	35
Miscellaneous Interior				
Acoustical ceiling tiles or panels	8	10	12	15
Built-in mail boxes, etc.	12	15	20	25
Cabinets	15	20	25	35

LIFE EXPECTANCY GUIDELINES

REPLACEABLE COMPONENTS

COMPONENT	LOW	AVG	GOOD	EXCL
Miscellaneous Interior (Continued)				
Countertops, laminates	10	15	20	25
solid materials	20	25	30	35
Doors, hollow core	18	20	22	25
solid	25	32	40	50
shower	5	9	15	25
Drapery	6	8	10	12
Elevators, escalators and chairlifts	18	20	23	26
dumbwaiter	13	16	20	25
Partitions, demountable	16	20	25	30
fixed	20	25	30	40
folding	8	10	12	15
Paint	3	5	7	10
Tiles, glazed	20	25	35	45
Wallpaper	7	10	13	18
Heating, Ventilating And Air Conditioning				
Electric heaters, radiant	9	11	15	19
Forced-air heat and heat pumps	10	12	16	20
Hot water or steam heat	17	21	25	30
Package heating and cooling	5	8	13	20
Package refrigeration	5	7	10	15
Refrigerated coolers, window	7	9	11	14
Solar-heating systems	5	7	10	15
Unit heaters and thru-wall units	8	10	14	18
Wall or floor furnaces	10	13	16	20
Evaporative coolers	5	6	8	10
Exhaust and ventilating fans	6	9	12	18
Air ducts, galvanized steel	17	20	25	30
aluminum	15	19	25	32
fiberglass	14	17	22	28
duct insulation	12	15	19	24
Ancillary items				
Controls, electric or electronic	9	11	13	16
pneumatic	14	16	18	20
Fans and motors	14	16	18	20
Heating and cooling coils	10	12	14	17
Humidifiers and air washers	11	13	15	18
Boilers	15	17	20	24
Steel oil storage tanks	25	27	28	30
Water evaporative condensers	9	12	15	20

LIFE EXPECTANCY GUIDELINES

REPLACEABLE COMPONENTS

COMPONENT	LOW	AVG	GOOD	EXCL
Electrical				
Emergency generators	22	25	27	30
Light fixtures, residential	15	20	26	35
commercial grade	7	10	14	20
Service wiring, residential	25	30	37	45
Security alarm systems, residential	10	12	15	18
Plumbing				
Plumbing fixtures	17	20	25	30
enameled steel	5	7	10	14
fiberglass	10	13	16	20
Faucets and valves	8	10	13	16
Water heaters, residential	3	5	7	12
commercial grade	8	11	15	20
Pumps, sump and well	8	10	12	15
Pipes, galvanized	12	16	22	30
copper	20	25	30	35
plastic	15	20	25	33
Sprinkler and fire protection systems	20	23	26	30
residential smoke detectors	10	12	14	17
smoke and heat detectors	13	15	17	20
fire hoses and misc. equip.	7	9	11	13
Miscellaneous pumps, motors, controls	3	4	7	10
Miscellaneous				
Awnings and window screens	3	5	7	9
Canopies and patio covers	12	14	16	19
Exterior paint	3	4	5	7
sealers, silicone, etc.	1	2	3	5
Fireplaces, chimneys, masonry	35	40	47	55
metal	20	25	30	35
Shutters	3	4	5	7
Storm windows	8	10	12	14
Roofing				
Built-up tar and gravel	10	13	16	20
Composition shingles	12	16	22	30
Elastomeric	12	15	20	25
Metal	13	20	30	45
Slate or copper	-----	-----	50	60
Tile, concrete or clay	30	36	42	50
Wood shakes	20	24	29	35
Wood shingles	16	20	24	30
Exposed insulation	19	20	22	24
Gutters and downspouts	10	15	20	30

LIFE EXPECTANCY GUIDELINES

REPLACEABLE COMPONENTS

COMPONENT	LOW	AVG	GOOD	EXCL
Site Improvements				
Bulkheads, concrete	30	34	36	40
steel	25	29	31	35
wood	20	24	26	30
Culverts, concrete	30	34	36	40
steel	10	14	18	25
Curbing, concrete	15	19	21	25
Fencing, chain-link	13	15	17	20
masonry walls	20	25	30	35
wood	6	8	10	12
wind screens	4	5	6	7
Flagpoles	16	20	25	30
Landscaping, decorative shrubs, trees, etc.	7	10	14	20
Outdoor furniture	3	5	7	10
Outdoor lighting fixtures	10	13	16	20
Parking lot bumpers	3	4	5	7
guardrails	7	9	11	13
Paving, asphalt	5	8	11	17
concrete/brick	10	13	16	20
gravel	3	5	7	10
Signs	8	10	12	14
Snow-melting systems	8	10	12	14
Sprinklers, galvanized pipes	10	14	18	25
plastic pipes	15	18	22	28
controllers and pumping systems	8	9	11	13
Stairways and decks, wood	7	9	12	15
cement composition	12	15	20	25
Swimming pools, commercial, concrete	15	20	25	30
stainless steel	25	30	35	40
mechanical equipment	10	12	15	20
Swimming pools, residential, aboveground	2	5	10	15
vinyl-lined, sand supported	10	15	20	30
fiberglass	15	20	25	30
concrete, gunite	15	20	25	35
mechanical equipment	4	5	7	10
vinyl liners	3	5	7	10
Spas	3	5	8	12
Solar pool equipment	7	10	14	20
Synthetic sports surfaces	3	4	6	8
play yards	10	13	16	20
Tennis courts	18	20	22	25
asphalt/colored concrete resurfacing	3	4	5	7
nets	1	2	2	3
Underground sewer and water lines	22	25	28	32

TYPICAL LIFE EXPECTANCY IN YEARS

Effective Age In Years	70	60	55	50	45	40	35	30	25	20	Effective Age In Years
					DEPRECIATION – PERCENTAGE						
1	0%	0%	1%	1%	1%	1%	2%	2%	3%	3%	1
2	1	1	2	2	2	3	4	4	6	7	2
3	1	2	2	3	3	4	5	6	9	11	3
4	2	3	3	4	4	5	7	9	12	15	4
5	2	4	4	5	6	7	9	12	15	20	5
6	3	4	5	6	7	9	11	14	18	24	6
7	4	5	6	7	8	10	13	17	22	28	7
8	4	6	7	8	10	12	15	19	25	33	8
9	5	7	8	10	11	14	17	22	29	38	9
10	5	8	9	11	13	16	20	25	32	43	10
11	6	9	10	12	14	18	22	28	36	48	11
12	7	10	11	13	15	20	24	31	40	53	12
13	8	11	12	15	17	22	26	34	44	57	13
14	8	12	13	16	19	24	29	37	48	61	14
15	9	12	15	17	21	26	32	40	52	66	15
16	10	13	16	19	23	28	34	43	55	70	16
17	10	15	17	20	25	30	37	46	59	73	17
18	11	16	19	22	27	32	40	50	63	76	18
19	12	17	20	24	28	34	43	53	67	78	19
20	13	18	21	25	30	37	45	56	71	79	20
21	13	19	22	26	32	39	48	59	74	79	21
22	14	20	23	28	34	42	51	62	76	80	22
23	15	21	24	29	36	44	54	65	77		23
24	16	23	26	31	38	47	57	68	79		24
25	17	24	27	33	40	50	60	71	80		25
26	18	25	29	35	43	52	62	74	80		26
27	19	26	31	37	45	55	65	75			27
28	20	28	33	39	47	57	68	77			28
29	21	29	34	41	49	59	70	78			29
30	22	31	36	44	52	62	71	79			30
31	23	32	38	46	54	64	72	79			31
32	24	34	40	47	56	67	74	80			32
33	25	35	42	49	58	69	75				33
34	27	37	44	51	60	71	77				34
35	28	38	45	53	62	72	78				35
36	29	40	47	55	65	74	79				36
37	30	41	49	57	67	75	79				37
38	32	43	51	59	69	77	80				38
39	33	45	53	61	70	78					39
40	35	47	55	63	72	79					40
41	36	49	57	64	73	79					41
42	38	51	59	66	75	80					42
43	39	52	60	67	76						43
44	41	54	62	69	77						44
45	42	55	63	70	78						45
46	44	57	65	72	79						46
47	45	59	66	73	79						47
48	46	61	68	75	80						48
49	47	62	69	76							49
50	49	64	71	77							50
51	51	65	72	78							51
52	52	66	73	78							52
53	54	68	75	79							53
54	55	69	76	79							54
55	57	70	77	80							55
56	58	71	78								56
57	60	72	78								57
58	61	72	79								58
59	63	73	79								59
60	64	74	80								60
61	65	75									61
62	67	76									62
63	68	76									63
64	70	77									64
65	71	78									65
70	76	80									70
75	80										75

LIFE CYCLE CHART

RESIDENTIAL PROPERTIES

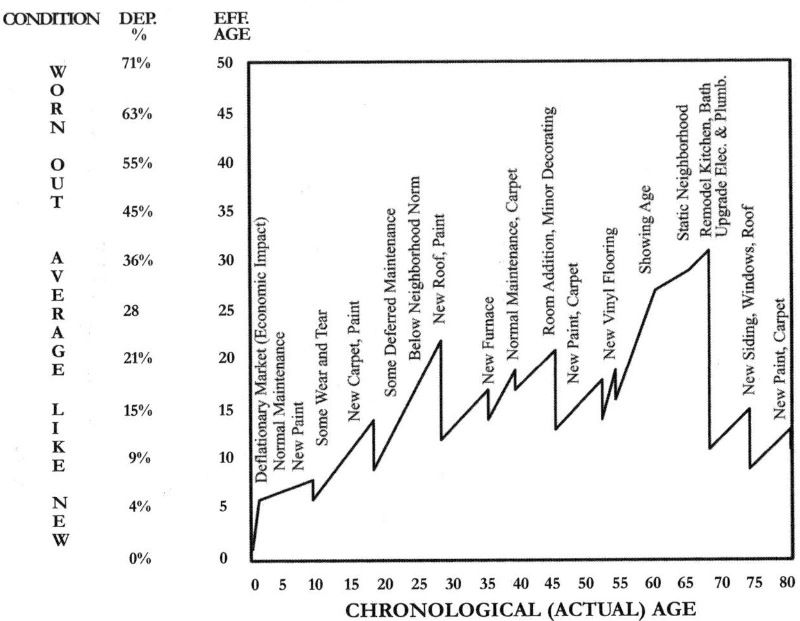

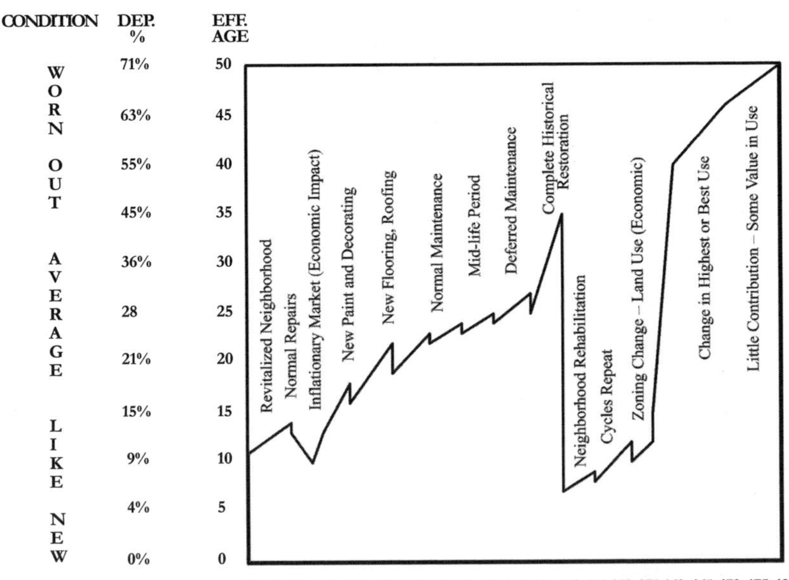

LOCAL MULTIPLIERS

- DEFINITIONS

- UNITED STATES MULTIPLIERS

- CANADIAN MULTIPLIERS

DEFINITIONS

Local Multipliers:

Reflect local cost conditions and are designed to adjust the costs to each locality. They are based on weighted labor and material costs most commonly found in the chapter specified. Local multipliers apply to all costs in the manual. In some cases, local building problems and practices must be considered. When applied to the total cost, local multipliers will adjust for variations in component costs as a whole, for a particular geographic area. But they may not adequately adjust when applied to specific components. In some cases, local building problems and practices must be considered.

Special Local Conditions:

Normally, smaller cities and suburbs near larger cities generally fall under the same cost influence as the larger city. However, local wage scales, inspection practices, licenses, codes and fees may vary and you should consider these possible deviations. Within a large city, costs will often vary by distance from sources of materials. Local multipliers apply only to typical conditions prevailing.

Remote Locations:

If a building or other structure is far removed from labor and material supplies or if its location is accessible with difficulty, requiring higher material freight charges, noncompetitive conditions for labor or materials, labor per diem charges or unusual climatic conditions, some upward modification of the multipliers is appropriate. Examples are mountain, desert or resort locations and others not possessing reasonable, adequate transportation facilities. Refer to the component chapter to obtain the correct multiplier.

Identify the exact multiplier you need by locating the state and then the first three digits of the ZIP code of your address.

UNITED STATES

	Baths & Kitchens	Ceiling & Wall Finishes	Doors & Windows	Elect., Plumb., & HVAC	Sitework & Ext. Walls	Floor Finishes	Roofing	Spec. & Equip.
ALABAMA								
350	.85	.82	.85	.86	.84	.84	.88	.81
351	.85	.82	.85	.86	.84	.84	.88	.81
352	.86	.85	.86	.85	.86	.87	.89	.83
354	.85	.82	.85	.86	.84	.84	.88	.81
355	.86	.85	.86	.85	.86	.87	.89	.83
356	.84	.80	.85	.86	.83	.84	.88	.80
357	.85	.80	.87	.88	.82	.84	.88	.81
358	.85	.80	.87	.88	.82	.84	.88	.81
359	.85	.82	.87	.87	.83	.84	.89	.82
360	.86	.81	.87	.92	.83	.84	.88	.83
361	.86	.81	.87	.92	.83	.84	.88	.83
362	.85	.82	.87	.88	.84	.85	.89	.82
363	.86	.84	.85	.87	.86	.88	.91	.83
364	.86	.84	.85	.87	.86	.88	.91	.83
365	.84	.82	.83	.88	.83	.79	.84	.82
366	.84	.82	.83	.88	.83	.79	.84	.82
367	.85	.82	.86	.88	.84	.85	.88	.82
368	.85	.82	.87	.88	.84	.85	.89	.82
369	.84	.82	.83	.88	.83	.79	.84	.82
ALASKA								
995	1.25	1.30	1.29	1.16	1.29	1.35	1.36	1.26
996	1.25	1.30	1.29	1.16	1.29	1.35	1.36	1.26
997	1.35	1.37	1.38	1.33	1.34	1.45	1.45	1.36
998	1.36	1.33	1.32	1.34	1.37	1.38	1.38	1.36
999	1.36	1.33	1.32	1.34	1.37	1.38	1.38	1.36
ARIZONA								
850	.88	.84	.91	.88	.91	.94	.87	.85
851	.88	.84	.91	.88	.91	.94	.87	.85
852	.89	.85	.92	.88	.92	.95	.88	.85
853	.90	.86	.96	.91	.89	.89	.89	.87
855	.87	.83	.89	.88	.87	.89	.83	.82
856	.87	.83	.89	.88	.87	.89	.83	.82
857	.89	.85	.92	.88	.91	.93	.87	.84
859	.92	.89	.95	.89	.96	1.02	.93	.87
860	.92	.89	.95	.89	.96	1.02	.93	.87
863	.90	.86	.94	.89	.93	.96	.90	.86
864	.97	.95	.99	.95	1.01	1.01	.94	.96
865	.92	.89	.95	.89	.96	1.02	.93	.87

UNITED STATES

	Baths & Kitchens	Ceiling & Wall Finishes	Doors & Windows	Elect., Plumb., & HVAC	Sitework & Ext. Walls	Floor Finishes	Roofing	Spec. & Equip.
ARKANSAS								
716	.84	.80	.83	.86	.83	.85	.82	.78
717	.81	.77	.80	.84	.79	.81	.79	.76
718	.81	.77	.80	.84	.79	.81	.79	.76
719	.84	.80	.84	.87	.83	.84	.80	.79
720	.85	.81	.85	.86	.84	.86	.80	.79
721	.85	.81	.85	.86	.84	.86	.80	.79
722	.85	.81	.85	.86	.84	.86	.80	.79
723	.85	.80	.86	.89	.83	.82	.85	.81
724	.87	.81	.89	.91	.85	.83	.86	.84
725	.86	.81	.86	.90	.84	.84	.83	.82
726	.86	.81	.86	.90	.84	.84	.83	.82
727	.86	.82	.86	.90	.83	.86	.79	.81
728	.86	.81	.86	.91	.83	.86	.81	.82
729	.86	.81	.86	.91	.83	.86	.81	.82
CALIFORNIA								
900	1.11	1.15	1.13	1.07	1.15	1.11	1.09	1.12
901	1.11	1.15	1.13	1.07	1.15	1.12	1.09	1.12
902	1.11	1.15	1.13	1.07	1.15	1.12	1.09	1.12
903	1.11	1.15	1.13	1.07	1.15	1.12	1.09	1.12
904	1.11	1.15	1.13	1.07	1.15	1.12	1.09	1.12
905	1.11	1.15	1.13	1.07	1.15	1.11	1.09	1.12
906	1.11	1.15	1.13	1.07	1.15	1.11	1.09	1.12
907	1.11	1.15	1.13	1.07	1.15	1.11	1.09	1.12
908	1.11	1.15	1.13	1.07	1.15	1.11	1.09	1.12
909	1.11	1.15	1.13	1.07	1.15	1.11	1.09	1.12
910	1.11	1.15	1.13	1.07	1.15	1.11	1.09	1.12
911	1.11	1.15	1.13	1.07	1.15	1.11	1.09	1.12
912	1.11	1.15	1.13	1.07	1.15	1.11	1.09	1.12
913	1.11	1.14	1.13	1.06	1.14	1.12	1.09	1.11
914	1.11	1.14	1.13	1.06	1.14	1.12	1.09	1.11
915	1.11	1.14	1.13	1.06	1.14	1.12	1.09	1.11
916	1.11	1.14	1.13	1.06	1.14	1.12	1.09	1.11
917	1.11	1.14	1.13	1.06	1.14	1.12	1.09	1.11
918	1.11	1.14	1.13	1.06	1.14	1.12	1.09	1.11
919	1.06	1.09	1.04	1.03	1.09	1.09	1.03	1.06
920	1.06	1.09	1.04	1.03	1.09	1.09	1.03	1.06
921	1.06	1.09	1.04	1.03	1.09	1.09	1.03	1.06
922	1.08	1.12	1.09	1.05	1.12	1.10	1.07	1.09
923	1.09	1.13	1.11	1.05	1.14	1.10	1.10	1.11
924	1.09	1.12	1.10	1.05	1.13	1.10	1.09	1.10
925	1.09	1.13	1.10	1.05	1.13	1.10	1.08	1.10

	Baths & Kitchens	Ceiling & Wall Finishes	Doors & Windows	Elect., Plumb., & HVAC	Sitework & Ext. Walls	Floor Finishes	Roofing	Spec. & Equip.
CALIFORNIA (Continued)								
926	1.09	1.13	1.10	1.05	1.13	1.10	1.08	1.10
927	1.09	1.13	1.10	1.05	1.13	1.10	1.08	1.10
928	1.09	1.13	1.10	1.05	1.13	1.10	1.08	1.10
930	1.10	1.13	1.13	1.06	1.13	1.12	1.09	1.11
931	1.10	1.13	1.13	1.06	1.13	1.12	1.09	1.11
932	1.08	1.12	1.08	1.03	1.13	1.09	1.11	1.11
933	1.08	1.11	1.10	1.02	1.13	1.08	1.11	1.10
934	1.10	1.12	1.11	1.06	1.14	1.10	1.10	1.11
935	1.09	1.14	1.09	1.03	1.14	1.10	1.10	1.11
936	1.08	1.13	1.06	1.01	1.13	1.09	1.11	1.11
937	1.08	1.13	1.06	1.01	1.13	1.09	1.11	1.11
938	1.08	1.13	1.06	1.01	1.13	1.09	1.11	1.11
939	1.21	1.27	1.16	1.16	1.25	1.29	1.18	1.24
940	1.24	1.30	1.17	1.20	1.27	1.31	1.21	1.26
941	1.26	1.32	1.18	1.24	1.28	1.33	1.22	1.29
942	1.26	1.32	1.18	1.24	1.28	1.33	1.22	1.29
943	1.26	1.32	1.18	1.24	1.28	1.33	1.22	1.29
944	1.26	1.32	1.18	1.24	1.28	1.33	1.22	1.29
945	1.20	1.26	1.14	1.16	1.24	1.26	1.19	1.23
946	1.26	1.32	1.18	1.24	1.28	1.33	1.22	1.29
947	1.26	1.32	1.18	1.24	1.28	1.33	1.22	1.29
948	1.26	1.32	1.18	1.24	1.28	1.33	1.22	1.29
949	1.20	1.26	1.14	1.16	1.24	1.26	1.19	1.23
950	1.24	1.29	1.17	1.19	1.29	1.35	1.23	1.26
951	1.24	1.29	1.17	1.19	1.29	1.35	1.23	1.26
952	1.15	1.21	1.13	1.09	1.20	1.19	1.12	1.17
953	1.15	1.21	1.13	1.09	1.20	1.19	1.12	1.17
954	1.21	1.28	1.15	1.18	1.25	1.28	1.20	1.24
955	1.18	1.24	1.16	1.09	1.22	1.28	1.25	1.19
956	1.15	1.22	1.12	1.10	1.20	1.18	1.14	1.17
957	1.12	1.18	1.08	1.06	1.17	1.13	1.13	1.13
958	1.12	1.18	1.08	1.06	1.17	1.13	1.13	1.13
959	1.12	1.18	1.09	1.07	1.17	1.13	1.13	1.13
960	1.12	1.18	1.09	1.07	1.17	1.13	1.13	1.13
961	1.06	1.09	1.06	1.04	1.10	1.07	1.08	1.07
962	1.06	1.09	1.06	1.04	1.10	1.07	1.08	1.07
963	1.06	1.09	1.006	1.04	1.10	1.07	1.08	1.07
964	1.06	1.09	1.06	1.04	1.10	1.07	1.08	1.07
965	1.06	1.09	1.06	1.04	1.10	1.07	1.08	1.07
966	1.06	1.09	1.06	1.04	1.10	1.07	1.08	1.07

UNITED STATES

	Baths & Kitchens	Ceiling & Wall Finishes	Doors & Windows	Elect., Plumb, & HVAC	Sitework & Ext. Walls	Floor Finishes	Roofing	Spec. & Equip.
COLORADO								
800	.96	.94	.96	.97	.97	.98	.88	.91
801	.96	.94	.96	.97	.97	.98	.88	.91
802	.96	.94	.96	.97	.97	.98	.88	.91
803	.96	.94	.95	.97	.96	.98	.88	.91
804	.96	.94	.95	.97	.96	.98	.88	.91
805	.96	.93	.95	.97	.96	.98	.90	.91
806	.96	.94	.95	.97	.96	.98	.88	.91
807	.95	.92	.94	.98	.93	.98	.88	.90
808	.96	.94	.95	.97	.96	.98	.90	.91
809	.96	.94	.95	.97	.96	.98	.90	.91
810	.96	.94	.95	.97	.97	1.00	.92	.91
811	.97	.95	.97	.97	.97	.97	.85	.92
812	.97	.95	.97	.97	.97	.97	.85	.92
813	.97	.95	.97	.97	.97	.97	.85	.92
814	.93	.91	.93	.95	.94	.96	.95	.89
815	.90	.87	.93	.91	.89	.88	.91	.86
816	.97	.95	.97	.97	.97	.97	.85	.92
CONNECTICUT								
060	1.14	1.19	1.08	1.13	1.14	1.14	1.18	1.15
061	1.14	1.19	1.08	1.13	1.14	1.14	1.18	1.15
062	1.14	1.19	1.08	1.13	1.14	1.14	1.18	1.15
063	1.14	1.19	1.11	1.12	1.14	1.16	1.17	1.14
064	1.16	1.24	1.11	1.13	1.18	1.18	1.16	1.16
065	1.16	1.24	1.11	1.13	1.18	1.18	1.16	1.16
066	1.19	1.28	1.14	1.14	1.22	1.21	1.14	1.18
067	1.15	1.22	1.10	1.12	1.17	1.16	1.16	1.15
068	1.34	1.46	1.33	1.28	1.37	1.31	1.29	1.36
069	1.32	1.43	1.30	1.26	1.35	1.30	1.27	1.33
DELAWARE								
197	1.14	1.17	1.15	1.14	1.14	1.14	1.17	1.13
198	1.14	1.17	1.15	1.14	1.14	1.14	1.17	1.13
199	1.09	1.11	1.10	1.09	1.08	1.09	1.17	1.07
DISTRICT OF COLUMBIA								
200	.99	.97	1.00	1.02	.98	.93	1.09	.96
202	.99	.97	1.00	1.02	.98	.93	1.09	.96
203	.99	.97	1.00	1.02	.98	.93	1.09	.96
204	.99	.97	1.00	1.02	.98	.93	1.09	.96
205	.99	.97	1.00	1.02	.98	.93	1.09	.96

	Baths & Kitchens	Ceiling & Wall Finishes	Doors & Windows	Elect., Plumb., & HVAC	Sitework & Ext. Walls	Floor Finishes	Roofing	Spec. & Equip.
FLORIDA								
320	.88	.87	.88	.87	.90	.86	.89	.86
321	.87	.84	.86	.88	.86	.83	.89	.84
322	.87	.84	.86	.88	.86	.83	.89	.84
323	.86	.83	.88	.84	.88	.89	.85	.83
324	.86	.83	.86	.87	.86	.87	.88	.83
325	.85	.82	.83	.89	.83	.82	.86	.81
326	.88	.86	.88	.88	.90	.85	.89	.86
327	.88	.89	.89	.84	.92	.88	.89	.87
328	.88	.89	.89	.84	.92	.88	.89	.87
329	.88	.88	.89	.86	.91	.87	.89	.87
330	.87	.82	.92	.88	.85	.83	.95	.84
331	.87	.82	.92	.88	.85	.83	.95	.84
332	.87	.82	.92	.88	.85	.83	.95	.84
333	.87	.83	.91	.88	.86	.84	.94	.85
334	.88	.85	.91	.88	.88	.85	.92	.86
335	.89	.86	.89	.88	.91	.86	.90	.87
336	.90	.87	.89	.90	.93	.87	.89	.88
337	.89	.87	.89	.89	.92	.87	.89	.87
338	.89	.87	.89	.88	.92	.87	.89	.87
339	.89	.86	.90	.88	.90	.86	.91	.86
340	.87	.82	.92	.88	.85	.83	.95	.84
341	.89	.86	.90	.88	.90	.86	.91	.86
342	.89	.86	.89	.88	.91	.86	.90	.87
343	.89	.86	.89	.88	.91	.86	.90	.87
344	.89	.86	.89	.88	.91	.86	.90	.87
346	.89	.86	.89	.88	.91	.86	.90	.87
347	.88	.89	.89	.84	.92	.88	.89	.87
349	.88	.85	.91	.88	.88	.85	.92	.86
GEORGIA								
300	.87	.84	.89	.92	.85	.83	.89	.84
301	.87	.84	.89	.92	.85	.83	.89	.84
302	.89	.86	.90	.92	.87	.84	.89	.85
303	.89	.86	.90	.92	.87	.84	.89	.85
304	.84	.83	.83	.86	.84	.82	.88	.81
305	.88	.85	.89	.91	.86	.84	.88	.84
306	.88	.84	.89	.90	.86	.85	.88	.84
307	.87	.84	.89	.92	.85	.83	.89	.84
308	.84	.83	.83	.86	.84	.82	.88	.81
309	.84	.83	.83	.86	.84	.82	.88	.81
310	.87	.86	.86	.89	.86	.84	.89	.83
311	.89	.86	.90	.92	.87	.84	.89	.85
312	.88	.86	.88	.91	.87	.86	.89	.84
313	.85	.86	.80	.86	.86	.84	.93	.81
314	.85	.86	.80	.86	.86	.84	.93	.81
315	.86	.84	.85	.86	.87	.85	.90	.83
316	.86	.84	.87	.86	.87	.87	.87	.83
317	.87	.85	.88	.88	.87	.88	.88	.84
318	.88	.85	.88	.91	.86	.86	.89	.84
319	.88	.85	.88	.91	.86	.86	.89	.84

UNITED STATES

	Baths & Kitchens	Ceiling & Wall Finishes	Doors & Windows	Elect., Plumb., & HVAC	Sitework & Ext. Walls	Floor Finishes	Roofing	Spec. & Equip.
HAWAII								
967	1.34	1.45	1.45	1.22	1.40	1.34	1.39	1.38
968	1.34	1.45	1.45	1.22	1.40	1.34	1.39	1.38
IDAHO								
832	.92	.88	.94	.91	.92	.95	.88	.90
833	.98	.93	1.00	.96	.99	1.02	.93	.96
834	.93	.90	.97	.91	.93	.94	.88	.93
835	.94	.92	.94	.94	.96	1.00	.93	.92
836	.92	.88	.94	.90	.94	.99	.87	.92
837	.92	.88	.94	.90	.94	.99	.87	.92
838	.94	.92	.94	.94	.95	1.01	.94	.92
839	.94	.92	.94	.94	.95	1.01	.94	.92
ILLINOIS								
600	1.13	1.20	1.11	1.11	1.15	1.12	1.08	1.15
601	1.15	1.22	1.13	1.13	1.16	1.12	1.09	1.17
602	1.15	1.22	1.13	1.14	1.17	1.12	1.08	1.17
603	1.15	1.22	1.13	1.14	1.17	1.12	1.08	1.17
604	1.14	1.21	1.12	1.13	1.16	1.11	1.09	1.16
605	1.13	1.20	1.11	1.12	1.15	1.11	1.10	1.15
606	1.20	1.28	1.18	1.18	1.22	1.14	1.09	1.22
607	1.20	1.28	1.18	1.18	1.22	1.14	1.09	1.22
609	1.10	1.14	1.09	1.09	1.10	1.06	1.08	1.11
610	1.08	1.13	1.06	1.07	1.09	1.07	1.08	1.10
611	1.10	1.15	1.08	1.10	1.11	1.09	1.12	1.13
612	1.03	1.07	1.02	1.02	1.04	1.03	1.02	1.03
613	1.10	1.14	1.09	1.09	1.10	1.06	1.08	1.11
614	1.04	1.09	1.02	1.03	1.04	1.04	1.06	1.04
615	1.06	1.11	1.03	1.05	1.06	1.04	1.11	1.06
616	1.06	1.11	1.03	1.05	1.06	1.04	1.11	1.06
617	1.10	1.14	1.09	1.09	1.10	1.06	1.08	1.11
618	1.05	1.09	1.03	1.04	1.04	1.03	1.09	1.04
619	1.04	1.08	1.03	1.03	1.04	1.03	1.08	1.04
620	1.07	1.07	1.08	1.09	1.05	1.03	1.03	1.08
622	1.07	1.07	1.08	1.08	1.05	1.03	1.02	1.08
623	1.02	1.02	1.03	1.03	1.00	.99	1.03	1.02
624	1.02	1.03	1.02	1.02	1.01	1.02	1.02	1.02
625	1.04	1.09	1.01	1.04	1.04	1.06	1.03	1.04
626	1.04	1.09	1.01	1.04	1.04	1.06	1.03	1.04
627	1.04	1.09	1.01	1.04	1.04	1.06	1.03	1.04
628	1.06	1.04	1.09	1.05	1.05	1.05	.98	1.06
629	1.02	.99	1.05	1.04	1.01	1.00	.98	1.03

UNITED STATES

	Baths & Kitchens	Ceiling & Wall Finishes	Doors & Windows	Elect., Plumb., & HVAC	Sitework & Ext. Walls	Floor Finishes	Roofing	Spec. & Equip.
INDIANA								
460	1.02	1.00	1.07	1.04	1.00	.96	.93	1.02
461	1.02	1.00	1.07	1.04	1.00	.96	.93	1.02
462	1.02	1.00	1.07	1.04	1.00	.96	.93	1.02
463	1.10	1.14	1.09	1.10	1.11	1.06	1.04	1.11
464	1.10	1.14	1.09	1.10	1.11	1.06	1.04	1.11
465	1.00	1.01	.97	1.03	1.00	1.00	1.01	1.00
466	1.00	1.01	.97	1.03	1.00	1.00	1.01	1.00
467	.98	.94	1.01	.97	.97	1.01	1.00	.96
468	.98	.94	1.01	.97	.97	1.01	1.00	.96
469	.99	.97	1.02	1.01	.98	.96	.95	.98
470	1.00	.99	1.02	1.00	.99	.98	.97	.98
471	.95	.93	.99	.99	.92	.92	.95	.93
472	1.00	.99	1.02	1.00	.99	.98	.97	.98
473	.98	.96	.99	1.00	.96	.97	.95	.95
474	1.00	1.01	1.01	.99	.99	1.06	.98	.98
475	1.00	1.01	1.01	.99	.99	1.06	.98	.98
476	1.00	1.02	.98	1.01	.99	.99	1.06	1.00
477	1.00	1.02	.98	1.01	.99	.99	1.06	1.00
478	1.00	1.02	1.01	1.01	.99	1.02	1.00	.99
479	.97	.95	1.00	.99	.96	.95	.95	.96
IOWA								
500	1.00	.99	.98	1.02	.99	1.03	.95	.99
501	1.00	.99	.98	1.02	.99	1.03	.95	.99
502	1.00	.99	.98	1.02	.99	1.03	.95	.99
503	.99	.97	.96	1.02	.97	.99	.91	.97
504	1.02	1.04	1.01	1.01	1.02	1.08	.99	1.02
505	.97	.97	.97	.98	.96	1.00	.94	.96
506	.99	.97	.96	1.02	.97	.99	.91	.97
507	.99	.97	.96	1.02	.97	.99	.91	.97
508	1.00	.97	.98	1.02	.97	.99	.94	.98
509	1.00	.97	.98	1.02	.97	.99	.94	.98
510	.91	.87	.92	.95	.88	.85	.88	.87
511	.91	.87	.92	.95	.88	.85	.88	.87
512	.94	.93	.96	.94	.92	.95	.93	.91
513	.94	.93	.96	.94	.92	.95	.93	.91
514	.95	.92	.92	.98	.92	.98	.90	.90
515	.95	.92	.92	.98	.92	.98	.90	.90
516	1.00	.97	.98	1.02	.97	.99	.94	.98
520	1.03	1.06	1.02	1.03	1.03	1.05	1.03	1.04
521	1.02	1.04	1.01	1.01	1.02	1.08	.99	1.02
522	.98	.97	.97	.98	.97	1.06	.98	.97
523	.98	.97	.97	.98	.97	1.06	.98	.97
524	.98	.97	.97	.98	.97	1.06	.98	.97
525	1.00	.99	.98	1.00	.99	1.03	.96	.99
526	1.02	1.04	1.00	1.01	1.02	1.05	1.01	1.01
527	1.03	1.07	1.02	1.02	1.04	1.04	1.03	1.03
528	1.03	1.07	1.02	1.02	1.04	1.04	1.03	1.03

UNITED STATES

	Baths & Kitchens	Ceiling & Wall Finishes	Doors & Windows	Elect., Plumb., & HVAC	Sitework & Ext. Walls	Floor Finishes	Roofing	Spec. & Equip.
KANSAS								
660	.98	.97	1.00	1.00	.96	.96	.99	.97
661	.98	.97	1.00	1.00	.96	.96	.99	.97
662	.98	.97	1.00	1.00	.96	.96	.99	.97
664	.91	.90	.93	.93	.89	.91	.97	.89
665	.91	.90	.93	.93	.89	.91	.97	.89
666	.91	.90	.93	.93	.89	.91	.97	.89
667	.91	.90	.91	.93	.89	.91	.89	.86
668	.91	.90	.91	.93	.89	.91	.89	.86
669	.95	.97	.93	.97	.93	.97	.85	.87
670	.87	.82	.86	.90	.84	.86	.82	.81
671	.87	.82	.86	.90	.84	.86	.82	.81
672	.87	.85	.87	.91	.84	.84	.78	.81
673	.87	.83	.87	.91	.84	.86	.85	.83
674	.95	.97	.93	.97	.93	.97	.85	.87
675	.92	.91	.90	.95	.89	.91	.83	.84
676	.93	.92	.91	.96	.90	.94	.86	.86
677	.96	.92	.93	.99	.92	.99	.90	.90
678	.91	.89	.89	.96	.88	.90	.83	.84
679	.89	.85	.88	.92	.85	.89	.84	.82
KENTUCKY								
400	.95	.91	.99	1.00	.90	.90	.94	.92
401	.95	.91	.99	1.00	.90	.90	.94	.92
402	.95	.91	.99	1.00	.90	.90	.94	.92
403	.91	.88	.93	.93	.91	.87	.98	.90
404	.91	.88	.93	.93	.91	.87	.98	.90
405	.91	.88	.93	.93	.91	.87	.98	.90
406	.95	.91	.99	1.00	.90	.90	.94	.92
407	.87	.83	.91	.89	.87	.87	.93	.85
408	.87	.83	.91	.89	.87	.87	.93	.85
409	.87	.83	.91	.89	.87	.87	.93	.85
410	.98	.99	.98	.97	.98	.98	1.02	.97
411	1.01	1.05	1.02	.99	1.02	.98	1.03	1.01
412	1.01	1.05	1.02	.99	1.02	.98	1.03	1.01
413	.87	.83	.91	.89	.87	.87	.93	.85
414	.87	.83	.91	.89	.87	.87	.93	.85
415	.97	.97	1.00	.96	.97	.95	.99	.96
416	.97	.97	1.00	.96	.97	.95	.99	.96
417	.87	.83	.91	.89	.87	.87	.93	.85
418	.87	.83	.91	.89	.87	.87	.93	.85
420	.95	.88	.97	.99	.92	.92	.95	.94
421	.91	.86	.91	.96	.89	.89	.93	.91
422	.91	.86	.91	.96	.89	.89	.93	.91
423	.94	.96	.96	.96	.92	.91	1.01	.94
424	.96	.96	.97	.98	.94	.94	1.02	.96
425	.91	.88	.93	.94	.90	.88	.96	.89
426	.91	.88	.93	.94	.90	.88	.96	.89
427	.94	.91	.96	.98	.90	.90	.95	.92

UNITED STATES

	Baths & Kitchens	Ceiling & Wall Finishes	Doors & Windows	Elect., Plumb., & HVAC	Sitework & Ext. Walls	Floor Finishes	Roofing	Spec. & Equip.
LOUISIANA								
700	.84	.79	.83	.88	.82	.83	.86	.79
701	.84	.79	.83	.88	.82	.83	.86	.79
703	.84	.81	.82	.87	.82	.84	.85	.79
704	.84	.81	.82	.87	.82	.84	.85	.79
705	.83	.80	.80	.85	.82	.85	.81	.77
706	.83	.82	.80	.84	.82	.86	.82	.78
707	.84	.82	.82	.86	.83	.85	.85	.78
708	.84	.83	.82	.84	.83	.87	.85	.78
710	.81	.76	.77	.85	.79	.77	.80	.76
711	.81	.76	.77	.85	.79	.77	.80	.76
712	.80	.75	.80	.83	.77	.80	.77	.74
713	.81	.74	.78	.86	.80	.82	.76	.76
714	.81	.74	.78	.86	.80	.82	.76	.76
MAINE								
039	1.00	.98	1.03	1.01	.99	.99	1.14	.99
040	1.00	.98	1.03	1.01	.99	.99	1.14	.99
041	1.00	.98	1.03	1.01	.99	.99	1.14	.99
042	1.01	.98	1.01	1.06	.98	1.01	1.14	1.00
043	1.01	.98	1.01	1.06	.98	1.01	1.14	1.00
044	1.00	.99	.99	1.00	.99	1.08	1.08	.97
045	1.01	.98	1.01	1.06	.98	1.01	1.14	1.00
046	1.00	.99	1.00	1.02	.99	1.04	1.11	.98
047	1.00	.99	1.01	1.02	.99	1.04	1.11	.98
048	1.01	.98	1.01	1.06	.98	1.01	1.14	1.00
049	1.00	.99	.99	1.00	.99	1.08	1.08	.97
MARYLAND								
206	.98	.96	1.00	1.02	.97	.94	1.05	.96
207	.98	.96	1.00	1.02	.97	.94	1.05	.96
208	.98	.96	1.00	1.02	.97	.94	1.05	.96
209	.98	.99	1.04	1.04	.98	.96	1.05	.98
210	1.01	.99	1.04	1.04	.98	.96	1.05	.98
211	1.01	.99	1.04	1.04	.98	.96	1.05	.98
212	1.01	.98	1.03	1.04	.98	.95	1.05	.98
214	1.00	.98	1.00	.97	.99	.99	1.07	.97
215	.98	1.02	1.05	1.05	1.01	.99	1.09	1.00
216	1.03	.95	.099	.96	.95	.97	.94	.95
217	.96	1.13	1.12	1.11	1.09	1.08	1.14	1.10
218	1.10	.98	1.03	1.04	.98	.95	1.05	.98
219	1.00	.93	1.00	1.00	.94	.92	1.00	.94

UNITED STATES

	Baths & Kitchens	Ceiling & Wall Finishes	Doors & Windows	Elect., Plumb., & HVAC	Sitework & Ext. Walls	Floor Finishes	Roofing	Spec. & Equip.
MASSACHUSETTS								
010	1.10	1.19	1.06	1.07	1.11	1.13	1.15	1.10
011	1.10	1.19	1.06	1.07	1.11	1.13	1.15	1.10
012	1.09	1.14	1.05	1.08	1.09	1.09	1.12	1.09
013	1.15	1.21	1.12	1.12	1.14	1.18	1.19	1.15
014	1.15	1.21	1.12	1.12	1.14	1.18	1.19	1.15
015	1.10	1.16	1.08	1.09	1.10	1.15	1.16	1.10
016	1.18	1.25	1.16	1.15	1.18	1.20	1.20	1.19
017	1.18	1.25	1.15	1.15	1.18	1.20	1.21	1.20
018	1.13	1.20	1.09	1.11	1.13	1.17	1.20	1.14
019	1.20	1.29	1.16	1.17	1.21	1.21	1.24	1.23
020	1.21	1.29	1.18	1.17	1.21	1.22	1.23	1.23
021	1.21	1.29	1.18	1.17	1.21	1.22	1.23	1.23
022	1.21	1.29	1.18	1.17	1.21	1.22	1.23	1.23
023	1.20	1.28	1.18	1.17	1.21	1.22	1.22	1.23
024	1.20	1.28	1.18	1.17	1.21	1.22	1.22	1.23
025	1.18	1.24	1.16	1.15	1.18	1.21	1.21	1.20
026	1.18	1.24	1.16	1.15	1.18	1.21	1.21	1.20
027	1.18	1.24	1.17	1.15	1.18	1.21	1.21	1.20
MICHIGAN								
480	1.11	1.12	1.13	1.12	1.11	1.08	1.06	1.12
481	1.09	1.10	1.06	1.11	1.08	1.05	1.07	1.09
482	1.09	1.10	1.06	1.11	1.08	1.05	1.07	1.09
483	1.11	1.12	1.13	1.12	1.11	1.08	1.06	1.12
484	1.08	1.07	1.07	1.12	1.06	1.03	1.08	1.07
485	1.08	1.07	1.07	1.12	1.06	1.03	1.05	1.06
486	1.08	1.07	1.07	1.12	1.06	1.03	1.05	1.06
487	1.08	1.08	1.07	1.12	1.07	1.03	1.08	1.07
488	1.03	1.02	1.02	1.07	1.02	.99	1.03	1.01
489	1.03	1.02	1.02	1.07	1.02	.99	1.03	1.01
490	1.00	.99	.98	1.04	.99	.98	.99	.99
491	1.00	.99	.98	1.04	.99	.98	.99	.99
492	1.06	1.07	1.03	1.09	1.06	1.03	1.06	1.07
493	.99	.98	.97	1.02	.98	.99	.98	.97
494	.99	.98	.97	1.02	.98	.99	.98	.97
495	.99	.97	.97	1.02	.97	.98	.95	.96
496	.99	.97	.98	1.01	.97	1.02	1.03	.96
497	1.04	1.01	1.04	1.10	.99	1.07	.98	1.00
498	1.03	1.05	1.01	1.03	1.04	1.07	1.04	1.03
499	1.03	1.05	1.01	1.03	1.04	1.07	1.04	1.03

UNITED STATES

	Baths & Kitchens	Ceiling & Wall Finishes	Doors & Windows	Elect., Plumb., & HVAC	Sitework & Ext. Walls	Floor Finishes	Roofing	Spec. & Equip.
MINNESOTA								
550	1.08	1.12	1.08	1.06	1.09	1.12	1.05	1.09
551	1.08	1.12	1.08	1.06	1.09	1.12	1.05	1.09
553	1.10	1.14	1.10	1.07	1.11	1.12	1.06	1.11
554	1.14	1.19	1.13	1.11	1.15	1.14	1.08	1.16
555	1.10	1.14	1.10	1.07	1.11	1.12	1.06	1.11
556	1.06	1.08	1.06	1.05	1.06	1.08	1.07	1.05
557	1.06	1.08	1.06	1.05	1.06	1.08	1.07	1.05
558	1.07	1.08	1.09	1.06	1.07	1.09	1.05	1.06
559	1.06	1.09	1.04	1.07	1.06	1.10	1.02	1.06
560	1.00	1.05	1.02	.95	1.02	1.13	1.02	1.00
561	1.00	1.05	1.02	.95	1.02	1.13	1.02	1.00
562	.98	.99	1.00	.97	.98	1.01	.99	.97
563	1.04	1.07	1.04	1.03	1.05	1.03	1.04	1.04
564	1.06	1.07	1.00	1.06	1.07	1.11	1.12	1.05
565	1.06	1.07	1.00	1.06	1.07	1.11	1.12	1.05
566	1.06	1.07	1.00	1.06	1.07	1.11	1.12	1.05
567	1.06	1.07	1.00	1.06	1.07	1.11	1.12	1.05
MISSISSIPPI								
386	.85	.80	.85	.89	.84	.83	.86	.81
387	.86	.81	.84	.89	.85	.87	.90	.80
388	.83	.78	.83	.85	.81	.81	.86	.78
389	.85	.80	.84	.88	.83	.83	.87	.80
390	.82	.78	.80	.84	.80	.83	.79	.76
391	.82	.78	.80	.84	.80	.83	.79	.76
392	.83	.80	.83	.86	.82	.81	.84	.78
393	.84	.80	.82	.85	.84	.84	.88	.78
394	.84	.81	.82	.88	.83	.81	.85	.79
395	.85	.80	.82	.90	.83	.81	.84	.78
396	.84	.81	.82	.88	.83	.81	.85	.79
397	.81	.76	.81	.83	.79	.81	.86	.76

UNITED STATES

	Baths & Kitchens	Ceiling & Wall Finishes	Doors & Windows	Elect., Plumb., & HVAC	Sitework & Ext. Walls	Floor Finishes	Roofing	Spec. & Equip.
MISSOURI								
630	1.02	1.01	1.04	1.04	1.00	.99	1.03	1.03
631	1.08	1.08	1.10	1.11	1.06	1.01	1.04	1.10
633	1.02	1.01	1.04	1.03	1.00	.99	1.03	1.02
634	1.02	1.01	1.03	1.03	1.00	.99	1.03	1.02
635	.97	.94	.98	.98	.95	.98	.97	.96
636	1.05	1.03	1.07	1.07	1.03	1.01	1.00	1.06
637	1.02	.98	1.04	1.04	1.00	.99	.98	1.02
638	1.02	.98	1.04	1.04	1.00	.99	.98	1.02
639	.96	.91	.98	1.00	.93	.90	.94	.95
640	1.04	1.03	1.08	1.05	1.02	.99	1.04	1.05
641	1.04	1.03	1.08	1.05	1.02	.99	1.04	1.05
644	1.02	1.00	1.04	1.03	1.00	.98	1.01	1.02
645	.99	.98	1.01	1.01	.97	.97	1.00	.98
646	1.00	.98	1.03	1.02	.98	.97	1.00	1.00
647	.98	.94	1.00	1.01	.95	.94	.98	.97
648	.87	.81	.86	.92	.83	.86	.82	.83
650	1.01	1.00	1.04	1.03	1.00	.98	1.03	1.02
651	.96	.92	.99	.99	.93	.93	.99	.96
652	.95	.90	1.00	.96	.92	.93	1.02	.94
653	1.01	1.00	1.04	1.03	1.00	.98	1.03	1.02
654	.97	.94	.99	1.01	.94	.94	.97	.97
655	.97	.94	.99	1.01	.94	.94	.97	.97
656	.89	.85	.90	.93	.87	.89	.88	.87
657	.89	.85	.90	.93	.87	.89	.88	.87
658	.89	.83	.86	.97	.85	.88	.84	.87
MONTANA								
590	.92	.88	.91	.95	.89	.97	.88	.89
591	.92	.88	.91	.95	.89	.97	.88	.89
592	.91	.87	.91	.92	.90	.95	.88	.87
593	.91	.87	.91	.92	.90	.95	.88	.87
594	.93	.86	.93	.94	.92	1.00	.96	.88
595	.93	.88	.93	.94	.91	1.01	.93	.88
596	.93	.88	.93	.93	.92	1.04	.95	.88
597	.93	.90	.93	.92	.93	1.07	.93	.89
598	.91	.87	.89	.91	.90	1.03	1.00	.87
599	.92	.88	.91	.92	.91	1.03	.97	.88

UNITED STATES

	Baths & Kitchens	Ceiling & Wall Finishes	Doors & Windows	Elect., Plumb., & HVAC	Sitework & Ext. Walls	Floor Finishes	Roofing	Spec. & Equip.
NEBRASKA								
680	.95	.92	.92	.99	.93	1.00	.90	.91
681	.95	.92	.92	.99	.93	1.00	.90	.91
683	.94	.92	.92	.97	.92	.98	.91	.90
684	.94	.92	.92	.97	.92	.98	.91	.90
685	.94	.92	.92	.97	.92	.98	.91	.90
686	.94	.91	.91	.96	.91	.98	.92	.90
687	.93	.91	.91	.95	.91	.97	.93	.90
688	.94	.91	.93	.97	.91	.97	.90	.89
689	1.00	.96	.97	1.04	.98	1.09	.97	.95
690	1.00	.96	.97	1.04	.98	1.09	.97	.95
691	1.00	.96	.97	1.04	.98	1.09	.97	.95
692	1.00	.96	.97	1.04	.98	1.09	.97	.95
693	.91	.87	.91	.93	.89	.93	.85	.86
NEVADA								
890	1.04	1.03	1.04	1.02	1.08	1.04	.97	1.06
891	1.04	1.03	1.04	1.02	1.08	1.04	.97	1.06
893	1.06	1.02	1.08	1.04	1.08	1.12	1.03	1.04
894	.99	.96	1.02	.99	1.01	.97	.96	.99
895	.99	.96	1.02	.99	1.01	.97	.96	.99
897	1.06	1.02	1.08	1.04	1.08	1.12	1.03	1.04
898	1.06	1.02	1.08	1.04	1.08	1.12	1.03	1.04
NEW HAMPSHIRE								
030	1.04	1.09	1.00	1.04	1.03	1.12	1.14	1.02
031	1.04	1.09	1.00	1.04	1.03	1.12	1.14	1.02
032	1.04	1.09	1.00	1.04	1.03	1.12	1.14	1.02
033	1.04	1.09	1.00	1.04	1.03	1.12	1.14	1.02
034	1.04	1.09	1.00	1.04	1.03	1.12	1.14	1.02
035	1.04	1.09	1.00	1.04	1.03	1.12	1.14	1.02
036	1.04	1.09	1.00	1.04	1.03	1.12	1.14	1.02
037	1.05	1.09	1.01	1.05	1.05	1.10	1.14	1.04
038	1.06	1.09	1.03	1.05	1.07	1.13	1.17	1.06

UNITED STATES

	Baths & Kitchens	Ceiling & Wall Finishes	Doors & Windows	Elect., Plumb., & HVAC	Sitework & Ext. Walls	Floor Finishes	Roofing	Spec. & Equip.
NEW JERSEY								
070	1.36	1.49	1.35	1.31	1.38	1.33	1.31	1.38
071	1.33	1.46	1.31	1.29	1.34	1.32	1.28	1.34
072	1.33	1.46	1.31	1.29	1.34	1.32	1.28	1.34
073	1.41	1.54	1.41	1.34	1.44	1.36	1.36	1.44
074	1.38	1.51	1.38	1.32	1.41	1.34	1.33	1.41
075	1.38	1.51	1.38	1.32	1.41	1.34	1.33	1.41
076	1.41	1.54	1.41	1.33	1.44	1.36	1.36	1.44
077	1.38	1.51	1.37	1.32	1.40	1.33	1.34	1.41
078	1.37	1.49	1.37	1.31	1.39	1.34	1.33	1.39
079	1.37	1.49	1.37	1.31	1.39	1.34	1.33	1.39
080	1.24	1.30	1.23	1.21	1.25	1.24	1.23	1.24
081	1.24	1.30	1.23	1.21	1.25	1.24	1.23	1.24
082	1.21	1.28	1.20	1.18	1.21	1.19	1.22	1.22
083	1.19	1.24	1.18	1.16	1.19	1.18	1.21	1.18
084	1.27	1.38	1.25	1.22	1.28	1.22	1.25	1.29
085	1.28	1.37	1.27	1.24	1.29	1.27	1.25	1.29
086	1.28	1.37	1.27	1.24	1.29	1.27	1.25	1.29
087	1.36	1.48	1.35	1.30	1.38	1.31	1.32	1.39
088	1.37	1.49	1.37	1.31	1.39	1.34	1.32	1.39
089	1.37	1.49	1.36	1.31	1.39	1.34	1.32	1.39
NEW MEXICO								
870	.87	.83	.87	.91	.85	.85	.87	.84
871	.87	.83	.87	.91	.85	.85	.87	.84
872	.87	.83	.87	.91	.85	.85	.87	.84
873	.88	.84	.88	.93	.85	.89	.87	.85
874	.88	.84	.89	.94	.86	.92	.87	.85
875	.89	.85	.88	.95	.86	.86	.87	.85
877	.89	.85	.88	.95	.86	.86	.87	.85
878	.87	.83	.87	.91	.85	.85	.87	.84
879	.87	.83	.87	.91	.85	.85	.87	.84
880	.86	.81	.86	.92	.83	.82	.80	.83
881	.87	.84	.86	.91	.84	.88	.86	.82
882	.89	.84	.92	.93	.86	.93	.84	.84
883	.89	.84	.92	.93	.86	.93	.84	.84
884	.87	.84	.86	.91	.84	.88	.86	.82

UNITED STATES

	Baths & Kitchens	Ceiling & Wall Finishes	Doors & Windows	Elect., Plumb., & HVAC	Sitework & Ext. Walls	Floor Finishes	Roofing	Spec. & Equip.
NEW YORK								
090	1.49	1.63	1.51	1.39	1.54	1.41	1.44	1.55
091	1.49	1.63	1.51	1.39	1.54	1.41	1.44	1.55
092	1.49	1.63	1.51	1.39	1.54	1.41	1.44	1.55
093	1.49	1.63	1.51	1.39	1.54	1.41	1.44	1.55
094	1.49	1.63	1.51	1.39	1.54	1.41	1.44	1.55
095	1.49	1.63	1.51	1.39	1.54	1.41	1.44	1.55
096	1.49	1.63	1.51	1.39	1.54	1.41	1.44	1.55
097	1.49	1.63	1.51	1.39	1.54	1.41	1.44	1.55
098	1.49	1.63	1.51	1.39	1.54	1.41	1.44	1.55
100	1.49	1.63	1.51	1.39	1.54	1.41	1.44	1.55
101	1.49	1.63	1.51	1.39	1.54	1.41	1.44	1.55
102	1.49	1.63	1.51	1.39	1.54	1.41	1.44	1.55
103	1.49	1.63	1.51	1.39	1.54	1.41	1.44	1.55
104	1.49	1.63	1.51	1.39	1.54	1.41	1.44	1.55
105	1.37	1.49	1.36	1.30	1.40	1.33	1.32	1.40
106	1.37	1.49	1.36	1.30	1.40	1.33	1.32	1.39
107	1.37	1.49	1.36	1.30	1.40	1.33	1.32	1.39
108	1.37	1.49	1.36	1.30	1.40	1.33	1.32	1.39
109	1.37	1.49	1.36	1.30	1.40	1.33	1.32	1.39
110	1.46	1.60	1.48	1.37	1.50	1.39	1.42	1.51
111	1.46	1.60	1.48	1.37	1.50	1.39	1.42	1.51
112	1.46	1.60	1.48	1.37	1.50	1.39	1.42	1.51
113	1.46	1.60	1.48	1.37	1.50	1.39	1.42	1.51
114	1.46	1.60	1.48	1.37	1.50	1.39	1.42	1.51
115	1.46	1.60	1.47	1.37	1.50	1.39	1.41	1.51
116	1.46	1.60	1.48	1.37	1.50	1.39	1.42	1.51
117	1.46	1.60	1.47	1.37	1.50	1.39	1.41	1.51
118	1.46	1.60	1.47	1.37	1.50	1.39	1.41	1.51
119	1.46	1.60	1.47	1.37	1.50	1.39	1.41	1.51
120	1.05	1.07	1.03	1.06	1.03	1.03	1.06	1.04
121	1.05	1.07	1.03	1.06	1.03	1.03	1.06	1.04
122	1.05	1.07	1.03	1.06	1.03	1.03	1.06	1.04
123	1.06	1.10	1.04	1.07	1.05	1.06	1.08	1.06
124	1.21	1.29	1.20	1.18	1.23	1.19	1.19	1.23
125	1.24	1.33	1.23	1.20	1.26	1.22	1.22	1.26
126	1.24	1.33	1.23	1.20	1.26	1.22	1.22	1.26
127	1.24	1.33	1.23	1.20	1.26	1.22	1.22	1.26
128	1.05	1.08	1.03	1.05	1.04	1.06	1.10	1.04
129	1.02	1.02	1.00	1.03	1.01	1.06	1.12	1.00
130	1.01	1.01	.97	1.04	1.00	1.04	1.06	1.00
131	1.01	1.01	.97	1.04	1.00	1.04	1.06	1.00
132	1.01	1.01	.97	1.04	1.00	1.04	1.06	1.00
133	1.02	1.03	.99	1.04	1.01	1.04	1.06	1.01
134	1.02	1.03	.99	1.04	1.01	1.04	1.06	1.01
135	1.02	1.03	.99	1.04	1.01	1.04	1.06	1.01
136	1.04	1.06	1.00	1.05	1.03	1.06	1.06	1.03
137	1.00	1.02	.98	1.02	1.00	1.06	1.06	1.00

UNITED STATES

	Baths & Kitchens	Ceiling & Wall Finishes	Doors & Windows	Elect., Plumb., & HVAC	Sitework & Ext. Walls	Floor Finishes	Roofing	Spec. & Equip.
NEW YORK (Continued)								
138	1.00	1.02	.98	1.02	1.00	1.06	1.06	1.00
139	1.00	1.02	.98	1.02	1.00	1.06	1.06	1.00
140	1.11	1.17	1.07	1.08	1.15	1.10	1.12	1.14
141	1.11	1.17	1.07	1.08	1.15	1.10	1.12	1.14
142	1.11	1.17	1.07	1.08	1.15	1.10	1.12	1.14
143	1.11	1.17	1.07	1.08	1.15	1.10	1.12	1.14
144	1.08	1.13	1.04	1.05	1.11	1.11	1.07	1.08
145	1.08	1.13	1.04	1.05	1.11	1.11	1.07	1.08
146	1.08	1.13	1.04	1.05	1.11	1.11	1.07	1.08
147	1.09	1.14	1.06	1.07	1.11	1.09	1.10	1.10
148	1.03	1.05	1.01	1.03	1.01	1.06	1.06	1.01
149	1.03	1.05	1.01	1.03	1.01	1.06	1.06	1.01
NORTH CAROLINA								
270	.87	.82	.92	.85	.87	.87	.87	.83
271	.87	.83	.92	.86	.87	.87	.88	.84
272	.87	.82	.92	.85	.87	.87	.87	.83
273	.87	.82	.92	.85	.87	.87	.87	.83
274	.87	.82	.92	.85	.87	.87	.87	.83
275	.87	.84	.92	.87	.86	.84	.86	.83
276	.88	.85	.92	.89	.86	.82	.85	.83
277	.87	.84	.92	.87	.86	.84	.86	.83
278	.88	.84	.91	.90	.87	.83	.87	.85
279	.88	.84	.91	.90	.87	.83	.87	.85
280	.86	.81	.90	.85	.86	.85	.87	.83
281	.86	.81	.90	.85	.86	.85	.87	.83
282	.86	.81	.90	.85	.86	.85	.87	.83
283	.87	.83	.92	.87	.86	.84	.86	.83
284	.86	.82	.91	.85	.86	.86	.87	.82
285	.87	.84	.90	.87	.87	.83	.87	.83
286	.87	.81	.91	.87	.86	.86	.89	.84
287	.86	.80	.91	.89	.85	.86	.90	.83
288	.86	.80	.91	.89	.85	.86	.90	.83
289	.86	.80	.91	.89	.85	.86	.90	.83
NORTH DAKOTA								
580	.93	.87	.92	.94	.94	.98	.95	.90
581	.93	.87	.92	.94	.94	.98	.95	.90
582	.98	.97	.94	.98	.99	1.06	1.02	.95
583	.95	.92	.94	.96	.96	1.01	.98	.92
584	.96	.92	.94	.96	.96	1.01	.98	.92
585	.93	.86	.94	.95	.92	.92	.92	.90
586	.93	.86	.94	.95	.92	.92	.92	.90
587	.95	.90	.99	.97	.94	.99	.97	.91
588	.92	.86	.94	.94	.91	.94	.92	.89

UNITED STATES

	Baths & Kitchens	Ceiling & Wall Finishes	Doors & Windows	Elect., Plumb., & HVAC	Sitework & Ext. Walls	Floor Finishes	Roofing	Spec. & Equip.
OHIO								
430	.98	.98	.96	1.01	.96	.99	.98	.96
431	.98	.98	.96	1.01	.96	.99	.98	.96
432	.98	.98	.96	1.01	.96	.99	.98	.96
433	.98	.98	.96	1.01	.96	.99	.98	.96
434	1.03	1.04	.99	1.06	1.03	1.01	1.04	1.04
435	1.03	1.04	.99	1.06	1.03	1.01	1.04	1.04
436	1.03	1.04	.99	1.06	1.03	1.01	1.04	1.04
437	1.01	1.02	1.00	1.03	.99	1.02	1.06	1.00
438	1.01	1.02	1.00	1.03	.99	1.02	1.06	1.00
439	1.03	1.03	1.03	1.04	1.01	1.03	1.11	1.01
440	1.07	1.10	1.05	1.08	1.07	1.05	1.10	1.09
441	1.06	1.10	1.04	1.06	1.05	1.05	1.12	1.07
442	1.05	1.07	1.03	1.05	1.04	1.04	1.10	1.05
443	1.05	1.07	1.03	1.05	1.04	1.04	1.10	1.05
444	1.05	1.07	1.04	1.05	1.04	1.04	1.11	1.04
445	1.05	1.07	1.04	1.05	1.03	1.04	1.11	1.03
446	1.05	1.07	1.04	1.05	1.03	1.04	1.12	1.04
447	1.05	1.07	1.04	1.05	1.03	1.04	1.12	1.04
448	1.03	1.05	1.01	1.04	1.02	1.02	1.06	1.03
449	1.02	1.03	.99	1.04	1.01	1.01	1.04	1.01
450	.97	.98	.98	.96	.98	.96	1.01	.97
451	.97	.98	.98	.96	.98	.96	1.01	.97
452 . . .	.99	1.00	.98	.97	1.00	1.00	1.03	.98
453	.98	.98	.99	.98	.98	.99	1.00	.97
454	.98	.99	.98	.98	.98	.99	1.00	.97
455	.98	.99	.98	.98	.98	.99	1.00	.97
456	1.01	1.04	1.01	1.00	1.01	.99	1.03	1.01
457	1.01	1.03	1.01	1.01	1.00	.99	1.02	1.00
458	1.00	.99	.99	1.01	.99	1.00	1.01	.99
OKLAHOMA								
730	.86	.79	.85	.90	.85	.84	.87	.83
731	.86	.79	.85	.90	.85	.84	.87	.83
734	.85	.78	.84	.92	.82	.90	.87	.82
735	.86	.79	.85	.91	.84	.88	.88	.83
736	.86	.80	.85	.90	.85	.88	.88	.83
737	.87	.81	.86	.90	.86	.92	.89	.83
738	.86	.80	.85	.90	.85	.88	.88	.83
739	.86	.80	.85	.90	.85	.88	.88	.83
740 . . .	.85	.80	.85	.90	.83	.85	.83	.81
741	.84	.77	.85	.89	.81	.84	.82	.80
743	.85	.80	.85	.90	.83	.85	.83	.81
744	.85	.79	.85	.90	.82	.84	.82	.81
745	.85	.78	.85	.90	.82	.86	.85	.82
746	.85	.80	.85	.90	.83	.85	.83	.81
747	.84	.80	.83	.88	.83	.86	.87	.80
748	.85	.78	.85	.90	.82	.86	.85	.82
749	.85	.78	.85	.90	.82	.86	.85	.82

UNITED STATES

	Baths & Kitchens	Ceiling & Wall Finishes	Doors & Windows	Elect., Plumb., & HVAC	Sitework & Ext. Walls	Floor Finishes	Roofing	Spec. & Equip.
OREGON								
970	1.08	1.09	1.10	1.06	1.09	1.05	1.03	1.08
971	1.08	1.09	1.10	1.04	1.10	1.07	1.04	1.08
972	1.08	1.09	1.12	1.05	1.10	1.08	1.04	1.08
973	1.07	1.07	1.10	1.03	1.08	1.07	1.02	1.07
974	1.05	1.05	1.08	1.00	1.07	1.08	1.01	1.04
975	1.03	1.05	1.06	.99	1.05	1.10	1.03	1.04
976	1.07	1.07	1.11	1.07	1.06	1.03	1.00	1.07
977	1.07	1.07	1.11	1.07	1.06	1.03	1.00	1.07
978	.99	.97	1.00	.98	1.00	1.01	.93	.98
979	1.07	1.07	1.11	1.07	1.06	1.03	1.00	1.07
PENNSYLVANIA								
150	1.06	1.09	1.06	1.06	1.05	1.03	1.10	1.04
151	1.06	1.09	1.06	1.06	1.05	1.03	1.10	1.04
152	1.06	1.09	1.06	1.06	1.05	1.03	1.10	1.04
153	1.03	1.04	1.04	1.05	1.01	1.03	1.11	1.02
154	1.01	1.02	1.03	1.02	1.00	1.01	1.08	1.00
155	1.01	1.02	1.03	1.02	1.00	1.01	1.08	1.00
156	1.03	1.04	1.04	1.04	1.02	1.02	1.09	1.01
157	1.01	1.02	1.03	1.02	1.00	1.01	1.08	1.00
158	1.01	1.03	1.03	1.02	1.00	1.02	1.08	.99
159	1.01	1.02	1.03	1.02	1.00	1.01	1.08	1.00
160	1.05	1.07	1.05	1.05	1.03	1.04	1.11	1.03
161	1.05	1.07	1.05	1.05	1.03	1.04	1.11	1.03
162	1.03	1.04	1.04	1.03	1.02	1.02	1.10	1.01
163	1.05	1.07	1.05	1.05	1.03	1.04	1.11	1.03
164	1.08	1.12	1.06	1.07	1.08	1.06	1.11	1.08
165	1.08	1.12	1.06	1.07	1.08	1.06	1.11	1.08
166	.96	.94	1.00	.98	.95	.95	1.00	.95
167	1.01	1.03	1.03	1.02	1.00	1.02	1.08	.99
168	1.01	1.03	1.03	1.02	1.00	1.02	1.08	.99
169	1.01	1.03	1.03	1.02	1.00	1.02	1.08	.99
170	1.00	.99	.98	1.02	.99	1.02	1.05	.97
171	1.00	1.00	.97	1.03	1.01	1.04	1.07	.98
172	.96	.94	1.00	.98	.95	.95	1.00	.95
173	1.02	1.02	1.03	1.05	1.01	1.01	1.07	1.00
174	.96	.94	1.00	.98	.95	.95	1.00	.95
175	1.02	1.02	1.03	1.05	1.01	1.01	1.07	1.00
176	1.02	1.01	1.02	1.04	1.00	1.01	1.07	.99
177	1.00	1.01	1.01	1.02	.96	1.03	1.06	.97
178	1.00	.99	.98	1.02	.99	1.02	1.05	.97

	Baths & Kitchens	Ceiling & Wall Finishes	Doors & Windows	Elect., Plumb., & HVAC	Sitework & Ext. Walls	Floor Finishes	Roofing	Spec. & Equip.
PENNSYLVANIA (Continued)								
179	1.00	.99	.98	1.02	.99	1.02	1.05	.97
180	1.09	1.13	1.07	1.09	1.10	1.14	1.13	1.09
181	1.09	1.13	1.07	1.09	1.10	1.14	1.13	1.09
182	1.00	1.02	.96	1.01	1.00	1.06	1.08	1.01
183	1.09	1.13	1.07	1.09	1.10	1.14	1.13	1.09
184	1.00	1.02	.99	1.00	1.00	1.07	1.05	1.00
185	1.00	1.02	.99	1.00	1.00	1.07	1.05	1.00
186	1.00	1.02	.96	1.01	1.00	1.06	1.08	1.01
187	1.00	1.02	.96	1.01	1.00	1.06	1.08	1.01
188	1.00	1.02	.99	1.00	1.00	1.07	1.05	1.00
189	1.28	1.36	1.27	1.24	1.29	1.27	1.25	1.28
190	1.28	1.36	1.27	1.24	1.29	1.27	1.25	1.28
191	1.28	1.36	1.27	1.24	1.29	1.27	1.25	1.28
192	1.28	1.36	1.27	1.24	1.29	1.27	1.25	1.28
193	1.13	1.15	1.14	1.13	1.12	1.12	1.15	1.12
194	1.28	1.36	1.27	1.24	1.29	1.27	1.25	1.28
195	1.08	1.11	1.06	1.09	1.09	1.12	1.13	1.08
196	1.08	1.11	1.06	1.09	1.09	1.12	1.13	1.08
RHODE ISLAND								
028	1.17	1.18	1.18	1.15	1.15	1.21	1.18	1.18
029	1.17	1.18	1.18	1.15	1.15	1.21	1.18	1.18
SOUTH CAROLINA								
290	.85	.85	.83	.86	.84	.81	.89	.81
291	.85	.85	.83	.86	.84	.81	.89	.81
292	.84	.83	.83	.86	.83	.81	.87	.81
293	.85	.81	.88	.87	.84	.84	.86	.82
294	.86	.86	.84	.88	.84	.80	.91	.81
295	.86	.86	.84	.87	.86	.85	.90	.82
296	.84	.80	.85	.86	.83	.83	.84	.80
297	.86	.86	.84	.87	.86	.85	.90	.82
298	.85	.86	.82	.86	.85	.82	.91	.81
299	.85	.86	.82	.86	.85	.82	.91	.81
SOUTH DAKOTA								
570	.92	.88	.92	.94	.89	.91	.91	.88
571	.91	.86	.95	.93	.87	.89	.90	.87
572	.94	.91	.94	.95	.94	.99	.96	.91
573	.94	.91	.94	.97	.92	.98	.93	.90
574	.95	.92	.94	.95	.95	1.01	.98	.92
575	.93	.87	.93	.95	.92	.96	.91	.89
576	.95	.92	.94	.95	.95	1.01	.98	.92
577	.86	.80	.87	.87	.86	.89	.85	.84

UNITED STATES

	Baths & Kitchens	Ceiling & Wall Finishes	Doors & Windows	Elect., Plumb., & HVAC	Sitework & Ext. Walls	Floor Finishes	Roofing	Spec. & Equip.
TENNESSEE								
370	.90	.88	.91	.93	.87	.87	.92	.88
371	.90	.88	.91	.93	.87	.87	.92	.88
372	.87	.84	.90	.90	.84	.84	.87	.84
373	.85	.81	.87	.90	.81	.80	.89	.81
374	.85	.81	.87	.90	.81	.80	.89	.81
376	.87	.82	.91	.88	.86	.87	.90	.84
377	.88	.85	.90	.89	.88	.87	.95	.85
378	.88	.85	.90	.89	.88	.87	.95	.85
379	.88	.85	.90	.89	.88	.87	.95	.85
380	.86	.79	.87	.91	.83	.78	.85	.82
381	.86	.79	.87	.91	.83	.78	.85	.82
382	.94	.89	.97	.98	.92	.91	.93	.93
383	.89	.83	.91	.93	.86	.84	.89	.87
384	.89	.83	.91	.93	.86	.84	.89	.87
385	.88	.84	.89	.92	.85	.84	.90	.85
TEXAS								
750	.85	.79	.84	.89	.83	.87	.85	.81
751	.84	.80	.84	.87	.83	.86	.85	.80
752	.84	.81	.84	.85	.82	.85	.82	.79
753	.84	.81	.84	.85	.82	.85	.82	.79
754	.84	.80	.84	.88	.83	.86	.86	.80
755	.83	.79	.81	.86	.82	.81	.84	.78
756	.84	.81	.82	.86	.82	.82	.87	.79
757	.84	.81	.82	.86	.82	.82	.87	.79
758	.84	.81	.82	.86	.82	.82	.87	.79
759	.83	.80	.81	.86	.82	.81	.85	.79
760	.84	.79	.84	.87	.82	.86	.83	.79
761	.84	.79	.84	.87	.82	.86	.83	.79
762	.85	.79	.84	.89	.83	.87	.85	.81
763	.85	.78	.84	.89	.83	.86	.86	.81
764	.84	.79	.84	.87	.82	.86	.83	.79
765	.84	.80	.84	.87	.83	.86	.85	.80
766	.84	.80	.84	.87	.83	.86	.85	.80
767	.82	.78	.83	.84	.80	.82	.81	.78
768	.83	.78	.84	.85	.81	.84	.84	.78
769	.82	.77	.84	.84	.80	.83	.81	.77
770	.83	.79	.85	.85	.82	.81	.80	.80
771	.83	.79	.85	.85	.82	.81	.80	.80
772	.83	.79	.85	.85	.82	.81	.80	.80

UNITED STATES

	Baths & Kitchens	Ceiling & Wall Finishes	Doors & Windows	Elect., Plumb., & HVAC	Sitework & Ext. Walls	Floor Finishes	Roofing	Spec. & Equip.
TEXAS (Continued)								
773	.83	.79	.85	.85	.82	.81	.80	.80
774	.83	.79	.85	.85	.82	.81	.80	.80
775	.83	.79	.85	.85	.82	.81	.80	.80
776	.84	.79	.84	.87	.82	.86	.83	.79
777	.83	.80	.81	.85	.82	.84	.80	.78
778	.82	.78	.83	.84	.80	.82	.81	.78
779	.82	.78	.83	.84	.80	.82	.81	.78
780	.77	.72	.78	.82	.74	.77	.81	.74
781	.77	.72	.78	.82	.74	.77	.81	.74
782	.77	.72	.78	.82	.74	.77	.81	.74
783	.79	.76	.79	.79	.79	.81	.81	.73
784	.79	.76	.79	.79	.79	.81	.81	.73
785	.79	.76	.80	.81	.78	.80	.81	.75
786	.79	.75	.80	.82	.77	.79	.81	.75
787	.79	.75	.80	.82	.77	.79	.81	.75
788	.80	.76	.81	.83	.77	.80	.81	.76
789	.79	.75	.80	.82	.77	.79	.81	.75
790	.85	.81	.87	.87	.82	.85	.81	.79
791	.84	.81	.87	.86	.81	.84	.80	.78
792	.81	.75	.86	.83	.79	.82	.79	.76
793	.81	.75	.86	.83	.79	.82	.79	.76
794	.81	.75	.86	.83	.79	.82	.79	.76
795	.83	.78	.84	.85	.81	.84	.84	.78
796	.83	.78	.84	.85	.81	.84	.84	.78
797	.81	.79	.81	.83	.78	.82	.77	.76
798	.83	.80	.87	.82	.83	.87	.80	.78
799	.83	.80	.87	.82	.83	.87	.80	.78
885	.83	.80	.87	.82	.83	.87	.80	.78
UTAH								
840	.86	.82	.85	.88	.87	.92	.85	.83
841	.86	.82	.85	.88	.87	.92	.85	.83
843	.89	.85	.89	.90	.90	.94	.87	.86
844	.89	.85	.89	.90	.90	.94	.87	.86
845	.88	.84	.87	.89	.88	.91	.86	.84
846	.88	.84	.87	.89	.88	.91	.86	.84
847	.95	.92	.95	.93	.98	1.00	.92	.93

UNITED STATES

	Baths & Kitchens	Ceiling & Wall Finishes	Doors & Windows	Elect., Plumb., & HVAC	Sitework & Ext. Walls	Floor Finishes	Roofing	Spec. & Equip.
VERMONT								
050	1.01	.99	.99	1.03	1.00	1.06	1.13	.99
051	1.01	.99	.99	1.03	1.00	1.06	1.13	.99
052	1.01	.99	.99	1.03	1.00	1.06	1.13	.99
053	1.01	.99	.99	1.03	1.00	1.06	1.13	.99
054	1.01	.99	.99	1.03	1.00	1.06	1.13	.99
055	1.01	.99	.99	1.03	1.00	1.06	1.13	.99
056	1.02	1.03	1.00	1.03	1.01	1.06	1.12	1.01
057	1.05	1.07	1.02	1.05	1.04	1.07	1.11	1.03
058	1.03	1.05	1.00	1.04	1.03	1.09	1.14	1.02
059	1.03	1.05	1.00	1.04	1.03	1.09	1.14	1.02
VIRGINIA								
201	.96	.93	1.00	1.00	.94	.92	1.00	.94
220	.96	.93	1.00	1.00	.94	.92	1.00	.94
221	.96	.93	1.00	1.00	.94	.92	1.00	.94
222	.96	.93	1.00	1.00	.94	.92	1.00	.94
223	.96	.93	1.00	1.00	.94	.92	1.00	.94
224	.96	.93	1.00	1.00	.94	.92	1.00	.94
225	.96	.93	1.00	1.00	.94	.92	1.00	.94
226	.94	.87	1.01	1.00	.91	.89	.97	.92
227	.94	.87	1.01	1.00	.91	.89	.97	.92
228	.94	.87	1.01	1.00	.91	.89	.97	.92
229	.91	.86	.96	.95	.90	.88	.92	.90
230	.90	.82	.93	.93	.89	.86	.90	.88
231	.90	.82	.93	.93	.89	.86	.90	.88
232	.90	.82	.93	.93	.89	.86	.90	.88
233	.89	.85	.90	.92	.89	.83	.91	.87
234	.89	.85	.90	.92	.89	.83	.91	.87
235	.89	.85	.90	.92	.89	.83	.91	.87
236	.89	.85	.90	.92	.89	.83	.91	.87
237	.89	.85	.90	.92	.89	.83	.91	.87
238	.90	.82	.93	.93	.89	.86	.90	.88
239	.90	.82	.93	.93	.89	.86	.90	.88
240	.90	.88	.93	.90	.90	.89	.89	.87
241	.90	.88	.93	.90	.90	.89	.89	.87
242	.90	.88	.93	.90	.90	.89	.89	.87
243	.90	.88	.93	.90	.90	.89	.89	.87
244	.90	.88	.93	.90	.90	.89	.89	.87
245	.89	.85	.93	.90	.89	.88	.89	.87
246	.90	.88	.93	.90	.90	.89	.89	.87

UNITED STATES

	Baths & Kitchens	Ceiling & Wall Finishes	Doors & Windows	Elect., Plumb., & HVAC	Sitework & Ext. Walls	Floor Finishes	Roofing	Spec. & Equip.
WASHINGTON								
980	1.09	1.12	1.09	1.06	1.13	1.04	1.06	1.10
981	1.09	1.12	1.09	1.06	1.13	1.04	1.06	1.10
982	1.09	1.11	1.09	1.05	1.12	1.05	1.06	1.09
983	1.09	1.11	1.09	1.06	1.12	1.05	1.06	1.10
984	1.09	1.11	1.09	1.05	1.12	1.05	1.06	1.09
985	1.08	1.10	1.10	1.04	1.11	1.07	1.04	1.08
986	1.08	1.09	1.11	1.05	1.10	1.08	1.04	1.08
987	1.08	1.09	1.11	1.05	1.10	1.08	1.04	1.08
988	1.06	1.07	1.06	1.03	1.08	1.04	1.02	1.05
989	1.08	1.10	1.10	1.06	1.10	1.05	1.04	1.09
990	.97	.96	.97	.97	.99	1.00	.93	.95
991	.97	.96	.97	.97	.99	1.00	.93	.95
992	.97	.96	.97	.97	.99	1.00	.93	.95
993	1.03	1.04	1.04	1.02	1.05	1.02	.99	1.03
994	1.03	1.04	1.04	1.02	1.05	1.02	.99	1.03
WEST VIRGINIA								
247	.95	.93	.97	.94	.94	.93	.96	.93
248	.95	.93	.97	.94	.94	.93	.96	.93
249	1.00	1.01	1.01	.99	1.00	.98	1.01	.99
250	1.04	1.06	1.05	1.03	1.04	1.02	1.06	1.03
251	1.04	1.06	1.05	1.03	1.04	1.02	1.06	1.03
252	1.04	1.06	1.05	1.03	1.04	1.02	1.06	1.03
253	1.04	1.06	1.05	1.03	1.04	1.02	1.06	1.03
254	1.02	1.02	1.03	1.04	.99	1.02	1.10	1.01
255	1.01	1.04	1.02	1.00	1.02	.99	1.03	1.01
256	1.01	1.04	1.02	1.00	1.02	.99	1.03	1.01
257	1.01	1.04	1.02	1.00	1.02	.99	1.03	1.01
258	1.00	1.01	1.01	.99	1.00	.98	1.01	.99
259	1.00	1.01	1.01	.99	1.00	.98	1.01	.99
260	1.02	1.02	1.03	1.04	.99	1.02	1.10	1.01
261	1.02	1.04	1.04	1.02	1.02	1.01	1.07	1.02
262	1.02	1.02	1.03	1.04	.99	1.02	1.10	1.01
263	1.02	1.02	1.03	1.04	.99	1.02	1.10	1.01
264	1.02	1.02	1.03	1.04	.99	1.02	1.10	1.01
265	1.01	1.01	1.002	1.04	.98	1.01	1.08	1.01
266	1.02	1.02	1.03	1.04	.99	1.02	1.10	1.01
267	1.02	1.02	1.03	1.04	.99	1.02	1.10	1.01
268	1.02	1.02	1.03	1.04	.99	1.02	1.10	1.01

UNITED STATES

	Baths & Kitchens	Ceiling & Wall Finishes	Doors & Windows	Elect., Plumb., & HVAC	Sitework & Ext. Walls	Floor Finishes	Roofing	Spec. & Equip.
WISCONSIN								
530	1.06	1.11	1.03	1.05	1.07	1.10	1.05	1.06
531	1.06	1.11	1.03	1.05	1.07	1.10	1.05	1.06
532	1.07	1.11	1.05	1.05	1.08	1.11	1.03	1.08
534	1.09	1.14	1.07	1.08	1.10	1.09	1.09	1.11
535	1.09	1.14	1.07	1.08	1.10	1.09	1.09	1.11
536	1.09	1.14	1.07	1.08	1.10	1.09	1.09	1.11
537	1.08	1.14	1.06	1.07	1.09	1.09	1.08	1.10
538	1.09	1.14	1.07	1.08	1.10	1.09	1.09	1.11
539	1.09	1.14	1.07	1.08	1.10	1.09	1.09	1.11
540	1.09	1.14	1.07	1.06	1.11	1.10	1.09	1.09
541	1.04	1.07	1.01	1.04	1.05	1.08	1.04	1.03
542	1.04	1.07	1.01	1.04	1.05	1.08	1.04	1.03
543	1.05	1.08	1.01	1.04	1.06	1.09	1.04	1.04
544	1.06	1.11	1.03	1.04	1.08	1.10	1.07	1.07
545	1.06	1.10	1.04	1.04	1.08	1.09	1.07	1.06
546	1.05	1.08	1.02	1.03	1.06	1.09	1.05	1.05
547	1.08	1.15	1.03	1.03	1.11	1.09	1.12	1.08
548	1.09	1.14	1.07	1.06	1.11	1.10	1.09	1.09
549	1.06	1.11	1.03	1.05	1.07	1.10	1.05	1.06
WYOMING								
820	.90	.86	.89	.94	.87	.92	.85	.85
821	.90	.86	.89	.94	.87	.92	.85	.85
822	.90	.86	.89	.94	.87	.92	.85	.85
823	.90	.86	.89	.94	.87	.92	.85	.85
824	.93	.90	.94	.93	.92	.97	.89	.89
825	.90	.86	.89	.94	.87	.92	.85	.85
826	.94	.94	.96	.92	.95	.98	.92	.87
827	.91	.88	.92	.91	.90	.95	.89	.86
828	.92	.89	.92	.93	.90	.96	.89	.87
829	.90	.87	.91	.90	.90	.92	.89	.85
830	.90	.87	.91	.90	.90	.92	.89	.85
831	.90	.87	.91	.90	.90	.92	.89	.85

CANADA

	Baths & Kitchens	Ceiling & Wall Finishes	Doors & Windows	Elect., Plumb., & HVAC	Sitework & Ext. Walls	Floor Finishes	Roofing	Spec. & Equip.
ALBERTA	1.28	1.20	1.31	1.48	1.09	1.16	1.17	1.13
Calgary	1.32	1.21	1.33	1.57	1.09	1.07	1.16	1.14
Edmonton	1.28	1.20	1.32	1.47	1.09	1.11	1.15	1.12
Grande Prairie	1.30	1.24	1.37	1.46	1.11	1.18	1.21	1.16
Lethbridge	1.24	1.19	1.24	1.40	1.07	1.18	1.18	1.11
Medicine Hat ..	1.26	1.18	1.27	1.46	1.07	1.17	1.17	1.11
Red Deer	1.29	1.20	1.31	1.50	1.09	1.15	1.16	1.13
BRITISH COLUMBIA ..	1.31	1.25	1.38	1.49	1.11	1.17	1.24	1.17
Cranbrook	1.28	1.20	1.30	1.49	1.08	1.16	1.16	1.13
Kamloops	1.30	1.25	1.38	1.47	1.10	1.17	1.25	1.17
Kelowna	1.31	1.26	1.39	1.48	1.11	1.17	1.26	1.17
Nanaimo	1.33	1.28	1.40	1.50	1.13	1.16	1.28	1.18
Nelson	1.29	1.22	1.33	1.49	1.09	1.17	1.20	1.14
Penticton	1.31	1.26	1.39	1.49	1.11	1.17	1.26	1.17
Port Alberni ...	1.33	1.27	1.40	1.50	1.13	1.16	1.28	1.18
Prince George	1.31	1.26	1.40	1.44	1.13	1.24	1.22	1.18
Prince Rupert .	1.32	1.27	1.40	1.48	1.13	1.19	1.26	1.18
Trail	1.29	1.22	1.33	1.48	1.09	1.17	1.21	1.14
Vancouver	1.32	1.28	1.39	1.51	1.11	1.16	1.25	1.18
Victoria	1.34	1.28	1.42	1.50	1.16	1.15	1.31	1.18
MANITOBA ..	1.24	1.11	1.31	1.45	1.04	1.11	1.12	1.09
Brandon	1.25	1.13	1.31	1.44	1.06	1.11	1.12	1.10
Thompson	1.25	1.11	1.31	1.46	1.04	1.12	1.13	1.09
Winnipeg	1.23	1.09	1.31	1.45	1.01	1.11	1.10	1.07
MARITIMES ..	1.34	1.17	1.37	1.57	1.13	1.26	1.18	1.16
Bathurst	1.23	1.07	1.21	1.50	1.03	1.14	1.08	1.06
Cape Breton ..	1.31	1.16	1.33	1.50	1.14	1.31	1.14	1.16
Charlottetown .	1.32	1.13	1.26	1.60	1.13	1.25	1.18	1.13
Corner Brook .	1.40	1.30	1.36	1.56	1.24	1.41	1.19	1.23
Dartmouth	1.34	1.16	1.46	1.60	1.08	1.17	1.20	1.17
Edmundston ..	1.38	1.22	1.40	1.64	1.13	1.27	1.21	1.16
Fredericton ...	1.31	1.10	1.36	1.61	1.05	1.21	1.17	1.10
Gander	1.40	1.27	1.45	1.56	1.23	1.39	1.20	1.23
Halifax	1.33	1.16	1.46	1.59	1.07	1.16	1.19	1.17
Moncton	1.25	1.06	1.24	1.54	1.04	1.15	1.14	1.09
New Glasgow .	1.34	1.17	1.38	1.59	1.13	1.24	1.22	1.16
St John	1.31	1.13	1.34	1.60	1.08	1.23	1.12	1.09
St Johns	1.44	1.29	1.56	1.59	1.26	1.40	1.24	1.25
Sydney	1.31	1.16	1.33	1.50	1.14	1.32	1.13	1.16
Truro	1.36	1.20	1.44	1.58	1.15	1.27	1.26	1.18

CANADA

	Baths & Kitchens	Ceiling & Wall Finishes	Doors & Windows	Elect., Plumb., & HVAC	Sitework & Ext. Walls	Floor Finishes	Roofing	Spec. & Equip.
NORTHWEST TERRITORY								
Yellowknife . . .	1.30	1.22	1.35	1.49	1.10	1.17	1.17	1.14
ONTARIO	1.42	1.33	1.45	1.64	1.19	1.28	1.30	1.27
Barrie	1.42	1.33	1.48	1.67	1.17	1.23	1.34	1.27
Belleville	1.42	1.32	1.44	1.67	1.18	1.26	1.28	1.26
Brampton	1.43	1.35	1.44	1.67	1.21	1.29	1.31	1.30
Brantford	1.40	1.33	1.42	1.61	1.20	1.29	1.34	1.28
Brockville	1.44	1.33	1.47	1.68	1.20	1.31	1.30	1.23
Cambridge . . .	1.40	1.33	1.40	1.62	1.19	1.29	1.36	1.27
Guelph	1.41	1.34	1.41	1.63	1.20	1.30	1.35	1.28
Hamilton	1.41	1.34	1.43	1.61	1.21	1.33	1.33	1.30
Kingston	1.41	1.31	1.51	1.66	1.15	1.24	1.28	1.23
Kitchener	1.39	1.32	1.39	1.61	1.18	1.28	1.38	1.26
Lancaster	1.46	1.35	1.48	1.69	1.23	1.38	1.26	1.23
Lindsay	1.42	1.33	1.41	1.68	1.19	1.27	1.30	1.28
London	1.41	1.34	1.49	1.60	1.19	1.25	1.29	1.26
Niagara Falls .	1.42	1.34	1.47	1.62	1.21	1.26	1.30	1.29
North Bay	1.42	1.33	1.45	1.63	1.20	1.33	1.28	1.24
Orillia	1.43	1.34	1.45	1.68	1.19	1.25	1.32	1.28
Oshawa	1.43	1.34	1.43	1.67	1.21	1.27	1.29	1.29
Ottawa	1.38	1.29	1.39	1.60	1.17	1.23	1.21	1.23
Owen Sound . .	1.49	1.36	1.62	1.78	1.17	1.30	1.36	1.28
Peterborough .	1.41	1.32	1.38	1.67	1.17	1.27	1.29	1.26
Sarnia	1.41	1.32	1.49	1.61	1.19	1.27	1.29	1.26
Sault St Marie .	1.37	1.25	1.38	1.61	1.16	1.27	1.23	1.23
St Catharines .	1.41	1.33	1.49	1.60	1.20	1.24	1.29	1.28
Sudbury	1.36	1.28	1.39	1.55	1.17	1.27	1.21	1.23
Thunder Bay . .	1.42	1.31	1.53	1.61	1.21	1.28	1.31	1.28
Timmins	1.43	1.29	1.58	1.63	1.20	1.28	1.39	1.27
Toronto	1.46	1.37	1.42	1.71	1.24	1.30	1.28	1.32
Trenton	1.42	1.33	1.43	1.67	1.18	1.27	1.29	1.27
Waterloo	1.40	1.33	1.40	1.61	1.18	1.28	1.36	1.27
Windsor	1.40	1.31	1.38	1.61	1.21	1.30	1.20	1.27

CANADA

	Baths & Kitchens	Ceiling & Wall Finishes	Doors & Windows	Elect., Plumb., & HVAC	Sitework & Ext. Walls	Floor Finishes	Roofing	Spec. & Equip.
QUEBEC ...	1.46	1.35	1.45	1.69	1.23	1.39	1.32	1.22
Chicoutimi	1.48	1.38	1.46	1.74	1.24	1.37	1.40	1.23
Drummondville	1.47	1.36	1.43	1.70	1.24	1.44	1.31	1.22
Hull	1.52	1.38	1.51	1.78	1.27	1.46	1.42	1.24
Jonquiere	1.47	1.37	1.45	1.72	1.23	1.37	1.38	1.22
Laval	1.49	1.37	1.50	1.71	1.26	1.42	1.28	1.24
Montreal	1.49	1.36	1.49	1.71	1.26	1.40	1.28	1.25
Quebec	1.40	1.30	1.46	1.59	1.17	1.29	1.24	1.16
Rimouski	1.47	1.34	1.50	1.71	1.21	1.36	1.29	1.22
Rouyn	1.49	1.39	1.49	1.70	1.27	1.48	1.30	1.23
Sept Iles	1.34	1.18	1.35	1.61	1.10	1.24	1.18	1.13
Sherbrooke ...	1.46	1.39	1.42	1.67	1.25	1.43	1.40	1.22
Trois Rivieres .	1.45	1.36	1.34	1.70	1.24	1.44	1.37	1.22
Val D'or	1.47	1.38	1.48	1.70	1.25	1.43	1.31	1.23
SASKATCHEWAN	1.27	1.14	1.32	1.48	1.06	1.14	1.17	1.10
Moose Jaw ...	1.25	1.11	1.30	1.48	1.04	1.12	1.15	1.09
North Battleford	1.25	1.11	1.29	1.47	1.05	1.14	1.16	1.09
Prince Albert ..	1.27	1.10	1.32	1.50	1.05	1.13	1.19	1.09
Regina	1.26	1.10	1.31	1.49	1.02	1.11	1.13	1.08
Saskatoon	1.24	1.12	1.26	1.44	1.05	1.15	1.16	1.09
YUKON TERRITORY								
Whitehorse ...	1.32	1.27	1.40	1.48	1.13	1.19	1.26	1.18

GLOSSARY

- RESIDENTIAL CONSTRUCTION NOMENCLATURE

- DEFINITIONS

RESIDENTIAL CONSTRUCTION NOMENCLATURE

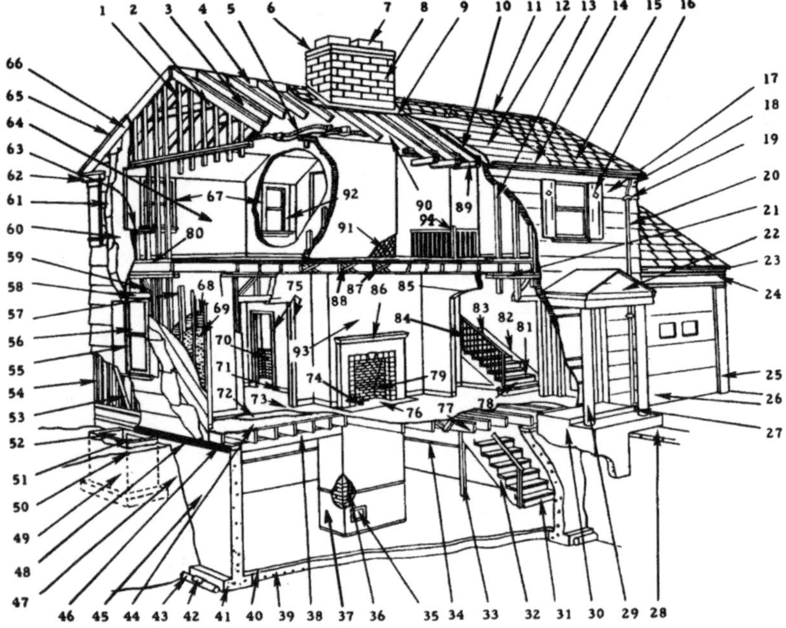

RESIDENTIAL CONSTRUCTION NOMENCLATURE

1. Gable stud
2. Collar beam/tie
3. Roof rafter
4. Ridgeboard
5. Cap/plate
6. Chimney wash
7. Chimney pot
8. Chimney
9. Chimney flashing
10. Insulation
11. Ridge
12. Roof sheathing
13. Stud
14. Eave trough or gutter
15. Roofing
16. Shutter
17. Horizontal board siding
18. Downspout or leader gooseneck
19. Downspout or leader strap
20. Downspout leader or conductor
21. Double plate
22. Entrance canopy
23. Garage cornice
24. Frieze
25. Doorjamb
26. Garage door
27. Entrance step
28. Sidewalk
29. Entrance canopy support column
30. Entrance platform
31. Basement stair riser
32. Stair stringer
33. Girder post
34. Chair rail
35. Cleanout door
36. Masonry chimney
37. Plaster over masonry
38. Furring strips
39. Cinder or gravel fill
40. Concrete basement floor
41. Footing for foundation wall
42. Filter mat
43. Foundation drain tile
44. Subflooring
45. Foundation wall
46. Mudsill
47. Backfill
48. Termite shield
49. Areaway wall
50. Grade line
51. Basement sash
52. Areaway
53. Corner brace
54. Corner studs
55. Window frame
56. Window light
57. Wall stud
58. Window header
59. Window cripple
60. Wall sheathing
61. Building paper
62. Frieze or barge board
63. Rough opening
64. Wall finish
65. Cornice molding
66. Fascia board
67. Window casing
68. Lath
69. Insulation
70. Wainscoting
71. Baseboard
72. Building paper
73. Finish floor
74. Ash dump
75. Door trim
76. Fireplace hearth
77. Floor joists
78. Stair riser
79. Fire brick
80. Sole plate
81. Stair tread
82. Finish stringer
83. Stair rail
84. Balusters
85. Plaster arch
86. Mantel
87. Floor joist
88. Bridging
89. Lookout/soffit framing
90. Attic space
91. Metal lath
92. Window sash
93. Chimney breast
94. Newel post

DEFINITIONS

EXPLANATION

The purpose of the following definitions is to provide a better understanding of key terms. It is not the intention of this section to serve as a comprehensive appraisal, architectural or construction dictionary.

Acoustical Ceiling

In general terms, a ceiling designed to lessen sound reverberation by absorption, blocking or muffling. In construction, the most common materials are acoustical tile and acoustical plaster.

Air Conditioning

The process of bringing air to a required state of temperature and humidity, and removing dust, pollen and other foreign matter.

Asphalt Shingles

A type of shingle made of felt, saturated with asphalt or tar pitch and surfaced with mineral granules or inorganic fiberglass saturated with asphalt and surfaced with ceramic granules. There are many different patterns, some individual and others in strips.

Asphalt Tile

A resilient floor covering laid in mastic, available in several colors. Standard size is 9" x 9". Asphalt is normally used only in the darker colors, the lighter colors having a resin base.

Backfill

Material used in refilling an excavation, such as for a foundation or subterranean pipe.

Backup

A lower-priced material in a masonry wall that is covered by a facing of more expensive and ornamental material, such as face brick, stone or marble.

Balcony

A railed platform projecting from the face of a building above the ground level, with an entrance from the building interior.

Baseboard Heating

Heating in which the radiant heating element, usually an electric resistance unit or forced hot water, is located at the base of the interior wall.

Batt Insulation

A type of blanket insulating material, usually composed of mineral fibers and made in relatively narrow widths for convenience in handling and applying between framing members.

Batten

A narrow strip of wood used to cover a joint between boards or to simulate a covered joint for architectural purposes.

DEFINITIONS

Bay Window

A window structure that projects from a wall. Technically, it has its own foundation. If cantilevered, it would be an oriel window; however, in common usage, the terms are often used interchangeably.

Beamed Ceiling

A ceiling with beams exposed. A false-beamed ceiling has ornamental boards or timbers which are not load-bearing.

Bearing Wall

A wall that supports upper floor or roof loads.

Bi-Level

A two-story residence with a split-foyer entrance. The lower level, partially above grade, is partially finished. Typically, the finish includes plumbing and electrical rough-ins with some partition wall framing for recreation room, bedroom, laundry area and bathroom. Other common terms for this type of construction are Raised Ranch, Hi-Ranch, Colonial and Split-Entry.

Blanket Insulation

A flexible type of lightweight blanket for insulating purposes. It is supplied in rolls, strips or panels, sometimes fastened to heavy paper of an asphalt-treated or vapor-barrier type. Blankets may be composed of various processed materials, such as mineral wool, wood or glass fibers.

B.T.U.

British thermal unit. A measurement of heat, i.e., the amount of heat required to raise one pound of water one degree Fahrenheit.

Building Permit

A certificate that must be obtained from the municipal government by the property owner or contractor before a building can be erected or repaired. It must be kept posted in a conspicuous place until the job is completed and passed by the building inspector.

Built-In Appliances

Those appliances that are permanent fixtures in the residence. They are not included in the base costs and should be added separately.

Caissons

Poured-in-place, reinforced concrete pilings.

Carport

An open automobile shelter. May be only a roof and supports or may be enclosed on three sides with one completely open side.

Cement Fiber (Asbestos) Shingles

A covering, consisting largely of portland cement and asbestos fiber, made into shingles.

Cesspool

A pit that stores liquid sewage, which is disposed of through seepage into the surrounding soil.

DEFINITIONS

Clerestory Window

A series or band of vertical windows set above the primary roof line.

Common Wall

A wall separating living area and a garage when the garage is attached, or a wall shared by two living areas in a multiple-family residence. In the latter, the wall can serve as a property line if separate ownership.

Condominium

Type of ownership of a multi-unit property in which the owner holds title to an individual unit and a percentage of common areas.

Crawl Space

A space of limited height sufficient to permit access to piping or wiring underneath the floor of a raised floor structure.

Curtain Wall

A nonbearing exterior wall supported by an independent structural frame of a building.

Detached Dwelling

A housing unit or garage with wall and roof independent of any other building, as opposed to an attached dwelling.

Dormer

A projection from a sloping roof to provide more headroom under the roof and allow the installation of dormer windows.

Double Glazing

A double-glass pane in a door or window, with an air space between the two panes, which may be sealed hermetically to provide insulation.

Double-Hung Window

A window with an upper and lower sash, each balanced by springs or weights enabling vertical movement in its own grooves.

Drywall

A finish material applied to an interior wall in a dry state, as opposed to plaster. Normally referred to as gypsum board or sheetrock.

Ducts

Enclosures, usually round or rectangular in shape, for distributing warm or cool air from the central unit to various rooms.

Electric Baseboard Heat

An electric heater installed as a baseboard, along a wall.

Electric Cable Heating

A heating system consisting of electrical coils installed beneath the surface of ceilings, walls or floors. It is commonly installed in ceilings of multifamily residences having a sprayed-on ceiling.

DEFINITIONS

Elevated Slab

A horizontal, reinforced, concrete structure that is formed and poured-in-place above the ground level.

Evaporative Cooler

An air conditioner that cools the air by water evaporation. Outdoor air is drawn through a moistened filter pad in a cabinet, and the cooled air is then circulated throughout the house. It is used in regions with low humidity.

Fenestration

Generally referred to as the arrangement of windows and doors in the walls of a building.

Finish Hardware

All exposed hardware in a house (door knobs, door hinges, locks and clothes hooks, etc.).

Floor Area

An area on any floor, enclosed by exterior walls and/or partitions. Measurement for total floor area should include the width of the exterior walls.

Forced-Air Heating

A warm-air heating system that circulates air by a motor-driven fan. It includes air-cleaning devices.

Formica

A trade name for a hard laminated plastic surfacing, often the name for all such finishes used on countertops.

Gable Roof

A ridged roof that slopes up from only two walls. A gable is the triangular portion of the end of the building, from the eaves to the ridge.

Gambrel Roof

A type of roof that has its slope broken by an obtuse angle, so that the lower slope is steeper than the upper slope; a roof with two pitches.

General Contractor

A builder who is responsible for all work in building a structure.

Gravity Heating

A warm-air system, usually located in a basement, which operates on the principle of warm air rising through ducts to the upper levels. Since it does not contain a fan, as does the conventional forced-air furnace, a larger burner surface as well as larger ducts are used.

Hardboard

A highly compressed wood fiberboard with many uses as exterior siding, interior wall covering or concrete forms.

DEFINITIONS

Heat Pump

A self-contained, reverse cycle, heating and cooling unit. On its cooling cycle it works like an air conditioner, collecting heat from inside and pumping to an outside coil where it is dissipated. On the heating cycle, heat is collected by the outside coil and pumped inside.

Hip Roof

A roof that rises by inclined planes from all four sides of a building. The line where two adjacent sloping sides of a roof meet is called the hip.

Hot Water Heating

The circulation of hot water from a boiler through a system of pipes and radiators or convectors, either by gravity or a circulating pump, allowing the heat to radiate into the room.

Humidifier

A device for maintaining desirable humidity conditions in the air supplied to a building.

Insulation

Any material used to obstruct the passage of sound, heat, vibration or electricity from one place to another.

Interim Money, Cost Of

Interest on financing during a normal period of construction, as well as an amount for servicing or handling of the loan. Bonuses (points) or discounts paid for securing the financing are not included in the costs.

Keene's Plaster

A quick-setting, white, hard-finish plaster that produces a wall of extreme durability and a smooth-finish coat.

Mansard Roof

A roof with two slopes, the lower slope very steep, the upper slope almost flat.

Masonry Construction

In building, a type of construction with concrete, concrete block or brick load-bearing exterior walls.

Mesh

Heavy steel wire welded together in a grid pattern, used as a reinforcement for concrete work.

Millwork

Wooden portions of a building that have been prebuilt and finished in a shop and brought to the site for installation, such as cabinets, door jambs, molding, trim, etc.

Modular Construction

Any building construction that is normally preassembled and shipped to the site in units.

DEFINITIONS

Monolithic
> One piece. Monolithic concrete is poured in a continuous process so there are no separations.

Overhead And Profit
> Overhead is a contractor's operating expense, including workers' compensation, fire and liability insurance, unemployment insurance, equipment, temporary facilities, security, etc., that cannot be prorated to any specific category of the construction. Profit is the compensation accrued for the assumption of risk in constructing the building only. These are not to be confused with a developer's or an owner's overhead and profit, associated with subdivision planning and administration.

Parameter
> Any characteristic of a statistical universe that is measurable. In construction: Square foot, cubic yard, board feet, etc., are cost parameters.

Parapet Wall
> The portion of a wall that projects above the roof line.

Perimeter
> The total length of all the exterior bearing walls of a building.

Pier
> The short, individual concrete or masonry foundation supports for the post and girder underpinning of a raised floor structure.

Pilaster
> A column usually formed of the same material and integral with, but projecting from, a wall.

Pilings
> Columns extending below the ground to bear the loads of a structure when the surface soil cannot. They may extend down to bearing soil or support the load by skin friction. Sheet piling is used to form bulkheads or retaining walls.

Plaster
> Portland cement mixed with sand and water to form a mortar-like consistency, used for covering walls and ceilings of a building.

Plumbing Fixtures
> Receptacles that receive and discharge water, liquid or waterborne wastes into a drainage system with which they are connected.

Porch
> A wood or concrete platform, often with a roof covering, found at the entrance of a building.

Precast Concrete
> Concrete structural components that are not formed and poured-in-place within the structure, but are cast separately either at another location or on site.

DEFINITIONS

Quantity Survey

A method of cost estimation that considers a detailed count of all materials going into a structure, together with the cost of labor to install each unit of material.

Radiant Heating

A system in which a space is heated by the use of hot-water pipe coils or electric resistance wires placed normally in the floor or ceiling, allowing the heat to radiate into the room.

Reinforcing Steel

Steel bars used in concrete construction for giving added strength; such bars are of various sizes and shapes.

Resilient Floor Covering

Floor covering products characterized by having dense, nonabsorbent surfaces, available in sheet or tile form. Among the various types are vinyl asbestos tile, asphalt tile, composition tile and linoleum.

Rough-In

Drain and water line hookups for laundry facilities or for future fixture installation.

R-Value

The standard measurement of resistance to heat loss related to a given thickness of insulation required by climatic demands.

Septic Tank

A watertight settling tank in which solid sewage is decomposed by natural bacterial action.

Shake

A shingle split (not sawed) from a bolt of wood and used for roofing and siding, or a manufactured imitation.

Skylight

An opening in a roof, covered with plastic or glass, for light and ventilation.

Slope

The ratio of rise to run, to express the angle of a roof pitch.

Storm Door

An extra outside or additional door for protection against inclement weather. Such a door also lessens the chill of a building's interior, making it easier to heat. It also helps to avoid the effects of wind and rain at the entrance doorway.

Storm Window

A window placed outside an ordinary window for additional protection against severe weather. Also called a storm sash.

Stucco

A coating for exterior walls in which cement is put on in wet layers and when dry becomes exceedingly hard and durable.

DEFINITIONS

Sump Pump

A suction device, usually operated to remove water or waste that collects at the sump pit or tank.

Terrazzo

A floor surface of marble chips in concrete. After the concrete has hardened, the floor is ground and polished to expose the marble chips. In epoxy terrazzo, the filler material is plastic.

Thermostat

An instrument, electrically operated, which automatically controls the operation of a heating or cooling device by responding to changes in temperature.

Tongue And Groove (Abbreviated T & G)

Any lumber, such as boards or planks, machined in such a manner that there is a groove on one edge and a corresponding projection on the other.

U-Factor

The heat transmission factor of a wall, roof or floor assembly measured in B.T.U.s per square foot per degree Fahrenheit.

Vapor Barrier

Material used to retard the passage of moisture through floors, roofs or exterior walls, thus preventing condensation with them; also called moisture barrier. See waterproofing below.

Veneer

A layer of material applied to another surface for ornamental or protective purposes. Masonry veneer refers to any masonry unit applied over wood-frame construction.

Vinyl Composition (Asbestos) Tile

A resilient floor covering laid in mastic that is available in many colors and textures. Standard size is 12" x 12".

Waterproofing

Any material designed to stop passage of moisture. Plastic sheets of treated papers and asphalt are used for membranes, while various chemical sealants and asphalt applications are used to seal pores or cracks.

Weather Stripping

Strips of felt, rubber, metal or other suitable material fixed along the edges of a door or window to keep out drafts and reduce heat loss.

Wood-Frame Construction

In building, a type of construction in which the structural members are wood or are dependent upon a wood frame for support. Same as frame construction.

INDEX

CONSTRUCTION COMPONENTS

NOTES

HOME REPAIR & REMODEL COST GUIDE WORKSHEET

COMPANY: ____

AGENT: ____

DATE: ___________________________ PHONE #: ___________________

PROPERTY ADDRESS: ____

SALE PRICE: ___________________________ FOR: ___________________

LINE	Improvement Required (Component)	Quantity		Unit Cost		Local Mult.		Total Cost
1			X		X		=	$
2			X		X		=	$
3			X		X		=	$
4			X		X		=	$
5			X		X		=	$
6			X		X		=	$
7			X		X		=	$
8			X		X		=	$
9			X		X		=	$
10			X		X		=	$

NOTES				
	11	Total Base Cost (Total of Lines 1 – 10)	=	$
	12	Depreciation % (If Required)	=	
	13	Depreciation Amount (Line 12 x 11)	=	$
	14	Depreciation Cost (Line 11 – 13)	=	$

NOTE: Space is provided on the back of this worksheet for sketches, computations and additional notes.

SKETCHES AND COMPUTATIONS

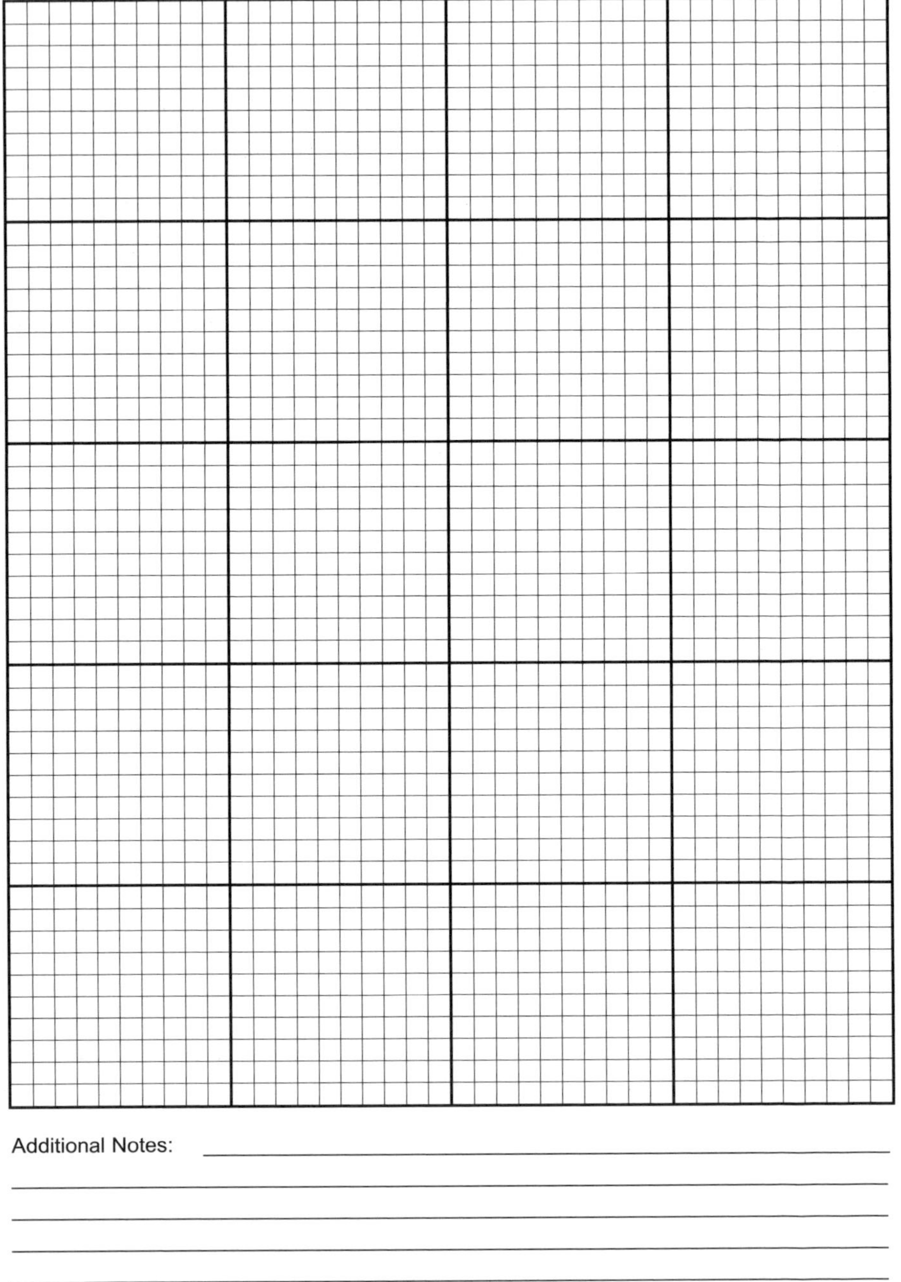

Additional Notes:

HOME REPAIR & REMODEL
COST GUIDE WORKSHEET

COMPANY: ____

AGENT: ____

DATE: _____________________________ PHONE #: _______________________

PROPERTY ADDRESS: ____

SALE PRICE: _____________________________ FOR: _______________________

LINE	Improvement Required (Component)	Quantity		Unit Cost		Local Mult.		Total Cost
1			X		X		=	$
2			X		X		=	$
3			X		X		=	$
4			X		X		=	$
5			X		X		=	$
6			X		X		=	$
7			X		X		=	$
8			X		X		=	$
9			X		X		=	$
10			X		X		=	$

NOTES				
	11	Total Base Cost (Total of Lines 1 – 10)	=	$
	12	Depreciation % (If Required)	=	
	13	Depreciation Amount (Line 12 x 11)	=	$
	14	Depreciation Cost (Line 11 – 13)	=	$

NOTE: Space is provided on the back of this worksheet for sketches, computations and additional notes.

SKETCHES AND COMPUTATIONS

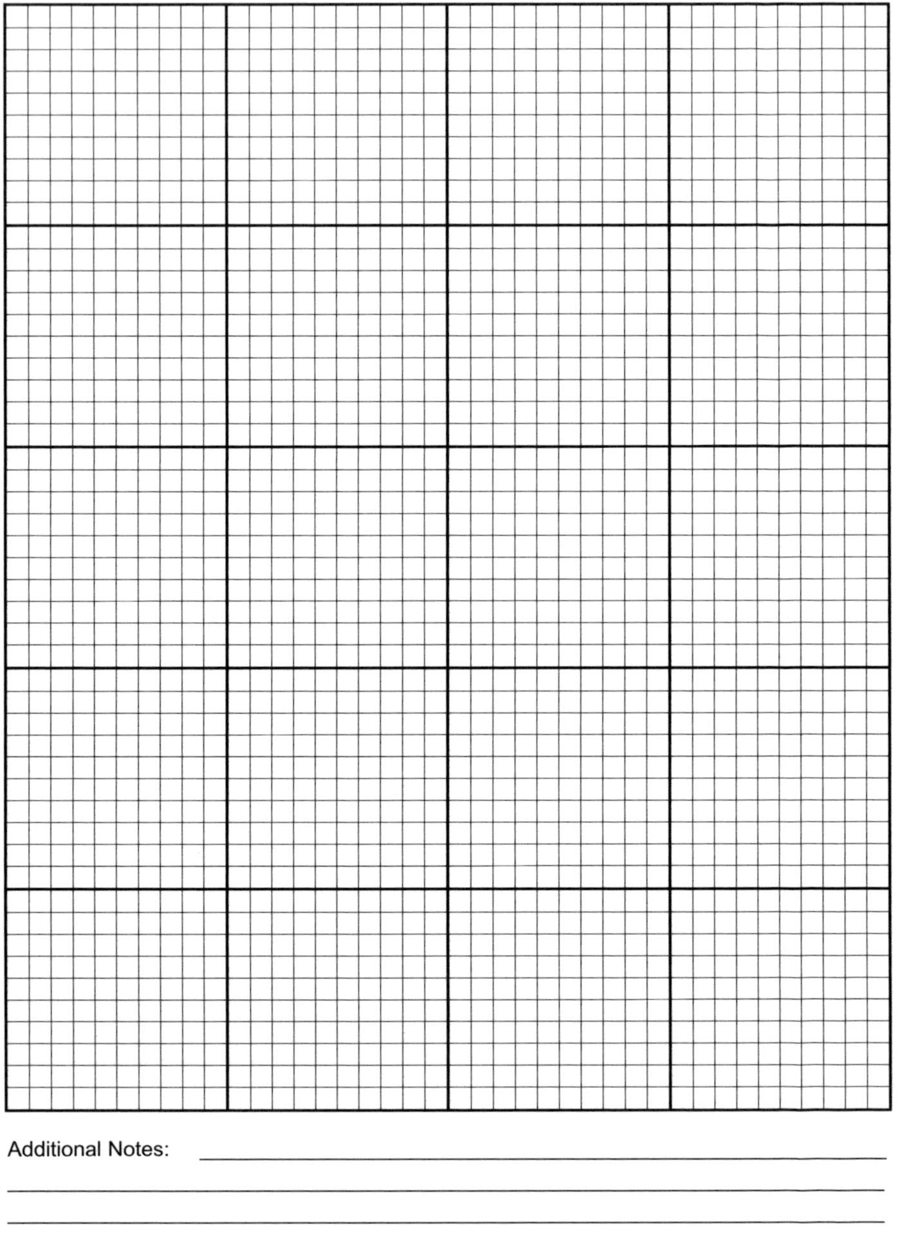

Additional Notes: ____

____

____

____

____

HOME REPAIR & REMODEL
COST GUIDE WORKSHEET

COMPANY: ____

AGENT: ____

DATE: _____________________________ PHONE #: _______________________

PROPERTY ADDRESS: ____

SALE PRICE: _____________________ FOR: _______________________

LINE	Improvement Required (Component)	Quantity		Unit Cost		Local Mult.		Total Cost
1			X		X		=	$
2			X		X		=	$
3			X		X		=	$
4			X		X		=	$
5			X		X		=	$
6			X		X		=	$
7			X		X		=	$
8			X		X		=	$
9			X		X		=	$
10			X		X		=	$

NOTES					
	11	Total Base Cost (Total of Lines 1 – 10)		=	$
	12	Depreciation % (If Required)		=	
	13	Depreciation Amount (Line 12 x 11)		=	$
	14	Depreciation Cost (Line 11 – 13)		=	$

NOTE: Space is provided on the back of this worksheet for sketches, computations and additional notes.

Additional Notes: _______________________________

____

____

____

____

HOME REPAIR & REMODEL
COST GUIDE WORKSHEET

COMPANY: ____

AGENT: ____

DATE: ______________________________ PHONE #: _______________________

PROPERTY ADDRESS: _______________________________________

SALE PRICE: ______________________ FOR: _______________________

LINE	Improvement Required (Component)	Quantity		Unit Cost		Local Mult.		Total Cost
1			X		X		=	$
2			X		X		=	$
3			X		X		=	$
4			X		X		=	$
5			X		X		=	$
6			X		X		=	$
7			X		X		=	$
8			X		X		=	$
9			X		X		=	$
10			X		X		=	$

NOTES				
	11	Total Base Cost (Total of Lines 1 – 10)	=	$
	12	Depreciation % (If Required)	=	
	13	Depreciation Amount (Line 12 x 11)	=	$
	14	Depreciation Cost (Line 11 – 13)	=	$

NOTE: Space is provided on the back of this worksheet for sketches, computations and additional notes.

SKETCHES AND COMPUTATIONS

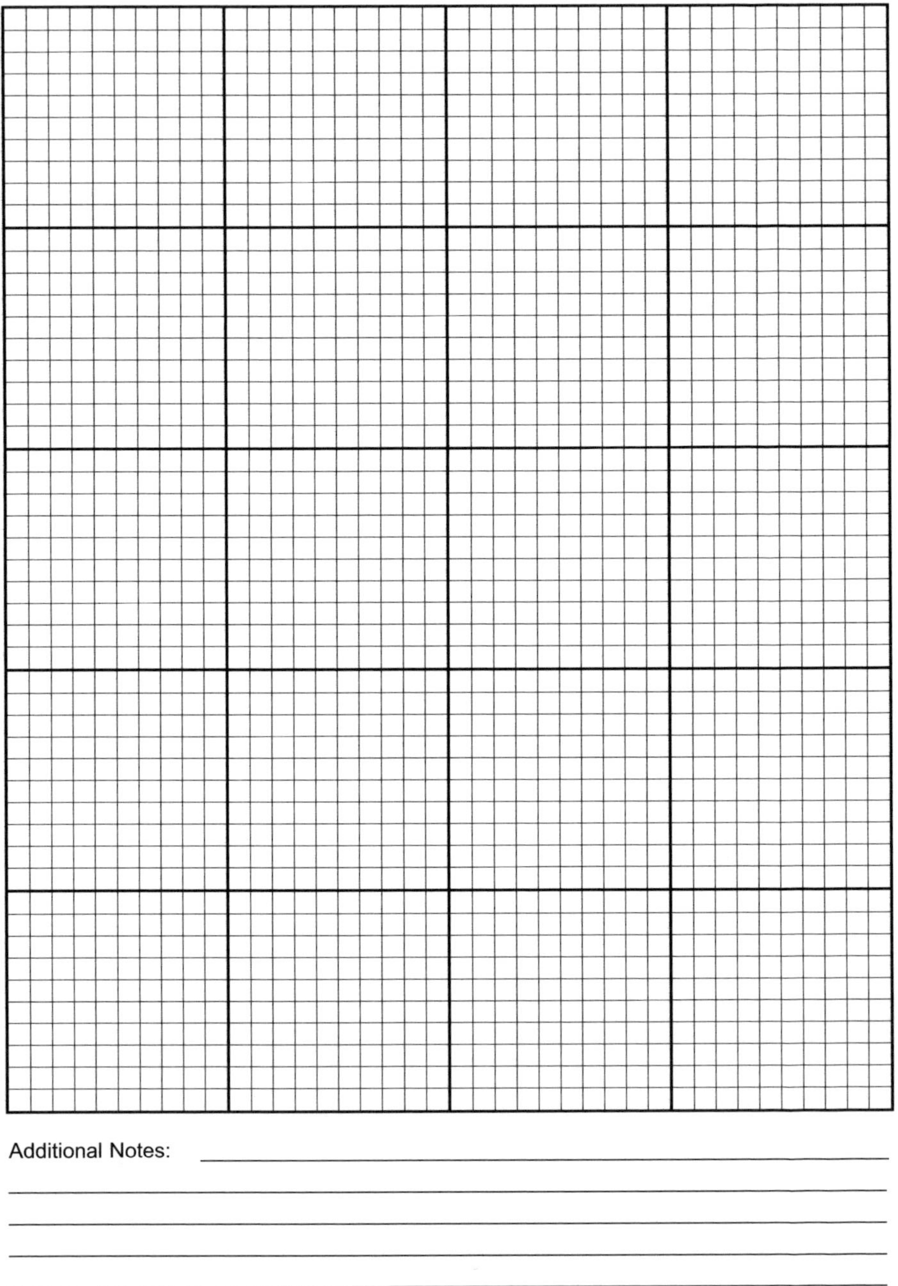

Additional Notes: ____

____

____

____

____

HOME REPAIR & REMODEL
COST GUIDE WORKSHEET

COMPANY: ____

AGENT: ____

DATE: ____________________________ PHONE #: ____________________________

PROPERTY ADDRESS: ____

SALE PRICE: ____________________________ FOR: ____________________________

LINE	Improvement Required (Component)	Quantity		Unit Cost		Local Mult.		Total Cost
1			X		X		=	$
2			X		X		=	$
3			X		X		=	$
4			X		X		=	$
5			X		X		=	$
6			X		X		=	$
7			X		X		=	$
8			X		X		=	$
9			X		X		=	$
10			X		X		=	$

NOTES				
	11	Total Base Cost (Total of Lines 1 – 10)	=	$
	12	Depreciation % (If Required)	=	
	13	Depreciation Amount (Line 12 x 11)	=	$
	14	Depreciation Cost (Line 11 – 13)	=	$

NOTE: Space is provided on the back of this worksheet for sketches, computations and additional notes.

SKETCHES AND COMPUTATIONS

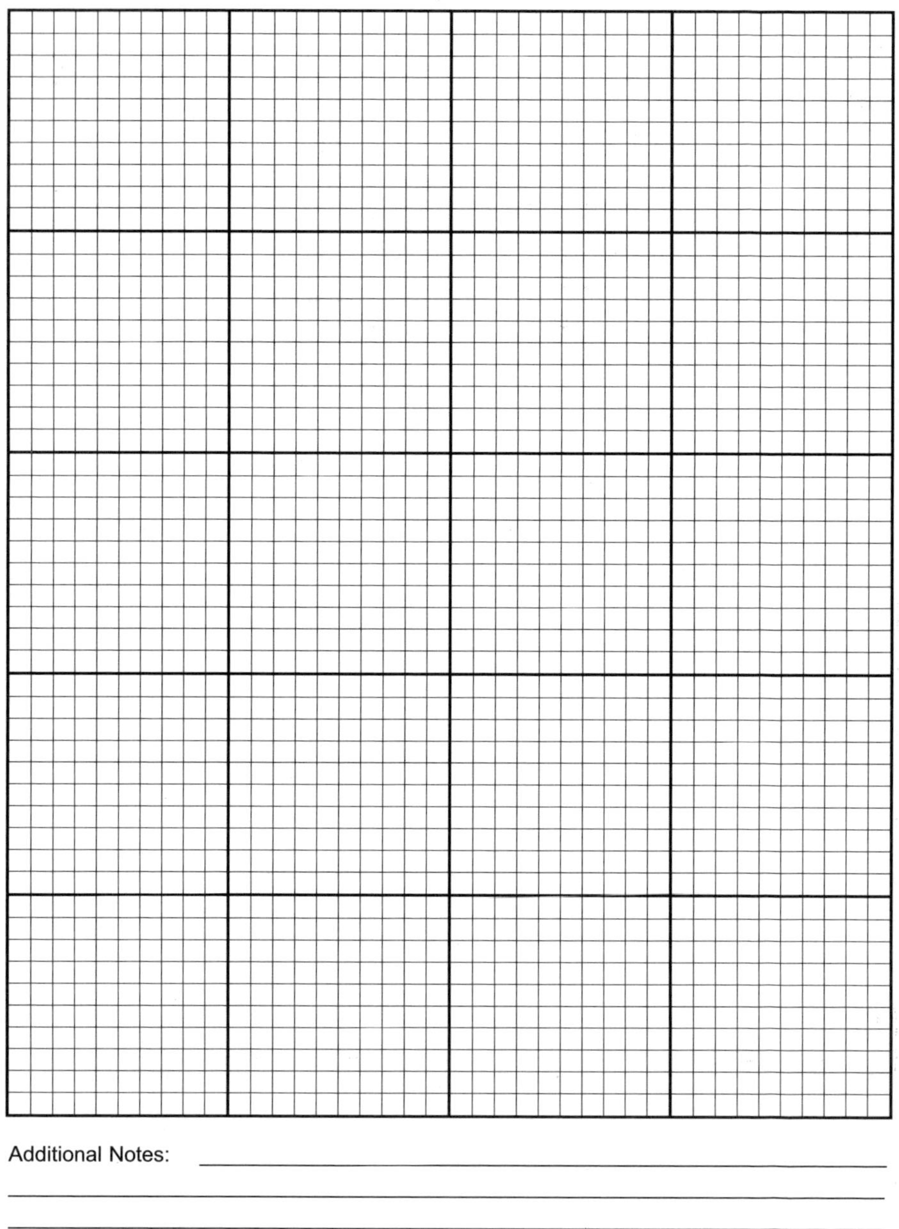

Additional Notes: ____

____

____

____

____